MAKING A KILLING

# Making a Killing

*States, Banks, and Terrorism*

IAN MICHAEL OXNEVAD

McGill-Queen's University Press
Montreal & Kingston • London • Chicago

© McGill-Queen's University Press 2021

ISBN 978-0-2280-0876-7 (cloth)
ISBN 978-0-2280-1001-2 (ePDF)
ISBN 978-0-2280-1002-9 (ePUB)

Legal deposit third quarter 2021
Bibliothèque nationale du Québec

Printed in Canada on acid-free paper that is 100% ancient forest free (100% post-consumer recycled), processed chlorine free

---

**Library and Archives Canada Cataloguing in Publication**

Title: Making a killing: states, banks, and terrorism / Ian Michael Oxnevad.

Names: Oxnevad, Ian M., author.

Description: Includes bibliographical references and index.

Identifiers: Canadiana (print) 2021023217X | Canadiana (ebook) 20210232226 | ISBN 9780228008767 (cloth) | ISBN 9780228010029 (ePUB) | ISBN 9780228010012 (ePDF)

Subjects: LCSH: Terrorism—Finance. | LCSH: Banks and banking—Corrupt practices. | LCSH: Banks and banking—Government ownership. | LCSH: Money laundering.

Classification: LCC HV6768 .O96 2021 | DDC 364.16/8—dc23

---

This book was typeset by Marquis Interscript in 10.5/13 Sabon.

To Marissa, John, Fariba, and Lou. Each of you helped me in more ways than you know.

This book is dedicated to the victims of the San Bernardino terrorist attack of 2 December 2015, and to all victims of terrorism. Your memory is motivation.

*Robert Adams*
*Isaac Amanios*
*Bennetta Betbadal*
*Harry Bowman*
*Sierra Clayborn*
*Juan Espinoza*
*Aurora Godoy*
*Shannon Johnson*
*Larry Daniel Kaufman*
*Damian Meins*
*Tin Nguyen*
*Nicholas Thalasinos*
*Yvette Velasco*
*Michael Wetzel*

# Contents

Figures and Tables   ix

Introduction   3

1  Enforcement Outcomes in Counterterrorist Financing   8

2  Bank of China   44

3  Al Rajhi Bank in Saudi Arabia   70

4  Halk Bank of Turkey   93

5  Institutional Independence and Regulatory Enforcement   121

Conclusion   153

Notes   165

Index   197

# Figures and Tables

## FIGURES

1.1 Phenomena of money laundering and terrorist financing  22
1.2 Independent variable: institutional linkage  34
1.3 Dependent variable: enforcement blockage  36
4.1 Halk Bank and the Turkish government  101

## TABLES

1.1 Potential cases (rule-of-law and regulatory quality data)  39
2.1 Timeline of anti-money-laundering regulatory adoption in China  59
2.2 PIJ/Hamas transfers conducted by Bank of China  65
5.1 Sample of Hamas members and Arab Bank accounts  146

MAKING A KILLING

# Introduction

International politics in the twenty-first century have thus far been largely characterized by terrorism and financial crisis. The new millennium's optimism came to an abrupt halt in September 2001, when Al-Qaeda operatives hijacked airline jets and crashed them into the World Trade Center towers in New York, and the Pentagon in Washington, DC, at a cost of nearly 3,000 casualties. Few at the time could have imagined that this literal fusing of capitalism's epicentre and religious fanaticism in a fireball would open a new era of financial regulation. This new era of financial rules and geopolitics regarding counterterrorist finance (CTF), which heralded the creation and expansion of a set of global financial institutions, was also driven by power politics and security considerations.

The expansion of financial regulations designed to counter terrorist financing served to further integrate different countries into the American-led international financial system and brought this liberalized system into direct conflict with the logic of national security. On the practical level, the expansion of these regulations brought the market-oriented world of financial institutions and bankers together with that of terrorists, spies, and law enforcement. Complicating matters further, the international prominence of the dollar and the origins of the CTF regime in a US legal system characterized by adversity brought other states and their banks into confrontation with complicated issues of jurisdiction and hegemony. This book is about the efficacy of these regulations; and, more importantly, the determinants of enforcement outcomes of these regulations when banks are suspected of financing terror.

Since 2001, the research on threat finance has grown substantially; however, research on anti-money laundering (AML) and CTF lacks both theoretical cohesion and a clear theoretical and analytical centre. Largely due to divisions within political science as a discipline, work on threat finance has either focused on the political economy of regulatory growth and harmonization, or on the financing and resource management of specific terrorist groups. With scholarly attention divided between the financial regulatory world and terrorism, developing a focus on banks and financial institutions as actors, and their relationships to terrorist groups, has been neglected. This inattention to banks leaves a theoretical blank spot for understanding the inner workings of counterterrorist financing institutions within the financial system. Banks connect the worlds of regulation and terrorist groups, and this connection warrants focusing upon them as a unit of analysis.

Criminal organizations and terrorist groups have long used financial institutions for holding wealth, moving it around the globe, and laundering it to keep money and illicit activity separate. Since the advent of AML/CTF rules in the 1970s, banks have taken on the additional role of serving as instruments of security for the states that regulate them. Tasked with following customer due-diligence rules, collecting data, adhering to sanctions regimes, and gathering financial intelligence, banks have emerged as the intersection point for criminal and terrorist organizations on the one hand, and the states seeking to counter them on the other. With banks comprising the central actors in the phenomenon of threat finance, the lack of scholarly focus on them as a unit of analysis leaves significant questions unanswered.

Regarding terrorist financing and CTF, literature focused on the regulatory side of the equation outlines a contradictory understanding of the effectiveness of such institutions. At the international level, an image emerges of profound regulatory harmonization and deepening. Beginning in the 1980s onward, great powers and financial centres pioneered the development of financial regulation as a means of advancing security against the threat of transnational crime and terrorism. Embodied first in the domestic regulatory regimes of the United States and the United Kingdom, such institutions quickly spread across the industrialized world, despite overall financial deregulation. In the 1990s, these regulations spread further internationally, with institutions such as the UN passing resolutions to combat money laundering and terrorist financing. The 1989 founding of the Financial Action Task Force (FATF) by states of the Group of Seven placed additional pressure on other states to adopt AML/CTF measures. After 2001, such regulations spread worldwide in a global effort to insulate the financial system from crime and to use financial regulation to combat terrorism.

Although the international CTF regime has proliferated and such regulations are now legally present in virtually every state,[1] little certainty exists as to their effectiveness. Aside from a few rogue states such as North Korea, Iran, and a handful of others, AML/CTF regulations have been adopted by states across the globe. Yet, even in states that are not rogue nations, the overall success of the international threat finance regime remains a mystery. One problem relates to the unknowable nature of how much illicit finance exists within the international banking system at any given time. Estimates consist largely of educated projections, but even approximated levels of laundered money and terrorist funds remain unknowable. Adding to this empirical challenge in assessing effectiveness is the uncertainty regarding the banks' level of commitment are to upholding the spirit of the AML/CTF regime. The incorporation of financial institutions operating under a profit motive into an extension of a state's security apparatus creates a number of conflicting interests. Unfortunately, to assess accurately the amount of illicit funds in the international financial system remains impossible, as does using this information as a metric for analyzing the CTF regime's effectiveness. However, some measures of effectiveness, such as enforcement outcomes once banks come under suspicion, can be tested.

The focus of this book is the outcome of enforcement efforts against banks that are suspected of and penalized for financing terrorism. This is a basic yet critical question that must be answered if any theory is to be developed regarding the determinants of success or failure on the part of AML/CTF regulations. Unlike the actual amount of illicit funds in the financial system and the true level of bank compliance, enforcement outcomes are observable and become analyzable once a bank comes under regulatory scrutiny for suspected terrorist financing. Furthermore, as the empirical record exhibits a range of outcomes for banks facing state pressures as the result of suspected terrorist financing, theories of enforcement outcomes become testable as a result.

This study tests the role of institutional linkages between a bank and its home state's regime as the determinant of enforcement outcomes against banks for suspected terrorist financing. If CTF regulations are widespread at the international level and have supposedly been adopted by most states around the globe, why are there such divergent degrees of enforcement? Why does a British bank in London face a level of enforcement for suspected terrorist financing similar to a Jordanian bank in Amman? Why does a bank in a rich tax haven like Luxembourg face closure for terrorist financing activities similar to those of a bank in a failed state such as Somalia?

This book answers these questions by positing an institutional theory of the linkage between a bank and its home state government as the determining factor in enforcement outcomes. Specifically, I hypothesize that an institutional link is necessary to block enforcement. My theory proposes that when a bank is institutionally linked to its home regime, it will escape attempted enforcement through active defences implemented by its home state.

The first chapter of this book discusses the emergence of financial regulations as a means of security against crime and terrorism, and pays particular attention to existing scholarly theories of regulatory compliance and effectiveness in this area in an effort to introduce readers to an otherwise obscure area of political economy. In this chapter, I also posit my theory of CTF enforcement outcomes and attempt to bridge the existing gaps in the literature by drawing upon theories of institutional change to explain this phenomenon. I hypothesize that in cases where a bank enjoys an institutional connection to its home state, the adoption of an AML/CTF regime will not overtake this existing relationship; and, by extension, any enforcement efforts deriving from these regulations will be blocked and misfire due to the overriding ability of the bank's home state.

This theory carries significant implications for the existing understanding of the international CTF regulatory regime, and indicates that the success or failure of these rules has less to do with regulatory harmonization than with the purview of the governments that must enforce them and the characteristics within national political economies. One possible implication of this theory is that regulatory outcomes may not be determined by a given regulatory regime's sophistication so much as by states pursuing their national interests. Certainly, if a state defends a bank that is institutionally linked to its ruling regime, the implication is that the bank is a means for the state to extend and fortify its own power.

The next three chapters test my theory using comparative case studies; and test for the causal role of institutional linkage in determining CTF enforcement outcomes against banks suspected of financing terrorism. This selection of cases controls for a number of rival explanations, such as the home state's membership in regulatory bodies, level of authoritarianism, the overall regulatory health of its economy, and rule of law. In accounting for institutional linkage, the case studies disaggregate this linkage by examining the bank's importance to the stability of its home state regime, as opposed to the bank's overall importance to the national economy.

For each positive case examined – that is, cases where banks enjoyed blocked enforcement – I first trace the origins of the bank in its home economy and establish its relationship to its home state regime. Next, I discuss to what degree the states in these positive cases have adopted the internationally driven AML/CTF institutions. In these positive cases of blocked enforcement, I demonstrate that the pre-existing relationships between bank and state perpetuate despite the adoption of fortified financial institutions. Last, I discuss the scandal phase as these banks came under regulatory pressure for suspected terrorist financing, and how enforcement was blocked by defensive measures taken by the bank's home state. Empirically, I examine the positive cases of the Bank of China in the PRC (chapter 2), Al Rajhi Bank in Saudi Arabia (chapter 3), and Turkey's Halk Bank (chapter 4).

An analysis of two negative cases serves as the focus of the final chapter. Here, I address potential rival causes such as authoritarianism, a state's status as a tax haven, and the effects of liberalization efforts, while further disproving the importance of de jure regulatory presence within a country for explaining enforcement outcomes. Each negative case exhibits banks where enforcement occurred and remained unblocked: Arab Bank in Jordan, and the Bank of Commerce and Credit International (BCCI). Finally, the book's conclusion recounts my theory and causal explanation, provides a brief review of my methods, and delineates the theory's implications for both policy and future research.

# I

# Enforcement Outcomes in Counterterrorist Financing

INTRODUCTION: ORIGINS AND EFFICACY OF THREAT FINANCE AND THE ANTI-MONEY LAUNDERING AND COUNTERTERRORIST FINANCING REGIME

When discussions of either international finance or terrorism arise, few observers connect the two phenomena conceptually. Scholars of terrorism who focus on financing have rarely left the metaphorical battlefield while producing a formidable corpus of non-theoretical, descriptive case studies of specific terrorist organizations and their funding. Conversely, scholars of international regulations who substantively address issues of terrorist financing have focused on institutional issues at the international level, such as regulatory harmonization and development. Despite the financial sector serving as the meeting point between CTF regulations and the terrorist groups themselves, little work has focused on banks as a unit of analysis, and little theory has developed as a result. This book bridges this gap in terrorist financing literature by focusing upon the bank as the primary unit of analysis and by testing the bank's connection with its home nation-state as the explanatory variable that explains when CTF enforcement measures are either blocked or carried out. Due to the esotericism of terrorist financing as a subject, this section first explains terrorist financing as a phenomenon, the growth of threat finance institutions, and the role of banks within them, while outlining the existing schism in the literature mentioned above.

While terrorism has increased over the past several decades, and the anti-money-laundering and counterterrorist finance (AML/CTF) regime has grown in conjunction with the threat it poses, the increase in depth and scope of threat finance regulation has occurred within an environment of overall deregulation and liberalization in international finance during the same era. It is worth establishing this frame of reference for the simple reason that it provides a jumping-off point for illustrating that state prerogative, rather than institutional harmony, has guided the growth of the AML/CTF regime worldwide. In other words, this spread of threat finance regulation grew out of states' concerns for traditional forms of security and power, rather than institutionally driven considerations. Beginning in the 1970s, banks and financial institutions helped the US and the UK catalyze the deregulation of the international financial sector; simultaneously, these same two states designed a system of financial regulation to safeguard their security interests against the threats of organized crime and terrorism.

Since the collapse of Bretton Woods in 1971, the international financial system has undergone a profound transformation in the direction of deregulation. International capital mobility and the banking sectors of major financial centres not only increased in magnitude and velocity, but did so in a manner that augmented the importance and role of the financial sector in the overall international economy. This deregulatory shift coincided with a steady fortification of the financial sphere in two important respects. First, despite the turn to deregulation and liberalization, banks themselves slowly became extensions of the state in efforts to monitor and combat the non-state threats of crime and terrorism. Second, both the deregulatory wave and the subsequent fortification of finance emerged out of the US and the UK before expanding worldwide in the post-Cold War era. Analyzing these trajectories will begin with the latter and then turn to the question of how banks became extensions of the state. Additionally, the concept of money laundering will be juxtaposed against terrorist financing.

The liberalization of international finance has often been portrayed as evidence of the erosion or ineptitude of state power when faced with the ostensible force of globalization and free capital flows. The collapse of Bretton Woods in 1971, and domestic turns toward neoliberalism in the United States and Britain in the following decades, foster this notion. Since the rescindment of Bretton Woods, the international economy has followed a trend of overall deregulation in the form of a removal of capital controls, privatization of state enterprises, and market liberalization. Scholars such as Susan Strange have theorized that the global economy essentially outgrew the authority of states, such that "markets are the masters of governments."[1] Regarding international finance in particular, Strange posited that whatever "international" regulatory system should emerge to deal with finance's incipient instability would have to be "national" in nature and that the United States, as the predominant power, would have to embrace its "national interest" in implementing international institutional controls on the financial system.[2] Also writing in the 1990s, Benjamin Cohen echoed Strange's assertion that "states have been thrown on the defensive" and that a "transcendent market" may indicate an "irreversible erosion of state authority" in light of such forces.[3] What neither Strange nor Cohen envisioned at the time was the emerging security dimension of international finance taking place over the same time span. For purposes here, the emergence of "fortified finance" is defined as the institutional and regulatory harnessing of financial institutions by states, the better to thwart the threats posed by terrorism, criminal organizations, and other states. Ironically, in the case of Strange's assertion, the United States *did* embrace its national interest in promoting a fortification of the financial sector. With the US leading the way, other states around the world followed suit.

## Competing Logics of Finance and National Security

The first problem with the propositions mentioned above by other scholars stems from overlooking the role that states played in fostering the new "globalized" financial order and the contingent national character of the firms within it. Helleiner notes that states, rather than passively accepting a new international financial structure, actually fostered the creation of the international neoliberal order by allowing greater freedoms to "market actors" and removing capital controls.[4] Helleiner notes that the US played a particularly important role in fostering this "new order" as it sought to preserve "policy autonomy" in the economic realm beginning in the 1970s.[5] American banks would benefit from domestic reforms at the same time, including the Federal Reserve's turn to monetarism under Volcker's chairmanship from 1979 into the 1980s.[6] Across the Atlantic, Britain underwent a similar shift with the coming to power of Margaret Thatcher in 1979 and the abolishment of exchange controls.[7] Helleiner mentions that London and New York, the premier banking centres, contended in liberalizing their regulatory structures to compete with one another.[8] Over the course of the 1980s, capital control liberalization would sweep the bulk of the industrialized world toward financial neoliberalism and offer "financial market operators" freedoms they had not yet seen in the postwar era up to that point.[9]

The shift to deregulation and liberalization in international finance spread at the behest of the Western powers and expanded with the end of the Cold War. This expanded liberalization has led some commentators to conceptualize international finance as nearly ungovernable, particularly in the wake of the financial crisis of 2008. Other scholarly observations assert that great powers and their firms remain central to the international financial sector. Drezner notes that in the realm of financial regulation, the production and dissemination of regulatory governance actually comprises a club good that is more the product of great powers than of international financial institutions.[10] Drezner's "great powers" are those governments who rule over large domestic markets; a "concert" of such powers, he notes, is a prerequisite for international governance.[11] In the case of "multinational firms," rather than functioning as unanchored economic mavericks in the global economy, Doremus et al. note that firms' domestic institutional and legal political economies influence their behaviours and operations.[12] In short, states continue to predominate in importance in international financial flows due to the embedding of firms in their national economies. Furthermore, it is the coordination among states that allows liberalized finance to flourish.

Despite the trend toward financial liberalization, both internationally and within major domestic financial sectors, security threats from non-state actors drove states to push for a fortification of finance in the form of new laws and regulations. Similar to the trajectory of liberalization, these new financial security regulations first formed in the US and the UK before spreading throughout the industrialized world, and then globally after 9/11. Additionally, as exchange-rate liberalization moved across states for the economic motivation of financial competitiveness, these fortified regulations would spread due to non-economic considerations of security.

It would be a mistake to conceive of the intersection between international finance, state security, and banking as a new phenomenon. The relationship between financial influence and security has existed since the first organized polities minted their own coinage to finance warfare. Yet, while the connection between the first two phenomena is relatively clear, the position of banks in this security matrix is more nebulous. In the lead-up to the First World War, notes Herbert Feis, "financial force" was often deployed as a method of building alliances, and "political calculation" often guided major bank lending between the European states, their respective allies, and their imperial holdings.[13] Indeed, Viner's account of the pre-First World War era in Europe concurs with Feis's assessment in that financial negotiations formed a part of "balance of power diplomacy."[14] Regarding the role played by bankers in this context, Viner asserts that financiers served as "passive" and often "unwilling instruments" of diplomats, given that bankers were primarily driven by profit motives rather than politics.[15] This early-twentieth-century observation on the banker's role in international politics echoed later findings by Kirshner that bankers are often risk-averse and supportive of "cautious national security strategies."[16] It must be noted that the pre-First World War era and its dynamics are far from apocryphal, particularly as the levels of capital mobility and integration before 1914 have much in common with those of the liberalized period that began in the 1980s.[17] In a similar parallel, the era from the 1970s to the present is one in which banks again serve as instruments of power politics – mechanisms by which states may advance their security interests. Contrary to the urbane conceptions of financial institutions that predominate in the subfield of political economy, banks are components of great power politics. Broadly speaking, discussions of such issues that intersect political economy and security fit into a phenomenological literature of "threat finance," a suite of concepts ranging from money laundering and corruption to terrorist financing, sanctions, and economic warfare. For the purposes of this book, threat finance refers to laws and institutions that states utilize to obtain a security goal.

The fortified finance regime that crystalized in the 1970s served the political purpose of linking states back to the US through financial mechanisms, despite the closing of the gold window. The US dollar's primacy as the international reserve currency, and the pricing of oil in dollars, virtually tied most of the world to the American financial sector despite the end of the Bretton Woods system. As fortified finance emerged, beginning with the US Bank Secrecy Act of 1970, American regulations designed to forestall tax evasion, money laundering, and eventually terrorism served as a new institutional mechanism for injecting power politics into the financial system.

Due to the primacy of the dollar in major bank transactions around the world, the adoption of the fortified finance regime by other states was virtually assured. Despite this "globalized" realm of international finance, with the US as its hub, national security concerns took on a new position of importance in the post-Bretton Woods world. Unlike in the gold-based system that predominated until 1971, banks and states in the emerging fortified financial system gradually adopted American and Western financial regulations to ensure their continued access to the US financial sector. Where gold-backed dollars had offered a buffer to states economically linked to the US, the new regulations became virtually mandatory for ensuring this connection. However, financial integration does not guarantee that states share mutual security interests. Indeed, this incongruity is pronounced given the near-universal adoption of the fortified finance regime and the divergent results achieved within it. Political affairs, and states pursuing their own interests, determine how this friction is negotiated.

## Terrorist Financing and the Fortified Finance Regulation

If, in the past, banking firms aided states in achieving security goals in the context of great power competition, they would be called on again to fight organized crime and terrorism. More specifically, states would effectively harness the financial sector to augment, via AML/CTF regulation, the generation of criminal evidence and intelligence. Furthermore, the use of financial regulation by great powers to combat these phenomena also corresponded to the evolving threats of terrorism and transnational crime as a whole.

Due in part to Hollywood movies and other popular conceptions of terrorist groups, many people perceive terrorist financing as existing outside of the formal financial sector. However, both terrorist financing and the closely related phenomenon of money laundering do involve otherwise ordinary banks and actors within the financial field. Since the regulatory institutions designed to curtail both phenomena are inextricably linked, it is worth noting where these phenomena align and diverge. Contrary to popular conceptions of terrorist organizations financing their operations through obscure channels separate from the mainstream economy, the financing of such groups relies, in part, on the formal banking sector for financial services. This is not to claim that terrorist financing is a straightforward or simple phenomenon. Rather, terrorist organizations operate as normal economic actors as much as they do as armed political groups. They raise funds through multiple means, which may include legal and illicit activities, and the transfer of non-cash instruments along with the formal movement of funds through mainstream financial channels. Timothy Wittig postulates that terrorist financing not only encapsulates both the "raising and spending" of money, but also the "capacity to move and store required resources" until needed by the group.[18] Wittig's conceptualization of terrorist financing extends beyond formal monetary vehicles, as the "transfer of value."[19]

For the purposes of this book, the definition of "terrorist funds" designates monies derived from licit or illicit sources and destined to facilitate violence against civilians perpetrated by a non-state actor for the achievement of a political purpose. Defined separately, "terrorist financing" is the provision, movement, transfer, integration, or obfuscation of the ownership or purpose of such funds.

The utility of disaggregating terrorist funds from terrorist financing is twofold. First, terrorist funds are often procured by the terrorists themselves through crime, fundraising, or state backing, even as counterterrorist financing (CTF) measures have been enacted to influence the behaviour of states and banks in order to prevent and monitor the movement of these funds in the international financial sector. Terrorist funds, legally obtained or not, are useless unless they can be effectively transferred, banked, and invested by actors into vehicles that can help meet an actor's financial needs. Here, "terrorist financing" does not mean the funds themselves but the handling and movement of such funds by banks and other financial actors.

The second reason for disaggregating terrorist funds from terrorist financing is to simplify the empirical reality that both the financing of terrorism and the efforts of law enforcement to curtail it often involve a series of actors whose efforts are concentric. For example, the entirety of a terrorist organization's financing often expands well beyond the activities of the organization itself, and may include banks operating under a profit motive, states seeking to strengthen their strategic position by backing various groups, corrupt regulators, and even international organizations and non-profits. Similarly, counterterrorist financing measures can include international organizations, coalitions of states, supranational entities, private transnational associations, national judiciaries, and various law enforcement and intelligence agencies.

Non-cash instruments, both licit and illicit, play a role in financing terrorism. Terrorist groups as a whole are remarkable in their ability to diversify their income, as funds from legitimate business activities, charitable donations, and sponsoring states often mix with revenues from an array of criminal activities ranging from human and drug trafficking to theft, blackmail, and fraud.[20] In theory, such portfolios may seem suspect given how inexpensive terrorist acts are to commit; however, the maintenance of a terrorist organization's support operations carries significant costs. The day-to-day expenses of a terrorist organization can include the provision of safe houses, recruitment, training, and propaganda operations as well as more mundane activities.[21] Indeed, rather than strictly cloak-and-dagger organizations driven by fanaticism, terrorist organizations exhibit a significant degree of banality in their financial operations and orientation. Additionally, a number of organizational, structural, and financial incentives exist that serve to drive terrorist groups to use the formal financial sector in conducting their financial affairs.

Terrorist groups are like any other organization that exhibits internal divisions over resource allocation and finances. Like any organization with limited resources and funds, a terrorist group can benefit from the efficiency and availability that banks provide. Shapiro notes that terrorist organizations face profound trade-offs that position managerial efficiency in the planning of violence and resource administration against considerations of operational security.[22] In other words, to ensure effective managerial control of a terrorist organization, terrorists must take steps to increase efficiency but necessarily increase their vulnerability in so doing. Shapiro and Siegel note that in terrorist organizations with more centralized hierarchies, leaders who seek efficiency will entrust tasks related to resource oversight to "middlemen" – mid-level managers who are often faced with the temptation to embezzle funds for private gain.[23] Contrary to the more grandiose or dangerous activities of terrorist combatants or others within their organizations, financial middlemen enjoy greater material payoffs, are seldom killed, and enjoy lower conviction rates upon arrest than their more martially oriented counterparts.[24] In short, contrary to popular misperceptions, the literature on terrorism indicates that groups have a number of rational incentives to turn to the formal financial system.

Terrorist groups obtain funds through a number of fronts, ranging from the self-funding opportunities afforded by outright fundraising through non-profit organizations and legitimate business enterprises to drug trafficking, crime, and soliciting state sponsorship. During the Cold War, terrorist funding derived predominantly from states. The

Soviet Union, for example, aided terrorist and guerilla groups in the Middle East, Europe, Africa, and Latin America.[25] While state-derived funding for terrorism has decreased since the 1990s, many of the self-funding techniques that terrorist organizations and criminals use today were learned by such groups under Soviet tutelage. For example, the Soviets actively advocated the use of narcotics trafficking by their non-state surrogates as a means of weakening the social fabric of the West, and most terrorist groups that arose under Soviet influence have made the drug trade a centrepiece of their operations.[26] The regulatory enlistment of financial firms for security in the United States began largely in response to the drug trade and has since expanded to combat the laundering of its illicit proceeds.

At the height of the Cold War in the 1960s, concerns arose in American regulatory circles about the production of criminal proceeds within the US and the role played by offshore tax havens.[27] Indeed, according to the gravity model developed by Walker in 1999 – one of the most reliable models for estimating illicit laundered finance to date – the United States serves as the top destination for such funds. Following the US are the Cayman Islands and then a combination of large, industrialized economies and offshore financial centres.[28] Estimates of illicit funds within US jurisdiction are by their nature impossible to quantify, though estimates have ranged from $100 billion to half a trillion dollars as of the early 2000s.[29] The Bank Secrecy Act (BSA) of 1970 initiated American efforts to combat the movement of such funds and imposed reporting requirements on US banks to file currency transaction reports (CTRs) with the US Department of the Treasury for transfers of funds in excess of $10,000.[30] It was the American BSA that sowed the seeds of future regulatory growth in fortified finance.

Within the US in particular, early fortified financial regulation expanded both the obligations imposed upon the private sector as well as the purview of state power related to the countering of illicit finance garnered by criminal activity. American counter-narcotics efforts in the 1980s and 1990s included the Money Laundering Control Act of 1986, the Annunzio-Wiley Anti-Money Laundering Act of 1992, the Money Laundering Suppression Act of 1994, and the Money Laundering and Financial Crimes Strategy Act of 1998.[31] Two elements of these legal and regulatory developments would later prove critical to CTF regulations. First, the Annunzio-Wiley Act mandated that banks file "suspicious activity reports" (SARs) with the

Department of the Treasury and that they monitor, surveil, and report financial behaviours that deviated from typical client profiles. Meanwhile, the 1998 law stipulated that both the Justice and Treasury departments improve linkages with the financial sector regarding AML efforts.[32]

Administratively, these US laws created the blueprint of a pipeline linking the government to the financial sector. Now mandated by law, banks and financial firms would collect information and intelligence relevant to criminal activity and channel it to the government. This institutional apparatus would be replicated in Europe and other Western countries before being widely adopted around the world after 2001. The US also augmented its fortification of the financial regime by opening violating banks to civil penalties. Under the Antiterrorism Act of 1990, US nationals who are victims of terrorism enjoy the option to sue banks suspected of financing terrorism.

By the late 1980s, regulatory anti-money-laundering efforts explicitly took on a security-related orientation with the Anti–Drug Abuse Act of 1988, which called for the creation of an "International Currency Control Agency" to institute and coordinate the collection of transaction reports around the world in an effort to combat money laundering.[33] While this agency never came to fruition, the Financial Action Task Force (FATF) – the premier AML/CTF institution to apply pressure to states and institute rules at the international level – was founded in 1989.[34]

That such US-led efforts emerged in the same time period as Reagan-era financial deregulation is not as surprising as it might seem, given that European states began implementing similar regulatory measures to counter terrorist threats west of the Iron Curtain. Italy, West Germany, and Spain all faced local leftist threats at the time in the form of the Red Brigades, the Baader-Meinhoff Gang, and Basque separatists, respectively. To counter these threats, Western European states began instituting AML laws in the mid-1980s under the auspices of the Council of Europe.[35] The United Kingdom implemented the Drug Trafficking Offences Act in 1986 (the same year as its US equivalent was implemented), effectively criminalizing money laundering in the British banking sector. Britain's plan to develop its own national CTF efforts also emerged during this period of financial deregulation – in this case as a means of counteracting, via its Terrorist Financing Unit, the financing program of the Irish Republican Army.[36] It is important to note that in the British context, such moves coincided with liberalization of the UK economy under Margaret Thatcher. If the 1980s ushered in an era in which Anglo-American banks could enjoy a freer reign, it also effectively deputized the banks as extensions of state security through AML and CTF regulations.

The liberal orientation of the Anglo-American political economic model is worth noting here, and is not inconsequential. If the global AML/CTF regime as it currently operates developed in these states with the intention to curtail banks from financing terrorism, the argument can be made that AML/CTF institutions were designed for banks operating in a liberalized financial sector.

The effectiveness of the international fortified finance regime is uncertain, as it is unclear how much illicit finance exists within the banking industry at any given time. However, financial regulations designed for banks within a liberal financial context are unlikely to work effectively in political economies with heavy state involvement or ownership in the banking industry. Yet, as liberalization has spread across the world (though with varying degrees of penetration) without fully disrupting the peculiarities of national political economies, so has the fortified finance regime. This is not merely a policy problem as to how well the fortified finance regime may function in locales far removed from where it originated. Rather, it is also an institutional problem concerning whether or not an imported institutional arrangement will effectively displace existing dynamics within a country's political economy.

These domestic changes within major financial centres, undertaken in the aim of countering the movement and integration of criminal funds in the financial system, were quickly followed by regulatory changes at the international level during the same timeframe. At the United Nations, the Vienna Convention of 1988 asserted that signatory states criminalize money from drug trafficking and enforce such measures through the tracking and freezing of proceeds from those activities.[37] At the bank level, the creation of the Financial Action Task Force and the imposition of rules by the Basel Committee on Banking Supervision would increase the pressure on financial firms to participate in the security arena. Additionally, while this participation would begin with AML efforts in the context of a "war on drugs," it would later prove instrumental in emplacing banks within counterterrorism efforts after 9/11.

At the heart of all AML/CTF institutions is the idea that banks know their customers. As such, "know your customer" (KYC) stipulations were introduced, mandating that banks have knowledge of the beneficial owner of each account and that they report suspicious activity and cooperate with police agencies in their respective jurisdictions. The effort to promote these customer due-diligence mandates was spearheaded by the US in 1986, when Federal Reserve chairman Paul Volcker pressed central bankers at the Bank for International Settlements.[38] Lending credence to Kirshner's finding that banks are loath to entertain notions of war, central bankers initially resisted such US efforts to fortify the financial sector against criminals and terrorists.[39] However, in 1988, the Basel Committee proposed mandates that banks certify the legitimacy of their customers' financial activity.[40] These international mandates effectively hybridized the Anglo-American anti-money-laundering model, ironically, with that of Switzerland by combining the "data gathering" component of the former with the "deep customer knowledge" approach of the latter.[41] In practice, banks are mandated as actors to surveil and discover nefarious activity on the part of criminals and terrorists. Once reported, the state then follows through with further investigations and, potentially, arrests and prosecutions. In theory, all countries that adopted the fortified finance regime follow this model of state-bank cooperation for reasons of security.

The founding of the FATF in 1989 would prove a turning point, at the level of international institutions, in fortifying the financial landscape. Established as a result of American and French pressure, the body published a list of "Forty Recommendations," outlining expected standards for international cooperation among member states. These recommendations, initially instituted in the context of the war on drugs, included creating or tasking national regulatory bodies as financial intelligence units (FIUs) to serve as go-betweens between private banks and national police forces or judicial agencies. Under such mechanisms, private banks (and later insurance firms, casinos, gold and diamond dealers, etc.) are tasked with gathering information on customers for the purpose of establishing a customer's "normal" behaviour, which can then be used to detect illicit activity.[42] In regard to the aforementioned French pressure, during the 1990s France was the primary target of Al-Qaeda for its involvement in assisting North African governments against the terrorist group.[43]

Structurally, the FIU is the central link for international coordination against money laundering and terrorist financing, and generally falls into four primary types. While all FIUs serve as a state's focal point for collecting data from financial firms and pursuing investigations of suspicious activity, they differ in terms of national importance depending upon where the FIU body is situated within the state bureaucracy. According to the International Monetary Fund, an FIU can be based in administrative functions, law enforcement, or the judiciary, or may exist as a hybrid of all three.[44] The administrative type is often found in finance ministries or central banks, and is the kind favoured by the private sector.[45] In contrast, the law enforcement FIU type is not only a regulator but also functions a law enforcement agency in its own right.[46] For example, the American Financial Crimes Enforcement Network (FinCEN) is administrative in nature and embedded in the Department of the Treasury, while the UK's National Criminal Intelligence Service is a law enforcement body. Worldwide, there are 152 states with FIUs, which coordinate the collection and sharing of financial intelligence to thwart money laundering and terrorist financing.[47]

Combined, the implementation of KYC standards for the financial sector and the implantation of state agencies to connect the private sector with the courts, the police, and intelligence agencies laid the groundwork for the fortification of the financial sector. After 2001, these institutions expanded around the world while also deepening their mandates beyond crime to include terrorism. As state sponsorship of terrorism around the world has decreased in scope, terrorists, in seeking greater levels of independent revenue and efficiency, have turned to crime as a means of augmenting funds received in the form of donations and what state backing remains in the twenty-first century.[48] As a result of this shift, banks became an even greater focal point for terrorists seeking to comingle illicit and legally obtained funds for the propagation of terrorist attacks and organizational capability.[49] This enlisting of banks for purposes of security, though seemingly novel, is neither new nor harmonious inasmuch as it pertains to the relationships between states and banks. While this tension and the divergence in terms of interests and outcomes between banks and states will be further explored in the theoretical section below, the incorporation of CTF measures into the overall institutional effort to combat illicit finance as it relates to terrorism must first be explored.

In practice, the banking system operates as a system of regulation in which banks and states cooperate in observing account activity for suspicious behaviour. Banks operate their own FIUs, which scrutinize account activity and file suspicious activity reports and currency transaction reports, as required, with another FIU operated by the government. While CTRs are mandated at specific currency amounts, SARs are more discretionary. For instance, if a bank account holder's spending or transactions suddenly begin to exhibit behaviour that deviates from the holder's typical activity or involves a high-risk jurisdiction, a compliance officer in the bank's FIU may choose to file a SAR to the government. Once filed, if the government's FIU – or FinCEN, in the case of the US – deems it worth further investigation, relevant law enforcement agencies then become involved. In sum, banks and governments cooperate in surveilling the financial system for malfeasance. In essence, compliance officers in banks serve a national security function despite their position in the financial sector.

The phenomena of money laundering and terrorist financing overlap both empirically and theoretically, despite their crucial differences. Both terrorist financing and non-political criminal proceeds are by their nature intended to be secret and withheld from public eye. In order to achieve such secrecy, terrorist and criminal funds share similar trajectories, as actors endeavour to obfuscate the true ownership of such funds while also attempting to integrate much of them into the normal economy. However, terrorist funds differ conceptually from criminal funds in two important respects. First, terrorist funds are often legally obtained through donations and charities, and are channelled only to terrorist activity.[50] Second, smaller amounts of terrorist funds obtained illegally through crime may never need to enter the financial sector at all if they are immediately directed toward terrorism, thereby negating the need to launder money in the first place.[51]

Conceptually, the movement of non-political criminal funds into the economy has been called "money laundering," while terrorist financing is *both* money laundering and "money dirtying," since terrorist funds directed toward an illegal activity may derive from a mix of legal and illegal sources. Anne Clunan conceptualizes terrorist financing as carrying "pre-crime" and "post-crime" components, such that the former is often comprised of legally derived funds that require no laundering, while the funds derived from criminal activity and destined for actual operations are more akin to traditional money laundering.[52] Grasping the difference between these two types of funds is critical to understanding the expansion of pre-existing anti-money-laundering efforts into strategies designed to counter the funding of terrorism. While AML goals are prohibitive in their aim to deprive criminals from enjoying the financial benefits of crime, preventing

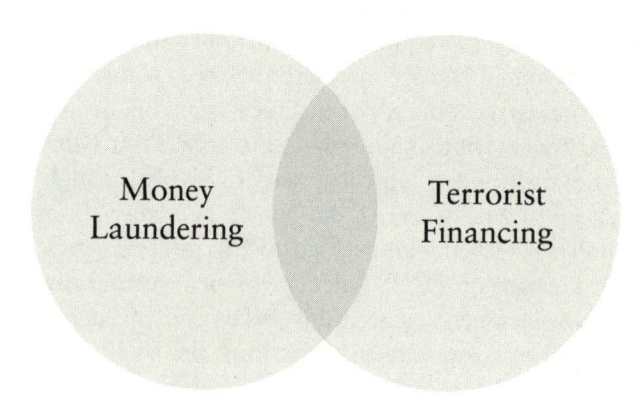

Figure 1.1 Phenomena of money laundering and terrorist financing.

terrorist activity is necessarily forward-looking and often warrants greater political consideration and proactivity on the part of states.

Prior to 9/11, and due in part to the older, historically predominant trend of terrorist groups operating with state backing, most countries used economic sanctions rather than financial regulation to parry the funding of terrorism.[53] Many well-known cases of economic sanctions, such as those against Iran, Libya, and other states, were designed largely to thwart terrorist activity. It was only when governments moved to address terrorist organizations' self-funding operations, as well as the operations of criminal organizations, that financial regulation began to be added to states' geopolitical arsenals to combat threats from non-state actors. International cooperation to counter terrorist financing began increasing in the 1990s, not under the auspices of the FATF but rather under the United Nations and its International Convention for the Suppression of the Financing of Terrorism (1999), as well as UN Security Council resolution 1267, which specifically targeted Al-Qaeda in Afghanistan.[54]

The 2001 attacks shifted the concerns of both international AML institutions and great powers from a crime-centric approach to one that fused pre-existing efforts to stop money laundering with a new approach designed to counter terrorism. At the international level, both the UN and the FATF extended new stipulations and regulations. The UN Security Council passed resolution 1373 just days after the 9/11 attacks thereby creating the Counter-Terrorism Committee, which requires states to seize and freeze the assets of terrorist groups within their jurisdictions and share information with other states.[55]

For the FATF's part, the organization published nine new special recommendations for states to counter terrorist financing, thus adding to its forty earlier recommendations against money laundering. At the national level, more than 100 countries passed laws to counter money laundering and terrorist financing, while 154 ratified the 1999 UN Convention for the Suppression of the Financing of Terrorism.[56] Largely through "naming and shaming" pressures on the part of the FATF, even tax havens have adopted AML and CTF statutes.[57] Switzerland, Luxembourg, and the Channel Islands, all notorious tax havens known for their bank-secrecy laws, nonetheless increased their regulatory rigour to combat the laundering of drug proceeds.[58] Other tax havens, such as the Cayman Islands and Jersey, complied with FATF recommendations by instituting the guidelines into law.[59]

If the 2001 terrorist attacks on the United States led to a diffusion of fortified financial regulation across with world (with the exception of a few rogue states), why do divergent enforcement outcomes in regard to terrorist financing continue to occur? Furthermore, in the post-2001 era, why do some banks enjoy protection from enforcement measures while others do not? Despite the nearly universal de jure presence of fortified financial regulation, scholars and practitioners alike decry the ineffectiveness of these widespread regulations. Observing the ubiquity of the AML/CTF regime around the world gives the impression that such regulations are effective by their very presence. Yet, scholarship of the same regulatory regime offers a number of diagnoses as to why they are inefficient at curtailing terrorism.

At the policy level, scholars such as Ibrahim Warde argue that the general US approach to combatting threat finance is divorced from the overall sociopolitical trends in which terrorist financing takes place.[60] More specifically, Warde argues that approaching the problem of terrorist financing from the "supply side" of terrorist funds, rather than addressing the demand, or support, that the terrorist organization enjoys, is the crux of CTF inefficacy.[61] Another issue raised by Warde, and echoed by Wittig, is the importance of the cultural context in which individuals conduct their financial affairs, and the need for CTF efforts to take such economic nuance into account.[62] Although critical scholars focus mostly on the US in the post-2001 era of CTF regulations and policy, the themes of power politics and domestic political will arise in other critiques of the overall institutional regime's ineffectiveness.

Warde and Wittig both note that formal banks are often not present or active in local economies in which terrorism exists. However, Juan

Zarate, former Assistant Secretary of the US Treasury for Terrorist Financing, notes that a number of banks were involved in facilitating financing for terrorist groups or sanctioned state sponsors of terrorism.[63] While Zarate views terrorist financing in the context of a state's overall acumen and ability to wage financial warfare, Gurule characterizes CTF efforts as a "dismal failure" in the sense of the legal regime's general inability to combat the phenomenon.[64] Gurule notes that criminal prosecutions against terrorist financiers in the US have been lacking, while asset freezes worldwide declined over the course of the 2000s.[65] In short, states are not following through on the necessary enforcement measures despite the widespread de jure presence of the threat finance regime across multiple jurisdictions. Sharman argues that states, even those without financial sectors,[66] adopted costly AML/CTF regulations from outside not to combat money laundering and terrorist financing so much as due to socially coercive pressures from outside powers.[67]

The literature on terrorist financing clearly indicates that state power matters not only in how the international AML/CTF regime emerged and spread but also to explain why the regulatory institutions are ineffective in curtailing terrorist financing. However, as the costly adoption of AML/CTF regulations has taken place across the majority of states, enforcement outcomes have nonetheless varied widely despite the presence of these regulations. In short, the international regulations designed to curtail threat finance are not only ineffective in precluding the entry of terrorist funds into the banking system, but the presence and de jure adoption of the AML/CTF regime is not enough by itself to ensure enforcement. The substantive question then remains as to what precludes enforcement from occurring, and why some banks get away with suspected terrorist financing while others are forcibly closed or fined as a result.

## THEORY

One of the challenges that studies of terrorist financing have faced is the conceptual separation of states, banks, and terrorist financiers. Rather than conceive of these three types of actors as inhabiting separate environments, my research includes them not as isolated entities so much as intimately connected actors within the same political and economic universe. States often do have close connections to their respective financial sectors or to specific banks. Similarly, terrorist financiers are not simply following the Hollywood cliché of carrying pallets of cash to and from remote locales so much as they are seeking financial efficiency. In recruiting banks and the finance industry as tools for fighting terrorism, states have effectively made banks the meeting point between governments, terrorist groups, and the financial sector as a whole. For this reason, it is critical to fill the existing void in the literature and focus on banks as a unit of analysis.

A second challenge in the literature of terrorist financing is the dearth of developed theory about the phenomenon that intersects the fields of comparative politics and international relations. Research on terrorist financing largely falls into three categories. The first category is descriptive case studies of specific groups, studies with little theoretical value outside of specific counterterrorism policies devoted to individual groups. The second encompasses critical studies of American efforts to develop legal frameworks devoted to countering terrorism and money laundering. The third category is comprised of institutional research-focused regulatory harmonization. Frustratingly, these literatures rarely address each other and offer little generalizable theory. In short, they do not congeal into a cohesive substantive focus. My research attempts to rectify this paucity and discord.

Unlike prior studies, my research conceptualizes states, terrorist financiers, and banks as cohabitants of the same institutional universe at the level of the national political economy. Furthermore, I posit a generalizable theory that transcends the aforementioned scholarly discord and asserts that institutional linkages between states and banks determine the process of enforcement outcomes.

## HYPOTHESIS

I hypothesize that a bank's institutional linkage to its home state enables the blocking of enforcement. Other factors may block enforcement once a bank comes under regulatory scrutiny for terrorist financing, but state-bank linkage remains a common structural institutional arrangement in national political economies around the world. Surely, banks may deflect enforcement through their own legal channels and without short-circuiting the regulatory regime. However, states ultimately hold the prerogative to acquiesce to international pressure, import regulatory institutions, determine to what degree they are followed and, ultimately, decide how to enforce them.

Stated simply, I hypothesize that the presence of an institutional linkage as the independent variable ($x$) will lead to an outcome of blocked regulatory enforcement ($y$). If an institutional linkage between a state and a bank is present, then CTF regulatory enforcement against that bank will be blocked. Conversely, if there is no linkage (~x), then enforcement will not be blocked once the bank is targeted (~y). In other words, enforcement fails if such a link is present.

Falsifying this conditional hypothesis requires testing to confirm that successful enforcement occurs in cases where a bank has institutional linkage with its state. For these cases, a chapter examining negative cases is employed drawing upon the same historical tracing of the independence of the banks in question. If enforcement ~y takes place in the presence of linkage x, then the state should not take up defensive measures in order to protect the bank. Additionally, it is imperative to demonstrate how institutional linkage x leads to blocked enforcement y. The rationale behind the hypothesis is simple in that it posits that when a bank is connected to a state, the state has a national interest in protecting it from a legal or geopolitical attack.

Falsifying and proving the role of institutional linkage in blocking enforcement requires first establishing that an institutional linkage is present and then demonstrating how that linkage leads to blocked enforcement. Establishing existing linkages and blocked enforcement between the targeted bank and its state requires scrutinizing the history of the bank and its role in the country's political economy. To establish such a history requires tracing the development of the bank in question and its relationship with its home government before, during, and after the country's importation of CTF regulations. Tracing this relationship between bank and state must account for any critical junctures separating the two, and determine whether the linkage was present at the time of the enforcement attempt.

Causally, I argue that a state's adoption of the regulatory regime does not fundamentally alter existing institutional relationships between the state and the bank or banks to which it is linked. If anything, the architecture of the regulatory regime, and its pipelines for information collection and surveillance between financial institutions and the government, actually *strengthen* existing linkages between the two actors. Then, once a bank comes under regulatory scrutiny, its home state's government and bureaucracies will actively negate enforcement attempts.

Regarding the diffusion and adoption of threat finance institutions, previous research clearly indicates that state power is critical in guiding the propagation of AML/CTF regulatory institutions around the world. The security interests of countries with major financial centres in the US and Europe provided the original impetus for CTF institutions. In turn, these regulations spread around the world and were copied by the majority of states at the national level. These multiple international mechanisms facilitate cooperation among states, such as UN conventions and resolutions, and comprise, together with the actions of the FATF, extensions of power by influential states.[68] Even the ability of many offshore tax havens to slither around AML statutes and institute lax enforcement is largely the result of such havens enjoying the backing of former colonial powers such as France and the UK, who in turn pressure international bodies against attempting to coerce their offshore surrogates.[69]

The puzzle, then, is why certain banks escape enforcement by the states in which they are embedded, and even in cases where these home states have adopted CTF institutions from abroad and integrated them into the national regulatory regime. Every country has its unique political economy, despite widespread notions of a single, globalized world. In essence, national characteristics matter. Karl Polanyi theorized long ago that economies remain "embedded" in their unique cultural environments.[70] Drawing from Polanyi's observation, it is only sensible that some critical link between a bank and its state should play a role in how CTF regulations fail amid certain relationship dynamics. This question is one of institutional theory as much as a state's security concerns and power politics. The findings of Warde, Sharman, and Wittig all portray the image of a hopeless situation with ever-increasing layers of CTF regulations, poorly crafted to local economic realities, piling upon pre-existing ones with ever-diminishing returns in stopping terrorist financing. However, the mystery as to why banks sometimes suffer and sometimes escape enforcement for suspected terrorist financing has not been explored.

In answering this question, I argue that when a bank exhibits an institutional linkage to their home state, incoming CTF institutions do not supersede these pre-existing connections. As a result, once the CTF regime targets that bank for financing terrorism, the home state will take measures to block the enforcement warranted by the CTF institutions, and these institutions will then misfire. More succinctly, when a bank is linked to its home state, enforcement attempts against it will be blocked by that state.

The development and spread of CTF institutions around the world over the past several decades illustrate profound institutional change in realm of financial regulations and of fortified finance in general.

Fortified finance developed and emerged first in major industrialized economies with formidable financial centres before being spread worldwide. At this time, however, the vast majority of states already had existing financial systems, complete with unique institutional arrangements suited to their national political economies. Pre-existing relationships between banks and their home states, if critical to that nation's political economy and regime stability, are not easily displaced by fortified financial regulations imported from abroad. In determining the outcomes of CTF enforcement, the degree of continuity or change within these pre-existing institutional arrangements between banks and their home states holds the key. If incoming CTF institutions are integrated only partially into existing institutional arrangements between banks and their home states, rather than transforming those arrangements, they will not be effective in penalizing banks that finance terrorism.

Literature on CTF regulations has neglected questions of institutional change at the domestic level in states with banks that finance terror, as well as questions as to enforcement outcomes. This neglect stems in large part from the ontological assumptions particular to the subfield of international political economy; namely, treating the international political economy as a single, cohesive system rather than as an aggregation of interactions between separate countries with their own, unique political economies. Indeed, the institutional matrix of regulations designed to keep banks from financing is "global" in its de jure intention. With the majority of states instituting financial intelligence units to monitor and enforce CTF compliance at the national level, the coordination of these efforts through international organizations like the Egmont Group and the FATF, the formation of regional compliance bodies, and coordination at the UN, the EU, and elsewhere, the international fortified finance regime is indeed global. However, in addition to such *global* institutional diffusion and adoption, the substantive area of the AML/CTF regime is also one of *national* security.

In historical terms, the fortified finance regime is new at the international level. In contrast, domestic political economies often contain old structural arrangements that predate the arrival of these regulations by many decades. Such pre-existing arrangements are not easily displaced once a state's economy has developed around specific arrangements (which indeed may have originated with the state's development). Just as a "global" political economy does not dissolve distinct national economic characteristics, it is doubtful that the fortified finance regime will dislodge relationships between states and the banks that are vital to them.

While fortified finance may predominate over the global financial system, the usefulness of these regulations is highly suspect. First, the fortified finance regime originated as a means of curtailing the wealth of apolitical criminal organizations. Unlike terrorist groups, the growth of profit-seeking criminal organizations is not often in the security interest of any state. In contrast, terrorism is elementally political, and states may support or combat such groups as befits their security interests. Yet, the post-2001 "globalization" of the fortified finance regime's CTF component functions on the assumption that states have no interest in supporting terrorist groups, rather in the same way that they are assumed to have no inherent interest in supporting criminal organizations. In short, the international CTF regime functions upon the assumption that states have a unified interest in curtailing terrorists from raising funds and banks from holding and transmitting them.

Following the Cold War, international relations research exhibited a new optimism as to the usefulness of institutions and their ability to facilitate cooperation and peace. Contrary to the assertions of scholars such as Francis Fukuyama,[71] however, the anticipated "global" world, characterized by cooperation, democracy, and capitalism, did not arrive. Certainly, the worldwide spread of neoliberalism lends itself to the notion of a highly integrated international financial system. In parallel, the rise and spread around the world of the post-2001 CTF regime offers the appearance of states acting decisively to make international finance safe from terrorism. However, states pursuing their own security and interests continue to characterize this international system well into the new millennium, and there is no reason to think that banks or other financial institutions are somehow immune to such pursuits.

In international relations, prior research by scholars and practitioners hammers home the notion that state power predominates over cooperative impulses among states. Realist scholars have long cast doubt on the efficacy of international institutions, with some such as Mearsheimer asserting that such institutions have no "independent effect" on state action and have import only "on the margins."[72] Historically, states in pursuit of their own interests have at times supported terrorist groups. By extension, there is no reason to believe that states will not support their local banks if threatened by regulatory moves from abroad. If a casual glance at the international threat finance regime shows a deep and unified regulatory effort to curtail terrorist financing, such a view glosses over differing goals of state security.

If states have diverging security interests, they also have different political economies. While the threat finance regime has spread de jure across the majority of states, and states have implemented FIUs and other mechanisms to curtail terrorist financing, the international regime lacks the flexibility to work effectively in unique political economic conditions at the national and local levels. Warde argues that in many states, particularly those in predominantly rural locales such as Afghanistan and parts of the Middle East and Africa, banks and other financial institutions are uniquely enmeshed within unique social, religious, and cultural contexts to which "US-style paperwork" is ill suited.[73] Indeed, Sharman notes that in the rush to jump on board with the international fortified finance regime, over 180 states adopted a "standard set" of policies and regulations in an effort to comply with dominant states in the aim of curtailing money laundering and terrorist financing.[74] In noting the mimetic approach that states have taken in adopting this fortified finance regime, together with the fact that this regime can vary from awkward to alien in terms of how it functions within local and national political economies, threat finance scholars uncovered a second macro-level problem facing international CTF institutions.

If the international CTF regime's first fundamental flaw stems from its outright rejection of the notion that states pursue their own security interests and thus that there is no unified global interest in curtailing terrorist financing, the second derives from its institutional design. The current AML/CTF regime originated and developed in states with advanced political economies characterized by financial liberalization throughout the period during which the regime emerged. Certainly, states such as Afghanistan, Somalia, and others cannot simply import financial regulations designed for banks in the West. However, this observation underscores a larger institutional problem in political economy; namely, that regulations from advanced liberal market economies are often ill-suited to institutional arrangements in political economies elsewhere.

If the international AML/CTF regime has been virtually uniform worldwide since the aftermath of 9/11, the political economic context in which it was developed has not. During the 1990s and into the 2000s, the situation of the post-Cold War international economy prompted debates about whether the distinct political economic models of the postwar era were "converging" toward a dominant model characterized by liberalized financial sectors. Questions arose as to whether longstanding institutional frameworks that comprised distinct national political economic models would persist in their unique differences.[75] More specifically, scholars questioned whether or not political economies dominated by bank-based financing would persist in an era in which capital markets played an increasing role.

Scholarship on comparative political economies indicates that convergence across models was elusive.[76] Berger argues that when institutional convergence does not take place, pre-existing institutions survive as the result of states or influential interest groups exerting "extramarket reinforcement" to protect or prolong the tenure of unique social and political economic configurations.[77] Indeed, in regard to external pressures on national political economies to converge, uniqueness will persist in order that "space for political vision and choice" remains.[78] While research on the persisting diversity in national political economies has centred mostly on advanced industrialized states, the principle is transferable to less developed countries and their economies.

The persistence of singular institutional configurations within national political economies relates to the question of why certain banks escape enforcement for financing terrorism. In piecing together any puzzle, it is first necessary to define the edges, or frame, before revealing the images at the centre. We know that banks are often the tools of states in pursuing their geopolitical objectives,[79] even though, as divined by Kirshner's research on banks and war, financial institutions are loath to be used in this way.[80] As political economies based upon bank financing have retained this characteristic despite market pressures to converge, we also know that the CTF regime that spread after 9/11 was adopted in a manner ill-suited to local conditions[81] and in a mimetic fashion whereby regulations were largely copied from existing rules prevalent in the developed liberal market economy of the United States.[82]

If CTF regulations were originally designed for financial sectors with a liberal market orientation, and if such regulations were adopted into political economies where banks are institutionally linked to states – where they serve as tools of those states while being shielded from market pressures – then we should assume that these banks will likewise be protected by those states when they finance terrorism. My theory is straightforward in that banks that are vitally linked to their home states will be protected once such banks come under regulatory scrutiny, and that CTF regulations will misfire as a result.

## VARIABLES AND CONCEPTUALIZATION

Though less common in the West, where the fortified finance regime developed, many financial institutions elsewhere in the world enjoy long-held relationships with the country in which they are embedded. For purposes of this book, an institutional linkage between banks and their home states is defined as a formal, structural relationship between a financial institution and the national government in whose political economy it is embedded. The reasons for such a linkage may include the bank serving as a coalition binder for the ruling regime, the state serving as the bank's predominant stakeholder, or deep career linkages between state and bank.

If a bank enjoys a relationship with its home state in the form of an institutional linkage, certain observable indicators will illustrate its presence. In the event that a state is a primary stakeholder in a given bank, such a bank may exhibit outright state ownership or cater to the state as its premier client and account holder. Similarly, if a state is the bank's premier stakeholder, that bank may operate as the primary lender for specific sectors of the economy in which the state is actively involved. Certain areas of business such as infrastructure, major corporate lending, energy investment, or the financing of state affairs (e.g., arms deals with other states or the dispensing of economic aid abroad) are liable to link a bank institutionally to its home state.

Depending upon the intimacy and proximity between a state's government and financial sector, a bank can exhibit institutional linkages to its state in the form of elite career ties. Namely, mid- and high-ranking corporate officers from the banking industry may spend one part of their career in the financial sector and another in the regulatory realm. Professional acumen in the regulatory realm and the financial world is often highly transferable given the need for banks to follow certain regulatory procedures and protocols, while officials in finance ministries and other governmental bodies are likely to enjoy greater pay and benefits in the corporate sector. Similarly, financial officers may easily traverse the bank-state divide through political appointments at higher levels as such elites, regardless of immediate employment, are likely to have matriculated from similar schools of higher learning.

If a bank as a corporate entity displays deep ties with its home state, that bank may operate as a coalition binder for a ruling party or cadre. If a country is at least semi-democratic, a bank may serve as a primary lender for a political party's electoral constituency. Similarly, authoritarian regimes reliant upon certain domestic interest groups, be they a primary ethnic or religious affiliation, the military, or a specific industry, may have key societal supporters who rely in turn upon specific banks in the country's economy. If a ruling government has such a key constituency linked in this manner to a certain bank, or maintains a set of financial institutions for purposes of lending or patronage running from the state to different parts of the populace, such linkages I conceptualize as coalition binders.

While I treat institutional linkage as a dichotomous variable, a spectrum of linkages may in fact exist that connect a bank to its home state in practice. One bank may be outright owned and operated entirely by the state through a specific bureaucracy or state-owned fund, while another linkage may be grounded in close personal relationships between a ruler and a specific constituency vital to that ruler's political survival. In many of the Arab monarchies, for example, tribal and familial ties can prove critical to a government's ability to function, even as no connection may be readily visible to the observer unfamiliar with the region. Developing a typology of linkages and testing them more closely is beyond the scope of this book, but provides fertile ground for future research.

Similarly, levels of privatization vary between the banks analyzed in this book. The Bank of China and Halk Bank both experienced varying degrees of privatization at different periods of their existence, despite state linkages remaining strong throughout the banks' existence. In the cases of Turkey and China, the banks never truly "privatized" in the Western sense of allowing for full private ownership and control. If anything, each bank simply allowed for infusions of private investment without an accompanying cession of governmental power.

Here it is worth distinguishing between what I conceptualize as an institutional linkage from corruption. Unlike a formalized structural relationship, corruption implies a circumvention of an established process or a perversion of an established set of rules. Studies of corruption often suffer for a lack of clear definition, although many acknowledge the use of public funds for private benefit. Shleifer and Vishny conceptualize corruption as "the sale by government officials of government property for personal gain."[83] Parallel definitions of

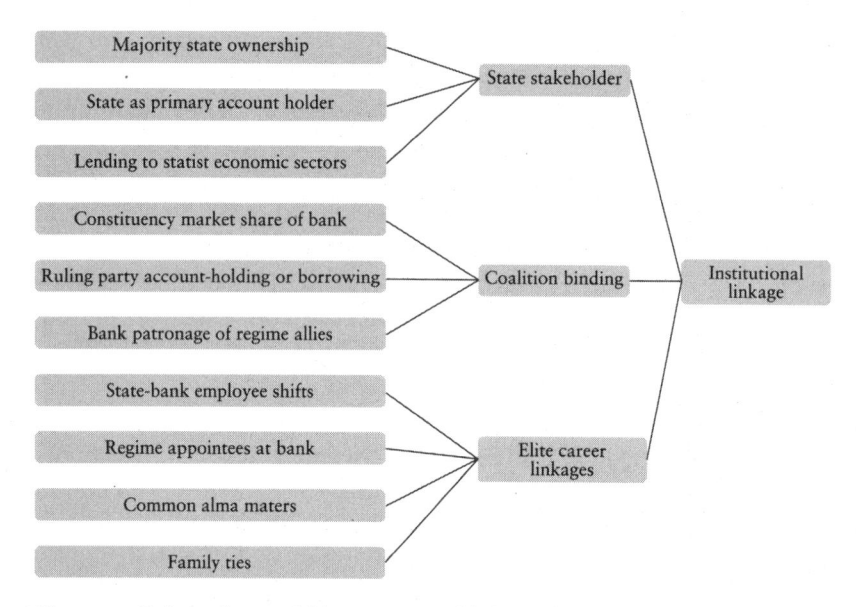

Figure 1.2 Independent variable: institutional linkage.

corruption abound, such as Svensson's assertion that corruption consists of "the misuse of public office for private gain" by which some "legal standard" is violated.[84] Shelley uses Transparency International's definition of corruption – that it comprises "the abuse of entrusted power for private gain" – but also acknowledges that a sole focus on corruption within the state overlooks areas where divisions between "state officeholders and private business" are scant at best.[85] With the circumvention of law or process in the form of bribery offering the clearest standard of measure, corruption alone cannot explain cases of regulatory misfire against terrorist financing.

Longstanding relationships between banks and their home states, some of which may date back decades into the state's formation, can hardly be considered "corrupt" in their interactions simply because they do not adhere to international norms. Corruption does not exist where such activities that would appear as corrupt to an outside onlooker are so ingrained as to comprise standard procedure or follow an established hierarchy. For an outside comparison, what may appear to be an illicit affair between two adults, due to the absence of a marriage certificate, cannot be considered to be such when the pairing is actually a common law marriage without a paper trail. Similarly, a state cannot be considered corrupt when it takes active diplomatic measures to protect a bank that it owns when it comes under foreign scrutiny. Rather, such state action is simply a government protecting its national interest and ensuring regime survival. Ultimately, as in the cases of Turkey and China, the state tasked with policing banks refused to police its own assets. Similarly, in the case of Saudi Arabia, Al Rajhi Bank can hardly be considered corrupt when government and business relationships are embedded in tribal ties and religious norms. While it may prove normatively reassuring to assert that the failures of governments to police their own assets and interests is simple corruption, the fact of the matter is that states as arbiters and enforcers of law ultimately do as they please.

While my causal variable for the misfire of a regulatory regime is institutional linkage between a bank and its home state, my dependent variable is the actual blockage of such enforcement efforts. Conceptually, "blocked enforcement" can manifest in the form of a home state's veto of the enforcement process, or its active deflection of enforcement efforts. A bank taking measures to defend itself, or altering its behaviour under pressure from an agreement of deferred prosecution, does not constitute evidence of blocked enforcement. Vetoes of enforcement and deflection are defences undertaken by a state for the purpose of defending a bank, and each measure has a number of potential observable indicators. A state's veto of the enforcement process is only possible at the *national* level, where a regime may engage in activities ranging from bureaucratic reshuffling and judicial interference to outright political intimidation of various domestic actors, pardons of suspected officials, or undermining external enforcement through state-backed financial support to the bank in question. In contrast, deflection implies action at the *international* level, where a bank's home regime may use organs of state to influence enforcement efforts abroad, at their source. If deflection is taking place, a state may rely on diplomatic means, intelligence agencies, or the threat of sanction as a means to dissuade potential enforcers from acting against a given bank.

## CASES AND METHOD

The unit of analysis for this study is the bank. As noted above, banks are where regulations, the financial system, and terrorist groups converge. These are case studies of banks within the unique political economies of the states in which they are embedded, and banks that

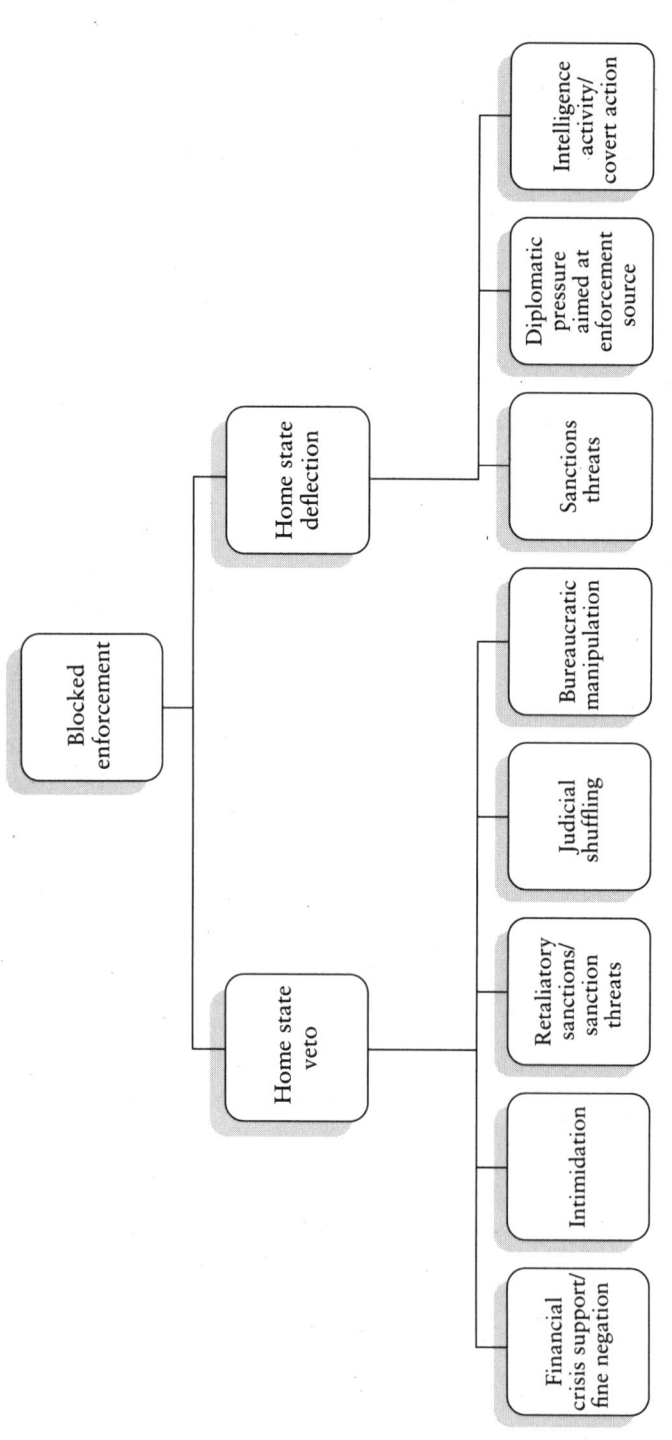

Figure 1.3 Dependent variable: enforcement blockage.

came under regulatory scrutiny for financing terrorism. In this regard, the unit of analysis incorporates the ensuing banking scandal that emerges once the bank is targeted, and examines how the institutional relationship between the state and its terrorist bank fares once this occurs.

While the true case universe of banks that finance terrorism cannot be known empirically, the universe of cases in which banks are caught or have been investigated for financing terrorism can be studied and analyzed. Theoretically, one of the main questions that this study seeks to address is why, in the face of broadening and deepening AML/CTF regulation around the globe, banks experience such divergent outcomes once these regulations are triggered. Due to the nature of the question, the universe of potential cases is temporally limited by the scope and condition of these regulations – not only their basic existence but also their spread and adoption by states that have banks that finance terror. Since such regulation has spread seriously and globally only during the past several decades, this universe of cases is fairly small and relatively new.

As noted above, the true population of banks that finance terrorism cannot be known. Dishonest banks tend not to profusely advertise their crimes to public scrutiny. However, the universe of banks that have come to public scrutiny for financing international terrorism is not only known and growing, but also quite dispersed around the globe. Fortunately, for two purposes, this spatial dispersion of cases, which ranges from rich OECD economies to failed states and spans multiple continents, offers greater leverage in controlling for variables related to economic development, political systems, and culture.

## RIVAL HYPOTHESES AND CASE CODING

Table 1.1 outlines a list of major terrorist financing cases in which banks have come under regulatory scrutiny. As noted in the table, the countries involved include industrialized economies, failed states, democracies, authoritarian regimes, and offshore tax havens. A number of rival hypotheses exist, such as poor rule of law, low state capacity, tax haven status, membership in a regulatory body, and authoritarianism. These rival hypotheses do not explain enforcement outcomes.

The first and most obvious rival hypothesis for blocked enforcement is a state's membership in a regulatory body. One of the startling aspects of the threat finance regulatory regime is the widespread diffusion that the regime has experienced since its initial conception in the US and Britain, and the slew of de jure adoptions of the regime after 2001. Not only is each country in this universe of cases involved in some sort of international regulatory body, enforcement occurred even for Somalia's Al-Barakat Bank, despite its home country's failed state status.

The second obvious rival hypothesis for blocked enforcement is authoritarianism. While each case of blocked enforcement took place in an authoritarian country, authoritarianism did not prevent enforcement against Arab Bank, in Jordan. Both Arab Bank and the Saudi banks, Al Rajhi and National Commerce Bank, inhabit similar regulatory and political environments. Additionally, both Jordan and Saudi Arabia exhibit similar levels of rule of law and regulatory quality. Both states are Sunni Arab monarchies in the same geographic region and both enjoy alliances with the United States. Yet, Arab Bank faced moderate enforcement for suspected terrorist financing – similar to the European cases of BNP Paribas and Standard Chartered – while Al Rajhi Bank and National Commerce Bank escaped enforcement.

Conversely, both Al Taqwa and the Bank of Commerce and Credit International (BCCI) faced severe enforcement and were shut down completely in their European tax-haven home states. Somalia's Al-Barakat experienced a regulatory shutdown identical to those of the banks in these Western tax havens. Banks surrounded by European norms such as rule of law, dense regulatory environments, high levels of state capacity, and liberal democracy effectively suffered similar penalization to a bank in a failed state. A cursory glance at table 1.1 indicates that some variable other than rule of law or state capacity is leading to the observed enforcement outcomes.

For this study, I examine five case studies. Three of these, coded as "positive," are cases in which a bank escaped enforcement due to defensive actions by its home state in blocking enforcement efforts. Two cases, coded as "negative," exemplify situations in which enforcement efforts were carried out by penalizing banks supposed to have financed terrorism. The three positive cases include the Halk Bank (Turkey), Al Rajhi Bank (Saudi Arabia), and the Bank of China (BOC). The negative cases include Arab Bank, in Jordan, and BCCI, now defunct but formerly based in the Cayman Islands and Luxembourg.

Every case except the Bank of China and BCCI centres on the Middle East, and all involve banks where regulatory enforcement for financing terrorism has at least been attempted. Among the positive

Table 1.1
Potential cases (rule-of-law and regulatory quality data)

| Bank | Link (bank and state) | Foreign policy importance of bank | Home state | Regulatory presence | Terrorist financing and enforcement outcome | Rule-of-law ranking for home state |
|---|---|---|---|---|---|---|
| Standard Chartered *Negative* | No | Yes | United Kingdom | · FATF member | Yes (moderate) | · Regulatory quality: 1.73<br>· Rule of law: 1.76 |
| HSBC *Negative* | No | Yes | United Kingdom | · FATF member | Yes (moderate) | · Regulatory quality: 1.73<br>· Rule of law: 1.76 |
| Al Rajhi Bank *Positive* | Yes | No | Saudi Arabia | · MENAFATF member<br>· FATF observer | No (non-enforcement) | · Regulatory quality: 0.183<br>· Rule of law: 0.25 |
| Bank of China *Positive* | Yes | Yes | People's Republic of China | · FATF member<br>· Eurasian Group member<br>· Asia/Pacific Group on Money Laundering member | No (non-enforcement) | · Regulatory quality: -0.217<br>· Rule of law: -0.328 |
| Al-Barakat Bank *Negative* | No | No | Somalia | · None | Yes (severe enforcement) – innocent | No data – failed state |
| Lebanese Canadian Bank *Negative* | No | No | Lebanon | · MENAFATF member | Yes (severe enforcement) | · Regulatory quality: 0.076<br>· Rule of law: -0.689 |
| Arab Bank *Negative* | No | Yes | Jordan | · MENAFATF member | Yes (moderate enforcement) | · Regulatory quality: 0.25<br>· Rule of law: 0.202 |

Table 1.1
Potential cases (rule-of-law and regulatory quality data) (Continued)

| Bank | Link (bank and state) | Foreign policy importance of bank | Home state | Regulatory presence | Terrorist financing and enforcement outcome | Rule-of-law ranking for home state |
|---|---|---|---|---|---|---|
| BCCI *Negative* | No | No | Luxembourg | · FATF member | Yes (severe enforcement) | · Regulatory quality: 1.687<br>· Rule of law: 1.831 |
| Al Taqwa *Negative* | No | No | Switzerland | · FATF member | Yes (severe enforcement) | · Regulatory quality: 1.64<br>· Rule of law: 1.76 |
| National Commercial Bank *Positive* | Yes | Yes | Saudi Arabia | · MENAFATF member<br>· FATF observer | No (non-enforcement) | · Regulatory quality: 0.183<br>· Rule of law: 0.25 |
| Halk Bank *Positive* | Yes | Yes | Turkey | · FATF member | No (non-enforcement) | · Regulatory quality: 0.38<br>· Rule of law: 0.117 |
| BNP Paribas *Negative* | No | Yes | France | · FATF member<br>· FATF Latin America observer<br>· MENAFATF observer<br>· Caribbean FATF observer | Yes (moderate enforcement) | · Regulatory quality: 1.31<br>· Rule of law: 1.41 |

*Sources:* On regulatory presence: Financial Action Task Force, "FATF Members and Observers: The 39 Members of the FATF" (Paris: FATF Secretariat, n.d.), accessed 5 September 2016, http://www.fatf-gafi.org/about/membersandobservers/. On rule-of-law ranking for home state: World Bank Institute, "Worldwide Governance Indicators for 2010" (Washington, DC: World Bank, n.d.), info.worldbank.org/governance/wgi/pdf/wgidatatables.pdf.

cases, while all three banks are based in authoritarian countries, authoritarianism itself does not determine the process of regulatory misfire. Jordan, where Arab Bank suffered penalties for financing Hamas, is based in an authoritarian Sunni Arab monarchy, similar to Saudi Arabia. However, Al Rajhi Bank, a Saudi bank with plausible historical links to Al-Qaeda, has suffered no penalty to date, despite efforts by regulators and the families of terror victims. Similarly, BCCI, once based in a tax haven with bank secrecy laws, experienced the counterintuitive penalty of complete closure for its illicit activity and financing of terrorism. Turkey's Halk Bank came under intense international scrutiny for laundering money for Iran, which had been sanctioned for its activities in financing terrorist groups like Hezbollah.

Regarding institutional linkage, it must be stressed that linkage does not necessarily connote total state ownership. Certainly, while both Turkey's Halk Bank and the Bank of China remain predominantly state-owned enterprises (SOEs), Al Rajhi Bank in Saudi Arabia has a downright cliquish and private history centred on ownership by a predominant Saudi family, traces its activities to the era of the kingdom's founding, and enjoys ongoing relationships with the royal family. In short, simple state ownership is not necessary to derail regulatory enforcement. This stipulation is also worth noting due to the theoretical observations of previous scholars who have decried the application of cookie-cutter CTF regulations around the world without taking into account local and national political economic circumstances.

Other rival causal explanations exist alongside institutional linkage, the most obvious two being a lack of a regulatory presence and poor rule of law within the banks' home states. China, Saudi Arabia, and Turkey all rank low on markers of rule of law. However, poor rule of law is not sufficient to explain regulatory misfire, particularly as Jordan ranks near to Saudi Arabia on this metric, despite the divergent regulatory outcomes for their banks.[86] Additionally, the very fact that Al-Barakat Bank in Somalia, a failed state without any official ranking of rule of law, suffered the same fate as BCCI in Luxembourg indicates that another variable must be present that accounts for allowing enforcement to proceed.

Regulatory presence, the strongest rival explanation, seems to play no role whatsoever in determining regulatory misfire. While Luxembourg became a Financial Action Task Force (FATF) member in 1990, and BCCI came under massive regulatory pressure a year later, in 1991, regulatory membership cannot explain Halk Bank's escape from enforcement despite its massive laundering of terrorist funds for Iran in the late 2000s, since Turkey has been an FATF member since 1991. The FATF is not the only international AML/CTF body in existence, but it does serve as a benchmark for measuring institutionalized fortified finance.[87] These rival explanations will be explored in chapter 5 for the negative cases of Arab Bank and BCCI.

## DATA

In establishing the existence of an institutional linkage between a bank and its home state, and then tracing this relationship through the adoption of CTF regulations and through the scandal phase in which enforcement is blocked or carried out, I employ data derived from documentary sources. As noted in the introduction, each of these cases is public knowledge and received widespread coverage including media reports, lengthy trials, and legislative hearings. In addition to documentary court data and government documents, I employ histories, memoirs, and other governmental and bank data to construct detailed histories of the banks being examined. Additionally, I use diplomatic material in the form of emails and cables from various government agencies, obtained and released by the whistleblower dissemination site Wikileaks.

For purposes of gathering data, few concise bank histories exist. With the exception of the Bank of China, little historical work has been done on the banks discussed in this book. Aside from accounting records, even the banks themselves have retained but few documents of their institutional past, which might shed light on their relations to the economies in which they are embedded. Documents such as annual reports, pertinent economic research on the country in question, bankers' memoirs, and media statements are used to construct the history of each bank and its relationship to its state. My documenting of the banks' institutional development also draws from earlier works on national political economies as well as research and data by previous scholars – economic historians and other political economists – on the specific banks in question.

Many of the banks I examine have long histories dating back deeply into the pasts of their home states. Some of the banks in question predate the modern countries in which they are based, and many of them have survived periods of profound internal and geopolitical upheaval. Furthermore, in each case, the country under examination is located in a region that experienced critical geopolitical flux during the twenty-first century. For these reasons, I endeavour to offer meticulous process tracing on the development of each bank. I seek to provide a detailed discussion of how each bank formed and how the links between it and its state developed in order to expose my analysis to scrutiny and pave the way for the use of these cases by other scholars interested in political economy and security in these countries.

Material from Wikileaks, enforcement bodies, and trial data is critical for analyzing the scandal phase during which the enforcement is attempted. This data provides additional background relevant to the suspected terrorist financing, and indicates that terrorist financing likely did occur. Additionally, trial data and the manner in which it was obtained reveals when a bank's home state cooperated with the regulatory action and when it assisted the bank by blocking enforcement. Documentary data from Wikileaks offers additional analytical benefits by affording the observer a look into diplomatic activity related to enforcement attempts.

# 2

# Bank of China

## INTRODUCTION

Perhaps the largest question in international politics in the new millennium is what role China will play in global affairs in the coming decades. Undergoing rapid and profound economic growth since the early 1980s, the contemporary People's Republic of China (PRC) bears little economic resemblance to its Maoist predecessor. As a result of the economic and financial reforms that first catalyzed the country's modern period of growth under Deng Xiaoping, Chinese banks comprised four of the world's five largest banks as of 2016.[1] China's banking industry remains the premier domain of the "Big Four": the Industrial Commercial Bank of China, the Bank of China, the China Construction Bank, and the Agricultural Bank of China.

Beginning in 2006, plaintiffs in the United States began filing suits against the Bank of China for its suspected laundering of money for Iranian-sponsored terrorism. These cases against the bank were dismissed in 2015. This chapter establishes, first, the longstanding linkages between the Bank of China and the Chinese state in its various manifestations since the late Qing dynasty. Next, China's "liberalization" and its adoption of fortified finance are discussed, along with how China's regulatory adoptions mixed with the formation of its domestic financial surveillance regime. Third, this chapter examines the Bank of China's involvement in suspected terrorist financing and how the adversarial nature of the American legal system was used by Israel to counter China's financing of terror. This last section explores how China used diplomatic leverage and a domestic bureaucratic veto to block enforcement actions against the bank.

## DEVELOPMENT OF THE BANK OF CHINA

Over the course of the bank's history, allegations of terrorist financing emerge as but a relatively minor crisis when compared to the upheavals that the bank has survived since its founding in 1911. Despite the cataclysms that have marked modern China's historical epochs since the decline of the Qing dynasty, the Bank of China has served as a tool of Chinese state policy since it opened. This institutional linkage between bank and state has not only survived critical junctures such as the Republican revolution, the Japanese occupation of the Second World War, and the Communist revolution, but has been maintained through Beijing's supposed "liberalization" of the financial sector and adoption of CTF regulations.

Since its genesis in the late Qing period, the Chinese state remained the perennial stakeholder in the Bank of China either through government function or outright ownership. While the state's status as primary stakeholder survived the collapse of the Qing, the Republican era on the mainland, Japanese occupation, civil war, and varying degrees of Communist and statist rule, the bank took on the additional role of securing Beijing's growth priorities through domestic lending to local government during the reforms of the late 1970s and 1980s. As I illustrate below, the state's role as primary stakeholder in the bank has deep roots in the bank's history and continues to the present day. While the state has long been a stakeholder in the bank, the bank has also served as a means of binding the Communist Party's coalition through domestic lending beginning in the 1980s. Both of these roles – coalition binding and state stakeholding – have survived China's financial "liberalization" and its importation of the international AML/CTF regime.

This chapter first outlines the role of state stakeholding in the bank over the course of its history, and then discusses the role the bank plays in domestic financing for local government. The bank's role in the various institutional changes made to the Chinese economy through the reform era of the late twentieth century is also discussed, and it is demonstrated that state stakeholding not only survived Beijing's supposed liberalization but also has served as an economic binding agent for the Chinese Communist Party's ruling coalition through domestic lending. The third section of this chapter discusses the banking scandal in which the Bank of China stood accused in US courts of financing terrorism, and the subsequent deflection of sanction which the bank enjoyed. Last, the Bank of China case is placed within the theoretical context predicated in the preceding chapter.

## *Origins of State Ownership*

Chinese banks and the role that they play within the country's modern statecraft cannot be understood without situating them in the context of Beijing's grand strategy. Facing rapid decline beginning in the nineteenth century, through the ensuing eras, and into the present, Chinese political thought of varying ideological orientations centred upon the notion of *fuguo qiangbing*, or "enrich the state and strengthen military power," as the state's guiding principle.[2] It was in this early era, as the waning Qing dynasty struggled to repel European and Japanese encroachment and contain civil unrest at home, that the Bank of China originated. It is worth noting here that the Bank of China, and perhaps large Chinese banks in general, give the lie to those scholars who assert that banks are loath to act as the instruments of states. In China, bank and state, if indeed they are distinguishable in management terms, are indistinguishable in their purpose of strengthening China's position in the world. The state's involvement in the Bank of China is long and deep, and the peculiar institutional linkages that connect state and bank have survived multiple eras of governance in China's modern political history.

In the late nineteenth century, banks in China were comprised of three types: the *piahao*, or "draft shops"; *qianzhuang*, or "native banks"; and *yinhang*, or "silver shops," which were Western banks operating in the country.[3] This early differentiation is critical to understanding the banks established by the Qing dynasty, particularly as the first major commercial banks bore the title of *yinhang*[4] and conceptually emulated the major Western banks present in China at the time of their founding. Prominent Chinese thinkers in the late nineteenth century such as Feng Guifen advocated that China "self-strengthen," or seek to understand and copy elements of what were seen at the time as Western strengths, notably in the areas of economic and financial development.[5]

Innovators within the Qing administration, under the influence of this self-strengthening movement, not only grappled with a number of foreign political pressures in the form of Western encroachment and a rising Japan, but also the economic difficulties derived from these pressures. Gluts of foreign exchange swamped the Chinese currency market following the Sino-Japanese War of 1894–95, and, because foreign currency exchanges remained the exclusive purview of foreign banks since the Opium Wars of the mid-nineteenth century, Chinese enterprise and the Qing administration began seeking mechanisms to promote the use of silver coins and "serve China with Chinese currency."[6] The founding of the "Treasury Bank" in 1905, later to be renamed the Da Qing Bank in 1908, was the fruit of such efforts. The Da Qing Bank's purposes were foundational and state-centred. By the dawn of the Republican period in 1911, the Da Qing Bank comprised thirty-five branches across China,[7] oversaw all government-related transactions, operated as the state's treasury and central bank, and issued official banknotes.[8] Uprisings that began in the 1890s finally culminated with the 1911 Revolution and the establishment of the Republic of China. The Da Qing Bank, due in large part to its unique relationship with the state, survived to become the Bank of China in 1912 when it forged a new relationship with the incoming government despite maintaining institutional continuity. Through various arrangements, this government ownership and oversight has persisted to the present day.

The Da Qing Bank was founded with hybrid ownership held in equal shares by the government and private shareholders within a single corporate structure.[9] The bank's founders formulated the institution as a stock company based on China's 1904 first real corporate statute (*gongsi lu*), a hybrid of characteristics which drew from British and Japanese models at the time.[10] Aside from its partial state ownership, the Da Qing Bank employed a unique dynamic of corporate governance that combined "government supervision with merchant management," and sought to use private business elites and their special expertise, often garnered from abroad, with active government support through policy and planning.[11] This mixture of institutional arrangements would translate, virtually in its entirety, from the Da Qing entity to the rebranded Bank of China shortly after the Nationalist takeover.

According to a 14 November 1911 report by the bank's Shareholders' Association, which represented the private equity interest in the bank, local revolutionaries often mistook Da Qing branches and the bank itself as being "wholly state owned" and as a result took to looting bank branches and, de facto, the Chinese treasury.[12] In reaction, the bank's private shareholders contacted the incoming Republican government and a "new" relationship between state and bank was forged.

## Ownership in the Republican Period

Shortly after the Republican government was founded in 1912, the new attorney general nominated Da Qing's managing director, Chen Jintao, to become the Republic's new finance minister.[13] It was under Chen Jintao's direction that the Da Qing Bank transitioned into the Bank of China as the central bank for the new republic.[14] Jintao not only advocated for this transition to the Republican government, he remained in the original bank's head office to oversee the transition. While the Qing government's equity in the bank was allocated to recuperating war-related costs, the Republican government took over management of the bank's properties and assumed an ownership share equivalent to that of the deposed Qing dynasty. This new arrangement continued the half-private, half-state ownership structure. Meanwhile, the private shareholders obtained an equivalent level of equity in the new Bank of China, soon to be the central bank. In late January 1912, Da Qing's shareholders formed the new bank and chose new board members. By mid-February 1912, the Bank of China opened and began opening branches in the same locations as the defunct Da Qing Bank.[15] The bank transitioned smoothly, maintaining a dual public-private model of joint ownership between private shareholders and the state as a stakeholder.

The continuity between the two banks was not limited to the figure of Chen Jintao. The bank remained a stock company with a half-government, half-private split in ownership and most private shareholders continuing to hold their respective shares in the new venture. Furthermore, the bank's staff, properties, and even banknotes remained unchanged. In the case of the latter, the only marked difference between the Bank of China notes and those of its Qing predecessor was the name of the issuing bank on the bill.[16] For the government's share, both the Qing and Nationalist governments owned and administered the state's half of the bank through the Ministry of Finance.[17] The relationship between ministry and bank served as the structural vehicle of government stakeholding until the Communist takeover, when the People's Bank of China (PBC) replaced this mechanism.

At first glance, to those unfamiliar with the Bank of China's history, the Communist takeover under Mao in 1949 appears as a complete, state-led takeover of the Chinese banks. In the case of the Bank of China, the Nationalist Kuomintang (KMT) had already seized control of the bank in the 1920s, such that the bank's transition saw continuous state control despite the change in government. The Nationalist takeover, and the bank's resistance to it, is worth discussing given the dynamics of private equity interests within the institution and the state's role in commandeering it for its own, insular political purposes. Additionally, it was during this period between the Republican revolution and the Communist takeover that the Bank of China took on certain characteristics that would later enable it to function as an international bank during the Maoist period and the later era of reform under Deng Xiaoping. The first such characteristic consisted of expansion and development, with the building of a Western-style form of professionalization under the guidance of a foreign-educated managerial class. The second, more lasting characteristic was the bank's premier role in China's foreign exchange business.

When the new Republican government officially seized control of China just prior to the First World War, the country's political situation was one of regional and national disarray. The young Nationalist government, in seeking to consolidate rule and secure its position against local warlords, required access to funds both for institution building and to contain ongoing regional resistance at the local level. Out of the need for survival, with its branches being looted by local warlords, the shareholders of the old Da Qing Bank petitioned the incipient Republican leadership, under Sun Yat-sen, to create a new bank-state relationship in which the bank would recast itself with a new fifty-fifty shareholder-state ownership split and a new purpose: to function as the central bank for the new Chinese republic. However, the Nationalists' unquenchable thirst for funds would stress the relationship between state and bank, leading to a brief fracture between the private shareholders and the government.

As noted previously, the Chinese term for "bank" – *yinhang* – was originally confined to foreign banks operating in the country. Only over time did this usage come to refer to newer Chinese banks founded in the early twentieth century. The Bank of China, in both its structure and management, drew from outside banking influences, and its private shareholders and managerial staff would test the institution's linkage with the state. This brief period, between 1916 and the Nationalist "bank coup" of 1935, allowed the Bank of China to develop a specific expertise in dealing with foreign exchange which would serve as its benchmark role throughout the "monobanking" Maoist era.

The new Bank of China's cozy relationship with the new government hit the rocks with the rise of the short-lived government of

Yuan Shikai in 1912. In seeking to secure the title of emperor for himself, Shikai made ever-increasing demands for funds from the bank, outstripping its reserve capital. In 1916, the government ordered the bank to cease the free convertibility of bank notes into silver and surrender its existing silver holdings to the government mandate under the threat of force.[18]

The Bank of China, based at its Shanghai branch, rejected the order out of fear of losing public and investor confidence, and undertook an endogenous restructuring to maintain the bank's financial integrity.[19] The bank's management curtailed their own arrests through legal action, and then undertook a number of restructuring efforts to weaken the government's hand through the expansion of private ownership of the bank and raising the political stakes of outright seizure by securing loans from foreign banks, thereby linking the Bank of China to other prominent Chinese financial institutions and lending houses. Ironically, it was thanks to the bank's conspiring with the new finance minister, Liang Qichao, who denounced Shikai's move to proclaim himself monarch, that the bank managed to reorganize itself as a more privatized institution under new internal corporate regulations.[20] This new internal mandate shifted the role of the Ministry of Finance within the bank, limiting its ability to appoint executives from among the existing board and removing the formal split between government and private shares that had existed since the Qing era.[21] This influx of private capital to the bank, the government's internal war efforts, and the ongoing selling of shares for cash shifted the ratio of private-state shares from 42 per cent government ownership in 1918 to less than 1 per cent in 1924.[22]

Two caveats are worth mentioning in regard to this historical period of privatization and the Bank of China's relationship to the state. First, in its efforts to maintain silver convertibility and undertake internal reorganization, the bank enjoyed the support of the finance minister, Ling Qichao. This support, together with the fractured nature of the Chinese state at the time – particularly during Shikai's fevered, unpopular play at monarchy – does not refute the argument that the Bank of China has remained virtually constant as a state-backed institution. Second, given the chaotic nature of Chinese politics at the time, it is arguable that little of the centralized state was functioning at all when the bank privatized. Regardless, the breathing room that the bank enjoyed in the period between its defiance of Beijing's silver mandate and the state's outright takeover of the bank under Chiang Kai-shek a few years later allowed the Bank of China to develop a specialty in conducting foreign exchange business and thereby adopting a greater role as an international Chinese bank.

Chinese politics at the time of the Bank of China's privatization were such that political instability prevailed until the Nationalist consolidation of the mid-1920s, a condition that necessarily restricted most of China's major banking activity to large cities such as Shanghai and Beijing, or foreign-controlled enclaves along the coast.[23] With the new ties between the Bank of China and prominent private individuals and other private banks similarly based in large cities, the Chinese banking industry enjoyed deepening liquidity and lending power until the eve of the Second World War.

Following Chiang Kai-shek's coming to power and the appointment of his brother in-law, T.V. Soong, as finance minister, in late 1928 the Bank of China received licence to begin operations as an international exchange bank. The bank's general manager, Zhang Jia'ao, travelled throughout Europe, the United States, and elsewhere, establishing correspondent banking relationships and setting up branches abroad. By 1936, the Bank of China's deposits had more than doubled and its deposits with the government's new central bank accounted for 57 per cent of the central bank's total holdings.[24] The state's inability to commandeer the Bank of China, as T.V. Soong had originally hoped, and the bank's recasting of itself as an international exchange bank, stemmed largely from the state's weakness at the time.[25] This is worth noting, particularly as it demonstrates the state's ongoing desire to control the Bank of China.

The Bank of China's golden age of privatization proved to be short-lived, however, as Chiang Kai-shek's regime essentially seized control of the bank in 1935. Despite the bank's success at establishing a notable presence in international finance through the late 1920s and early 1930s, and in spite of the Great Depression, the bank was abruptly seized by the government in 1935 through the mandated issuing of new shares to the state. This government control would characterize and dominate the bank's existence until the present.

If the government's shareholding in the Bank of China was essentially nil in 1924, its share rapidly rebounded as the state consolidated in the wake of Chiang Kai-shek's Northern Expedition, which quelled warlord resistance throughout much of the country. Perhaps drawing from the time he'd spent in Japan and the Soviet Union during his early career, Chiang Kai-shek set about implementing a number of fiscal and financial reforms designed to increase state control of the economy. In 1928, the government, through Chiang's finance minister and brother-in-law, T.V. Soong, sought to reabsorb the Bank of China as the state's central bank as it had originally functioned.[26] The bank, due to its considerable public credibility, was able to lobby against the move; it was thus able to limit the government's shareholding increase to 20 per cent,[27] but reauthorized the finance ministry to select the chairman of the board.[28]

The 1930s would witness the Chinese state's increasing intervention in the financial sector, and in the Bank of China in particular in the lead-up to the 1937 Japanese invasion. In 1935, the state issued new bonds and mandated the Bank of China to increase its available shares and sell stock to the government. This proclamation came from H.H. Kung, another brother-in law of Chiang Kai-shek. With the new funds from these bonds, the state increased its percentage of ownership back to 50 per cent.[29] On the eve of the Japanese invasion, the state owned 70 per cent of all assets within the Chinese banking industry and silver convertibility was suspended.[30] By 1943, the Chinese state would hold a 67 per cent stake in the Bank of China and enjoy the right to appoint the majority of its directors.[31] Although its overseas business continued, the Bank of China would exist as an extension of the state's activity against Japanese aggression during the Second World War and after the Communist takeover in 1949.

The notion that banks are loath to take part in war is the theoretical gleaning of Kirshner in his work on bankers and national security.[32] The Bank of China's operations during the Second World War pose serious challenges to this theory, however, particularly as the bank proved especially aggressive in its financial efforts to undermine the Japanese presence in the country and maintain business ties with friendly states. Perhaps in large part due to its outright control by the state, the Bank of China managed to play a role in supporting the war effort. Despite the Japanese military presence, the Bank of China worked with allied banks and embassies to smuggle silver holdings, maintain the republic's currency, and even engage in espionage activity against the Japanese-backed Central Reserve Bank of China, established by the puppet regime of Wang Jingwei.[33]

As mentioned above, it is a misconception to see the state's takeover of Chinese banks in 1949 as a uniquely Maoist phenomenon. The process of state control came to fruition slightly more than a decade prior to the end of the Chinese Civil War and just before Japanese incursion. Under Mao, rather than seek government control through shareholding, the state would cement itself as stakeholder of the Bank of China through the mechanism of the People's Bank of China (PBC). If the state maintained its stakeholder status from the prior era, it also continued in its role as the purveyor of foreign exchange and overseas finance during the era of monobanking that would define the Chinese banking industry until the era of economic reforms several decades later. Largely due to its overseas focus and its role of acting as China's financial presence abroad, the Bank of China during the postwar period must also be considered in the context of the PRC's foreign policy.

## The Monobank Era

From 1949 until the reforms of Deng Xiaoping that unwound China's banking sector, the People's Bank of China served as the only true bank operating within China and held all responsibilities for both central and commercial banking. The Bank of China continued to exist, as an extension of the PBC, serving largely as the state's financial window to the outside world. In 1953, the Bank of China regained its authorized status as a foreign exchange bank and served Chinese interests abroad. Prior to the Communist takeover, the finance ministry served as the state's tool to control the bank. Under the Maoist monobank model, the Bank of China operated as a foreign exchange specialty bureau under the PBC, the central bank.

Within the PRC's monobank structure between 1949 and 1979, the PBC sat directly beneath the State Council, which oversaw both the Bank of China and the Agricultural Bank of China. Urban development was funded either through the Bank of China or the People's Construction Bank, overseen by the Ministry of Finance. For its part, the Bank of China serviced local PBC branches, which in turn performed financial duties for the local economy.[34] Standing under the authority of the State Council, both the Ministry of Finance and the PBC operated the State Planning Commission, responsible for all planning within the centrally planned economy.[35] Although the Ministry of Finance controlled the state's funds and the PBC, it also oversaw the entirety of Beijing's "banking sector" at the time. Institutional power for decision making lay with the State Planning Commission. It is also worth noting that the relationship between local PBC branches and the state was replicated at the local level, with local state planning bodies overseeing local bank operations, and local governments taking guidance from the central government via the State Council.[36] Nonetheless, despite total state control, the Bank of China maintained its overseas presence, effectively operating as Beijing's commercial window and presence to the outside world.

Despite the bank's function as an organ of the Communist state, the institution retained at least a veneer of the professionalism that it had begun to garner as an international bank prior to its prewar seizure. From its early years, the Bank of China boasted an elite managerial staff replete with Chinese elites educated abroad who leveraged their multilingual business talents for the bank's overseas operations.[37] The Maoist revolution, with its base in the peasantry, lacked the human capital to effectively replace these elites. Indeed, for much of the Maoist period, the Chinese Communist Party continued to rely on experienced bureaucrats left over from KMT rule, since those with peasant backgrounds often lacked urban-based economic expertise.[38] What is notable is that foreign-educated, multilingual bankers affiliated with the Bank of China are recorded as meeting with representatives from international banks and foreign dignitaries at its overseas branches during the pre-reform era. With these elites maintaining the Bank of China's operations abroad, the PRC was able to use the institution as its economic window on the outside world.

*The Times* vividly describes the Bank of China's operations in the then-British enclave of Hong Kong in 1971, noting that the branch manager, Li Chao-chih, held the position of "vice-minister" and operated the bank with the assistance of a cadre of personnel "trained as economists in the West, and impressively at home in both English and the manners of the outside world."[39] It is also worth noting that despite its small scale as a single segment within the PRC's monobank of that era, the bank facilitated an inordinate amount of foreign exchange dealings for the state, a level out of correlation to its size.[40] Based out of its Hong Kong branch, the Bank of China served as the "foreign department" of the state's central bank, the People's Bank of China.[41] In acting as the state's "financing agent," the Bank of China would buy convertible foreign currencies that could then be sent to major banking centres overseas.[42] The bank's unique institutional position situated it to be the state's negotiating agency with foreign banks seeking to finance trade with the PRC. This often included the settling of foreign transactions in currencies other than the US dollar, largely due to Beijing's animus toward the US.[43]

The Bank of China's unwinding from the monobank arrangement of the Maoist era and into its current configuration began with the reforms instituted by Deng Xiaoping in the late 1970s. The state remained a stakeholder in the institution, but a new function relating to China's domestic economy would be added to the bank's importance as a foreign currency window between the PRC and the rest of the world. This new role in China's domestic economic development cemented the bank as a coalition binder for Beijing's efforts to renew political legitimacy.

At the time of Mao's death in 1976, the PRC faced a triad of domestic crises related (but not limited) to domestic economic rot, a crisis of legitimacy, and a struggle for succession. Economically, the PRC's potential remained bottled due an overemphasis on pure industrialization without a concurrent increase in consumer demand, a situation due in part to overly high prices on goods deemed "luxurious" and lagging levels of new employment.[44] Compounded with low levels of labour absorption in new industries[45] and a system of managerial promotion that favoured party loyalty over competence,[46] the PRC faced multiplying economic pressures as Deng Xiaoping assumed power.

## Reform and Continued State Control

At the microeconomic level, Deng's reforms mitigated the Maoist-era problem of labour absorption through the active encouragement of private business ventures[47] along with allowing competition for bank financing at the local level.[48] By the early 1980s, the PRC's monobank, through which all local funds were dispersed in the form of grants prior to reform, had been unwound to allow for the state's major banks to compete in making loans to localities and enterprises.[49] The four state banks involved in this devolution of lending power comprised contemporary China's "Big Four" and included the Bank of China.

The reorganization of the monobank model into separate state banks out from under the PBC's umbrella proceeded according to sector. The Bank of China, though unwound and made a separate state entity, retained the specialty it held since the 1920s as a bank devoted to foreign exchange and international finance.[50] The PBC, as China's central bank, was institutionally separated from the Ministry of Finance in 1978, when it was redesignated as its own ministry.[51] Later, in the 1990s, the PBC would come to house the PRC's financial intelligence unit.

The financial sector's reform, and the separation of the state bank into multiple entities did not in any way reduce the state's role as a stakeholder, a condition that continues to the present. Ironically, the massive financial reforms instituted under the guidance of Zhu Rongji, premier from 1998 to 2003, shifted the Bank of China's form of state stakeholding back to control through shareholding, the mode that had predominated during the Nationalist era. In the 1990s, when US president George H.W. Bush asked Zhu about the progress of privatization in the PRC, he responded bluntly that China was not privatizing so much as changing the form of state ownership.[52] Zhu's comments are telling in that they capture succinctly the nature of contemporary China's move to state control through the adoption and tailoring of international business models to Chinese needs.

The separation of the "Big Four" state banks from the PBC functionally divided China's financial sector into distinctive realms of commercial banking, each being the domain of one of the Big Four, while the PBC would serve solely as the state's central banking apparatus.[53] This separation, carried out in 1983, brought the banking sector closer, in part, to international institutional norms. By the mid-1990s, the PBC had joined the Bank for International Settlements and committed itself to the adoption of the Basel Accords (1996), cleaned the balance sheets of the Big Four through the removal of bad loans, and began seeking large foreign investors for the infusion of private equity into the otherwise state-owned banks.[54]

A number of factors in the late 1990s and early 2000s lent the PRC the appearance of moving toward normalcy in international finance. Joining the Bank for International Settlements in 1996, the repossession in 1997 of Hong Kong, an important financial centre, and joining the World Trade Organization in 2001 portrayed an image of China coming into line with international best practices and liberalization. However, even as it prepared to issue shares in its major banks for private ownership, China created institutional mechanisms to retain state control and oversight of the Bank of China and to create a regulatory structure that would survive the adoption of the fortified finance regime.

First, China's central bank, though now functionally separate from the PRC's commercial banking sector, remains politically tied to the State Council and senior leadership.[55] Unlike the international norm of central banks enjoying ostensible independence from political forces for the sake of financial stability, China's central bank remains a considerable outlier. This raises the question of how important the "norm" of central bank independence truly is, given that most of the largest banks in the world are supervised by a central bank tied firmly to Beijing's leadership. For the AML/CTF regime, this arrangement creates the problem of a state-controlled central bank effectively having to police banks owned by the state itself.

Second, in preparing the Bank of China for an initial public offering (IPO) and shifting the state's control back to the shareholding model of the Nationalist era, the government created two ownership vehicles: the Huijin Corporation, in 2003, and the China Investment Corporation (CIC), in 2007. The CIC, though created four years after Huijin, houses the Huijin Corporation as a subsidiary, which in turn owns more than 60 per cent of the Bank of China.

The Huijin Corporation, formally known as Central Huijin Investment Ltd, was founded in December 2003, the same year, and month, as the Bank of China's IPO.[56] Huijin describes its sole purpose as being to "perform obligations as an investor on behalf of the State ... with the goal of preserving and enhancing the value of state-owned financial assets."[57] In corporate governance, the State Council appoints all of Huijin's directors for three-year terms.[58] In the early 2000s, the PBC continually infused funds into Huijin, which, in turn, invested in the Bank of China.[59] With an initial investment of $22.5 billion, the state held a controlling share of the Bank of China, at 67.6 per cent.[60] In terms of personnel, Huijin's staff largely derives from the PBC.[61]

With the Bank of China's shares held by state-owned investment corporations, the bank has largely returned to the stakeholder dynamic that existed prior to the PRC's establishment in 1949. Interestingly, the bank's institutional arrangement has not modernized so much as returned to a previous model of state stakeholding, though government control of the bank's operations has remained virtually unchanged over the course of a century. Succinctly stated, the linkage between the Bank of China and its home state has proven both deep and resilient. If this linkage has survived multiple wars, decades of turmoil, and massive regulatory reforms, it is doubtful that the adoption of AML/CTF rules could dislodge such arrangements. The next sections address this regulatory adoption and its performance.

## CHINA'S FORTIFIED FINANCE REGIME

As the Bank of China retained the state as its premier stakeholder throughout China's financial reforms, the PRC banking industry's adoption of the international AML/CTF regime was a significant move.

In fact, most of these adoptions took place in the 1990s and in the immediate aftermath of 9/11, prior to the Bank of China's IPO and subsequent exposure to international investors. Ranging from de jure adoptions of fortified finance regulations to active prosecution, China has made considerable efforts to implement changes to its banking sector to curtail crime and terrorism. Table 2.1 outlines the steps that China has taken to implement fortified finance, both in terms of its internal adoption of AML laws and through its membership in multilateral regulatory bodies.

Two trends become noticeable upon close analysis of China's regulatory and legal changes as they pertain to fortified finance. First, China was not merely reacting to the global push, post-2001, to spread the AML/CTF regime. Domestically, China had made money laundering and terrorist financing into criminal offences in the late 1990s, and significantly expanded its penal code to do so. Passed in 1997, article 191 of the PRC's penal code effectively criminalized the laundering of criminally obtained funds from drugs and organized crime. Notably, terrorism was included in the statute and the obfuscation or transfer of such funds specifically deemed a criminal act.[62] In April 2001, prior to 9/11 and the subsequent wave of regulation it set in motion, Beijing began implementing "know your customer" (KYC) requirements for depositors throughout its financial sector, mandating that new account holders offer identification during the on-boarding process.[63] Beijing's KYC regulations were modelled on those of the US. These domestic legal changes to the PRC's criminal code place it in line with overall international AML regulatory trends at the time and, given the restructuring of Beijing's banking industry over the 1990s, indicate the country's proactivity in this arena. In June 2001 – again prior to 9/11 – the Bank of China formed its own internal anti-money-laundering bureau,[64] thus raising the possibility that the bank had functioned as a test run for Beijing when it established a national FIU two years later.

The second trend that stands out in China's adoption of threat finance regulation is the timing and context in which the PBC took up its new, additional role as Beijing's financial intelligence unit (FIU). Working under the mandate of the State Council in 2003, the PBC issued mandates to the Chinese banking sector stipulating the gathering of financial information and establishing reporting requirements for suspicious transactions. That same year, the State Council also shifted the Ministry of Public Security's AML mandate to the central bank.[65] With these new mandates and capabilities, the

Table 2.1
Timeline of anti-money-laundering regulatory adoption in China

| Adoption | Year | Type |
|---|---|---|
| Article 191 of Penal Code introduced, criminalizing laundering from drugs, organized crime, terrorism (FATF) | 1997 | Domestic law |
| Member and founder of Asia-Pacific Group on Money Laundering (APG) | 1997 | International membership |
| PBC becomes China's FIU and mandates monitoring of suspicious activity | 2003 | Domestic regulatory adoption |
| Member and founder of Eurasian Group (EAG) | 2004 | International membership |
| PBC issues new AML/CTF regulation expanding supervision and reporting mandates | 2007 | Domestic regulatory expansion |
| Member of Financial Action Task Force (FATF) | 2007 (observer since 2005) | International membership |

PBC established coordination mechanisms to facilitate the production and sharing of financial intelligence related to crime and terrorism throughout the Chinese financial system.[66] In 2004, one of these mechanisms emerged in the form of the PBC's AML Monitoring and Analysis Center (CAMLMAC), charged with operating as the FIU's monitoring centre within the central bank.

As noted in the previous section, the Bank of China remains a state bank, as it has nearly without interruption since its inception, with the government holding either outright control or the lion's share of ownership in the institution. Now owned by the state as a majority investor through sovereign investment funds, which in turn are financed, overseen, and staffed by the PBC, the state has effectively turned the Bank of China into an extension of its financial intelligence apparatus as of the early 2000s. Although such regulatory adoptions and legal changes have occurred de jure, the question remains as to how Beijing has implemented such regulations in practice. This consideration must first be addressed before considering the accusations against the Bank of China of financing terrorism and the subsequent blocked enforcement.

After the adoption of the fortified finance regime, China began centralizing the monitoring of its financial system. Following the creation of CAMLMAC within the PBC in 2004, Beijing implemented a computer network to link its banks. Within a year, above 90 per cent of Chinese banks were linked to this system.[67] Shortly after implementing these institutional capabilities and technical arrangements, reports of suspicious activity began to deluge the PBC's FIU. Between 2004 and 2008, CAMLMAC took in 93.62 million suspicious activity reports, with an additional 585 million large-volume transaction reports in the same period.[68] According to analysts within the PBC, 1,859 reports were sent to Chinese judicial and law enforcement from this surge of reporting.[69] This resulting flow of financial intelligence moves in three directions, depending upon the nature of the suspicious transaction in question. Under normal circumstances, a Chinese bank first reports the activity to its corporate headquarters, which in turn sends bulked reports, weekly, to the PBC's FIU.[70] If a bank branch suspects the activity pertains to a crime, it is mandated by law to send reports both horizontally and vertically by informing the nearest local branch of the PBC, local law enforcement, and its corporate headquarters.[71] For its part, and as a by-product of China's totalitarian composition, in 2004 the PBC began anti-money-laundering propaganda campaigns in consort with AML trainings in an effort to discourage bribery while fomenting greater levels of customer due diligence.[72] Local bank branches are also subject to inspection by PBC personnel from the central bank's nearby branches.[73] In 2004 alone, the PBC shuttered 155 underground banking operations and froze 460 accounts in conjunction with 274 arrests.[74] By the mid-2000s, the Chinese state had begun exercising its coercive capacity in accordance with the international AML/CTF regime. It was during these years that the Bank of China came to be accused of harbouring and transacting funds for terrorism.

In the realm of China's domestic AML/CTF financial regulations, the PBC significantly expanded its reporting requirements and best practices during the same period in which the Bank of China came under suspicion for terrorist financing. While the 2003 regulations established by the PBC mandated that banks operating in the PRC follow reporting requirements and stipulated penalties for executives found to be operating in contravention of these regulations, the regulations that took effect in 2007 added confidentiality clauses designed to maintain secrecy in the event of a bank violating the law. Based on article 7 of the new regulations, the PBC mandated that its personnel "shall keep all information obtained in fulfilling its anti-money laundering responsibilities confidential, and must not disclose [these] to outsiders in violation of regulations."[75] The new regulations also mandated that the PBC's FIU keep confidential the identities of account holders conducting large and suspicious transactions, and warned against the sharing of these identities with "any other organization or individual."[76] The timing of these regulatory expansions may have related to foreign suspicions regarding the Bank of China beginning in 2006.

China's adoption and development of fortified financial regulations has largely kept pace with the outside world. In fact, it can even be argued that Beijing's regulatory development in this area would have continued even if 9/11, and the wave of regulatory advancement that followed it, had not occurred. China's banking sector was already undergoing massive reform to increase its efficiency and attractiveness when these regulations were adopted. Efforts by Beijing to create sovereign investment vehicles to allow its banks to sell limited levels of private equity would have been contraindicated should its state banks not conform to some level of regulatory safeguarding, as was becoming the norm in the global financial sector. Additionally, it is questionable whether an authoritarian state such as China would forego such an opportunity to use its banks as a partial extension of its intelligence apparatus, particularly given the larger banks' size and scope.

## THE BANK OF CHINA
## AND BLOCKED ENFORCEMENT

In the mid-2000s, allegations began to arise that the Bank of China had financed terrorism for the Palestinian terrorist groups Hamas and Islamic Jihad. The scandal played out as a court case between plaintiffs seeking damages against the bank in American courts for terrorist acts carried out in Israel during this period. The regulations, based in the US, became a terrain for international power politics between Israel and China. Unfolding over the course of a decade, the Bank of China, with Beijing's backing, evaded enforcement through a combination of home-state veto through bureaucratic stalling and diplomatic deflection through external pressure on a third-party state.

The increasing intensity of great power competition between China and the US is well known. What is less well known is the role that China has played in the areas of terrorism and terrorist financing since the current era of international terrorism began in 2001, and the relations between Beijing and Jerusalem in this context. In Middle East politics, relations between the PRC and terrorist groups have a deep history in international affairs, one that often pits Israel (and the US) against Chinese designs in the region.

The PRC's foreign policy orientation of antagonism toward the US has its roots in Mao's conception of the US as the ultimate "imperialist" power following the Second World War, while holding at its core the Leninist notion of "imperialism as the highest form of capitalism."[77] After its break with the Soviet Union, Beijing's strategy in the Middle East sought to drive wedges between the superpowers and the newly independent Arab states in the region, shifting the latter away from a reliance on either Moscow (in the case of those countries ideologically sympathetic to the PRC) or Washington.[78] Beijing's stance on Israel during the Maoist era placed the two states on opposing sides of a covert war, with terrorist financing serving as a major source of strategic antagonism.

During the height of the Cold War, when many African states were gaining their independence, Israeli covert activity in that continent followed a strategy of thwarting China's Secret Intelligence Service from providing money laundering services to terrorist organizations seeking to strike at Israel.[79] Using Hong Kong as a base for money laundering operations in the 1960s and 1970s, the PRC used profits from drug dealing in the West, often working through Chinese gangs abroad, to finance covert operations in the developing world.[80] China's activities in Africa included the active transport and training of students from the continent to Beijing, where they were taught practical skills relevant to conducting terrorist attacks.[81] Centred in North Africa and based in Cairo, China's covert activities in Africa actively supported insurgent groups and provided political and logistical support for the Nasser regime's activities against Israel.[82] With drug money going to support Beijing's proxies in Africa and the Middle East, the Israelis and Chinese fought each other through their respective intelligence services in Africa, which served as the corridor through which Beijing funded its sponsored groups. It is worth noting that the Bank of China was the only financial institution connecting Beijing to the outside world at this time.

This antagonism between China and Israel resurfaced in the early 2000s, when suicide bombers began using explosives manufactured in China.[83] China's suspected role in supporting a number of terrorist organizations came to light in 2001 with the defection of a People's Liberation Army colonel, Xu Junping, to the United States. The intelligence gained by the US through Xu's defection concerned networks of Chinese support for rogue states such as Iran and North Korea, and terrorist groups throughout Latin America, as well as China's hosting of Osama bin Laden on three occasions prior to 9/11.[84] The link between regional terrorist groups operating in the Palestinian territories and Beijing was not limited to the procurement of explosives, but also included services provided by the Bank of China to a Palestinian Islamic Jihad trade-based money laundering operation. In turn, such services linked the group to its backers in Iran and subsequently empowered the group to carry out terrorist attacks in Israel.

Trade-based money laundering is a form of laundering that involves the transfer of value through goods. The FATF defines trade-based money laundering as "the process of disguising the proceeds of crime and moving value through the use of trade transactions in an attempt to legitimize their illicit origin."[85] John Cassara argues that trade-based money laundering constitutes a massive problem for countering illicit finance and that trade transactions are used by launderers of various types, including terrorists.[86] In the case of the Bank of China, seemingly innocent items with no apparent relation either to war or to terrorism were used in a trade scheme to finance terrorism.

In 2006, the Wultz family was the victim of a suicide bombing in Tel Aviv. Under stipulations provided by the US Anti-Terrorism Act of 1990, the family sued the Bank of China, alleging that the bank had funnelled money to the terrorist group Palestinian Islamic Jihad (PIJ) between 2003 and 2006.[87] The case, which relied on affidavits from Israeli intelligence officials, alleged that the Bank of China knowingly conducted business on behalf a PIJ and Hamas account holder, Said al-Shurafa, at its Guangzhou branch in China. More specifically, the plaintiffs asserted that the Bank of China knowingly conducted this business for PIJ after multiple meetings between delegations of Israeli intelligence officials and organs of the Chinese government including the Ministry of State Security, the People's Bank of China, the Ministry of Foreign Affairs, and other agencies – meetings in which the Israelis alerted their Chinese counterparts to the activities of al-Shurafa and other account holders.[88] Far from being an isolated encounter, these Chinese-Israeli meetings spanned a course of two years between 2005 and 2007.[89]

According to a declaration by one of the intelligence officials, Shlomo Matalon, filed with the US District Court in Washington, DC, in 2009, PIJ and Hamas leaders transferred millions of dollars in funds to terrorist operations in West Bank and Gaza via two Bank of China account numbers. Both accounts were held by al-Shurafa between July 2003 and early 2008.[90] The funds in question were not inconsequential; most were classifiable as large-volume and therefore would have been subject to reporting requirements. Table 2.2 outlines some of the sums involved. According to Matalon, the Bank of China continued to service these transactions despite having been notified by the Israelis of this activity.

The terrorist financing in which the Bank of China was suspected to have been involved consisted of a trade-based money laundering operation. Funds from the Syrian and Iranian regimes were sent to al-Shurafa's accounts at the Bank of China branch in Guangzhou. Monies from these accounts were then used by al-Shurafa to purchase innocent items such as clothing and toys that would then be sent to Gaza and the West Bank, where they were sold. In other words, the value of the money, through toys and clothing, crossed international borders in place of cash. The operation was devious, since stopping such goods at a border would appear as the cruel deprivation of civilians of peaceful consumer goods. Once the items sold, the proceeds were used to facilitate terrorist operations like the one that killed and injured members of the Wultz family in 2006.[91] The damage claim filed by the plaintiffs totalled $750 million.[92]

The case against the Bank of China was neither isolated nor even entirely an independent civil action by the plaintiffs alone.[93] Rather, the lawsuit served as one element in an Israeli strategy to use American civil law to counter the terrorist financing and thereby blunt terrorist operations against the Jewish state. Along with the interdiction of shipping containers of Chinese origin en route to Gaza, Israel supported lawsuits against banks that finance terrorism as part of a "national policy" to counter terrorism.

During the tenure of Meir Dagan as the director of Mossad (2002–10), Israel's foreign intelligence service and the Israeli National Security Council authorized the country's Terrorist Financing Task Force to begin providing information from intelligence sources on terrorist financing to lawyers and plaintiffs seeking to sue banks for financing terror.[94] Knowing that the Bank of China held branches in the US and conducted dollar transactions, Jerusalem assured the plaintiffs that both documentary and testimonial evidence would be offered in support of the suit. It was intended that this evidence would include testimony from Israeli intelligence officers who had been present at

Table 2.2
PIJ/Hamas transfers conducted by Bank of China

| Date of transfer | Amount |
| --- | --- |
| 5 December 2003 | $99,970 |
| 9 January 2004 | $99,960 |
| 18 February 2004 | $99,990 |
| 15 March 2004 | $99,970 |
| 19 March 2004 | $99,970 |
| 15 April 2004 | $100,000 |
| 9 October 2004 | $200,000 |
| 24 October 2004 | $199,965 |
| 7 December 2004 | $8,000 |
| 8 December 2004 | $8,000 |
| 17 December 2004 | $8,000 |
| 28 January 2005 | $100,000 |

Source: Declaration by Shlomo Matalon.

the meetings between Israel and China regarding the Bank of China.[95] The Israelis would later retract this offer due to diplomatic pressure from Beijing.

Over the course of the lawsuit, the Bank of China engaged in two lines of defence. First, the bank deployed its own bureaucratic countermeasures designed to thwart discovery efforts and prevent the court from accessing valuable documentary evidence. Second, Beijing used diplomatic pressure on Jerusalem to prevent Israel from allowing its intelligence officials to provide testimony. With these measures, the Bank of China managed to block enforcement.

In 2011, the plaintiffs requested that the Bank of China proffer documents related to Said al-Shurafa's accounts, along with documents pertaining to investigations into the bank and its dealings, as they concerned sanctions related to money laundering and terrorism.[96] The bank immediately turned to the PBC for guidance. Subsequently, the Bank of China then asked the court to send its discovery requests to the PBC, which the court did. Over a year passed without the court receiving a response from the Chinese FIU. Eventually, in August 2012, the court received documents consisting largely of copies of Chinese regulation manuals.[97]

On 29 October 2012, the New York district court ordered the Bank of China to produce documents related to AML/CTF investigations.

The bank initially claimed that the production of such material would violate Chinese bank secrecy laws.[98] Based on Chinese bank regulations instituted in 2007 (mentioned earlier in this chapter), the bank's arguments carried some validity. As such, the bank refused to comply with this first order to compel the production of evidence. Initially, the court remained hesitant to grant the plaintiff's motion to compel discovery, with the presiding judge noting that the "production of confidential documents created by the Chinese government" would "infringe on the sovereignty of the foreign state and violate principles of international comity."[99]

In May 2013, two years prior to the dismissal of the case, the court again ordered the Bank of China to produce documentary evidence pertaining to four aspects of the suit against it. First, the motion to compel the production of evidence sought to obtain documentation of communications between the Bank of China and the Chinese government regarding the al-Shurafa accounts. Second, the court sought access to reports and other information on "deficiencies" in the AML/CTF infrastructure at the bank's Guangzhou branch and corporate headquarters. Last, the court sought to procure evidence relating to visits between "foreign officials" and Chinese authorities related to al-Shurafa's financial activity.[100] This May 2013 order resulted in the production of a deluge of documents: 5,751 in number and more than 200,000 pages of material.[101] However, the plaintiffs asserted that this corpus of documents consisted of "filler," including publicly available material such as compliance manuals and information already produced by the bank.[102]

Malnourished in terms of documentary evidence, the plaintiffs eventually turned to Israel, which had empowered the suit, and others like it, to progress in the first place. Among the Israeli intelligence officers who had met with the Chinese government was a Mossad officer named Uzi Shaya. In February 2012, the Wultzes wrote to Israeli Prime Minister Benjamin Netanyahu requesting that Shaya be allowed to testify under oath about matters related to the case. In response to the plaintiffs' letter, hand-delivered by Ileana Ros-Lehtinen, a US congresswoman, the Prime Minister's office notified the Wultzes several months later that Shaya's testimony could proceed.[103]

Two years prior, in 2010, the Bank of China and Beijing had reached an agreement that neither the Chinese government nor the bank would be required to communicate with Jerusalem. Under the umbrella of "mutual trust," they assumed, the Israelis should not provide the courts with information on the meetings between their intelligence officials and the Chinese.[104] On 20 March 2013, Shaya wrote to the plaintiffs' attorneys that he was willing to testify, but with certain stipulations given the nature of his official status and the sensitivity of the subject matter.[105] Fearing the ramifications of Shaya's testimony, Beijing immediately began exerting diplomatic pressure on Israel.

In April 2013, the Chinese summoned Israel's ambassador in Beijing, Matan Vilnai, and threatened to cancel Netanyahu's May 2013 trip to China.[106] After the Shaya letter and prior to Netanyahu's visit, the Israelis assured Beijing that intelligence officers who were privy to information from the Israel-China terrorist financing meetings would not testify in the United States.[107] Netanyahu did travel to China in May of that year. He met with the Chinese in order to boost trade from $8 billion to $10 billion over three years, initiate free trade negotiations, and cement new ties with Xi Jinping.[108] It is worth noting that the diplomatic stakes for Israel were high at this time. Cooling relations between the Netanyahu government and the Obama administration, and the ongoing negotiations with Iran over its nuclear program (to which China was one of the permanent negotiating parties), provide some context to Israel's decision to retract the offer to allow Shaya to testify.

In reaction to the Israeli reversal, both the plaintiffs and US officials pressured Israel to recommit to its promise to allow testimony. A month after Netanyahu's China trip, a plaintiff from the Wultz case spoke with Israeli general Yaacov Amidror about the Bank of China case. Amidror mentioned that the Bank of China had promised to cease financing terrorism in the future, though it had done so willingly in the period up to the suicide bombings of the mid-2000s.[109] Furthermore, Amidror urged the plaintiffs to recognize that the bank had reversed its policy as a result of the legal assault waged against it in court.[110] With China increasing in financial status – and with the Bank of China, in particular, growing in stature in the banking industry – such a change in course could as easily have resulted from adopting regulatory institutions organically as from legal warfare. Despite additional pressure from Congresswoman Ros-Lehtinen, the Netanyahu government refused to allow Shaya's testimony. In late 2013, the Israeli government moved to quash. In August 2015, the case was dismissed.

## ANALYSIS

Throughout its history, the Bank of China has developed and maintained deep institutional linkages with the Chinese state. Since it opened at the turn of the twentieth century, the bank has in essence maintained the same relationship with the state, with the latter remaining the premier stakeholder in terms of bank ownership over the course of multiple regime types. State ownership began during the Qing era and expanded drastically under the Nationalist government, well before the Communist takeover in 1949. Serving as a financial extension of Beijing, the bank allowed the PRC to maintain a foreign exchange window to the outside world. Under subsequent restructuring beginning with Deng Xiaoping, the bank maintained this same status, with the state conserving its premier stakeholder status while absorbing private capital and increasing the scope of its operations.

This institutional linkage between bank and state survived not only the country's abundant political turmoil but also its adoption of the international threat finance regulatory regime. China began adopting the international AML/CTF regulations prior to 9/11 and the flood of regulatory adoptions that followed worldwide. Even in the midst of enforcement attempts, the threat finance regime continued to mature, with the PRC joining the FATF in 2007. However, the Bank of China's deep relationship with the state was not altered when the fortified finance regime was adopted. Rather, the AML/CTF regime simply grew up around this precedent structural configuration.

The Bank of China case encapsulates the moral hazard risk posed by a state seeking to effectively regulate a bank that it itself owns. The PRC had a vested interest in defending the Bank of China from regulatory sanction throughout the course of the lawsuit filed against it. Not only did the bank and its overseer, the People's Bank of China, bureaucratically choke off the production of evidence in the course of discovery, the PRC government also employed diplomatic pressure to coerce Israel into withholding testimony vital to the enforcement attempt carried out in US courts. This combination of bureaucratic foot-dragging and diplomatic deflection was sufficient to block enforcement against the bank.

This case not only offers an example of blocked enforcement but also underscores how the financial system comprises a strategic terrain in its own right. In the case of the Bank of China, Israel and the PRC engaged in a legal fight over regulatory malfeasance in a third country's legal system. Furthermore, the entire encounter was the result of a state using the adversarial legal system of the US to pursue geopolitical goals against a terrorist group. Of all the positive cases, the Bank of China arguably comprises the "easiest," as the bank itself was essentially a longstanding possession of the state. The case also highlights the centricity of the American financial and legal systems to the international regulatory system of fortified finance. Not only did Israel consciously approach the American legal system as a strategic terrain through which to pursue its security policy goals, but China leveraged its own status as a rising great power against Israel to dissuade it from using this American legal arena for this purpose.

# 3

# Al Rajhi Bank in Saudi Arabia

### INTRODUCTION

Saudi Arabia's volte-face relationship with Sunni jihadist groups is an open secret in international affairs. Fifteen of the nineteen hijackers who carried out the 2001 attacks on New York City and Washington, DC, were from Saudi Arabia, and significant amounts of terrorist financing have flowed through the kingdom despite Riyadh's close relationship with the West. According to investigative researcher Rachel Ehrenfeld, the 9/11 hijackers received funds from an Al-Qaeda financier in Europe named Mohammed Galeb Kalaje Zouaydi.[1] Arrested in Spain in 2002,[2] Zouaydi allegedly transferred funds to the terrorists from an account at the Saudi financial institution Al Rajhi Bank.[3] Al Rajhi Bank has yet to face regulatory or judicial penalty for its suspected involvement in financing terrorism, despite facing multiple attempts by plaintiffs in civil suits and American regulatory action.

This chapter traces the Al Rajhi Bank's deep roots in Saudi Arabia and its close institutional intertwining with the Saudi monarchy and royal family. In addition to this connection, the bank's relationship to the Saudi regulatory regime is explored for the period prior to the importation of the fortified finance regime. Next, the bank's suspected involvement in terrorism is outlined, together with an account of Riyadh's adoption of greater regulatory capacity. Last, the blocked enforcement phase is discussed, along with what transpired after the bank came under regulatory suspicion.

## AL RAJHI BANK, LEGITIMACY, AND REGIME BINDING

Al Rajhi Bank's institutional position in Saudi Arabia within dates back deep into the kingdom's past, with the Al Rajhi family to whom it belongs enjoying close relations with the monarchy. Tracing this history illustrates a relationship in which the monarchy has been unable to regulate a financial institution due its position as a coalition binder for the ruling family. The Al Rajhi family's supposedly close ties with jihadist elements in the kingdom, and the monarchy's reliance both upon this banking family and its relationship to certain religious authorities, effectively render the bank institutionally untouchable by the Saudi authorities due to the Al Rajhi family's importance to the Saudi regime's stability.

In order to understand the nature of the relationship between the Saudi monarchy and Al Rajhi Bank, it is necessary to understand the bank's unique history and its role in the Saudi economy. Unlike modern Western banks, or banks elsewhere that follow a Western business model, Al Rajhi Bank's origins lie in Saudi Arabia's deep past, as a money-dealing network that emerged in 1957 as the institution's first modern incarnation. The monarchy, the bank, and the money network that preceded it – as well as religious radicalism – are closely intertwined with the origins of the Saudi state and its composition as a tribal monarchy that relies heavily upon religious legitimacy.

The Saudi monarchy's reliance on religious influence dates to the mid-eighteenth century. Unlike other areas of the Middle East, the interior of the Arabian Peninsula in which the monarchy originated never experienced colonization, as neither regional nor global powers ever penetrated fully into the peninsula's harsh interior. Effectively isolated from much of the outside world, today's ruling Saudi monarchy developed a unique relationship with religious authority that would shape its banking and government institutions.

The fusion of the Saudi royal family's temporal authority with the religious zeal of the Hanbali Islamic juridical tradition traces to the 1740s, when the sheikh of the Ruwallah tribe, Muhammad ibn Saud, brokered a marriage between his son and the daughter of Muhammad ibn 'Abd al-Wahhāb.[4] The Hanbali tradition of Islamic jurisprudence, with its offshoots of Salafism and Wahhabism, serves as the religious basis for many Sunni jihadist movements around the world. In foreign relations, the binding of the Saudi monarchy with Wahhabism allows the kingdom to leverage considerable soft power in the Sunni world as a result of its considerable oil revenues and the presence of the holy cities of Mecca and Medina within its modern borders. Domestically, Wahhabism contributed directly to the consolidation of Saudi power within the Arabian Peninsula while also serving as a threat to the monarchy's security over the course of its modern history. Wahhabi groups' activities within the kingdom have intermittently threatened the monarchy's grasp on power, while Wahhabi jihadist groups have undermined the kingdom's relationships with outside powers.

Wahhabi influence has played a significant role in the kingdom's legal and institutional development, often leading to tensions between religiously motivated traditionalists and ambitious reformers. The contemporary Saudi state only came into being in 1932, after nearly a century of fluctuating Saudi tribal rule based in the Nejd region, in the heart of the peninsula. The Ikhwan, the Wahhabi militia that had helped the Saudi family consolidate its rule during the 1920s, had to be defeated by forces of Abdulaziz ibn Saud in 1930 before the monarchy could effectively exert royal authority over the religious elements in its midst.[5] Since 1932, the monarchy has engaged in an uneasy political balancing act with Wahhabi radicals in the kingdom. As the state matured in the 1940s and 1950s, schisms over the establishment of economic institutions would become a focal point of tension between the forward-looking monarchy and the religious traditionalists.

Economically, Saudi Arabia relied upon localized agriculture, pastoralism, and small commerce into the 1940s.[6] From the death of Ibn Saud in 1953 until the oil boom twenty years later, the Saudi political economy witnessed an enmeshing of relationships between the monarchy and the banking industry that would later result in the kingdom's inability to effectively regulate the lion's share of its financial sector. During the 1950s and 1960s, regional dynamics driven by political events elsewhere in the Arab world shook the Saudi sociopolitical landscape. Saudi workers trained in Egypt and Lebanon brought secular political mores back to the kingdom, while the proliferation of print periodicals and the introduction of radio and television prompted a backlash by conservative Wahhabis.[7]

Threatened by secularizing influences imported from Arab nationalist Egypt via modern media, and Saudi engagement in a proxy war with Cairo in Yemen, Wahhabi clerics in the country during this era pushed for the development of institutions that would provide modern mechanisms for the propagation and preservation of Wahhabi power. Such institutional developments would include the formation of religious universities, establishment of the World Muslim League, and a parallel and often contentious relationship between religious and state-based authority in the kingdom's legal system.[8] This legal double helix within Saudi Arabia led to Wahhabi considerations taking precedent in matters of commercial law. In business, legal developments took place in a context of competition between secular administrative bodies and religious authorities in the court system.

Until the foundation of the modern Saudi state, the west coast of the Arabian Peninsula, the Hejaz, remained outwardly oriented and cosmopolitan due to its access to foreign trade along the Red Sea and exposure to outside influences during the annual Hajj pilgrimage. The cosmopolitanism of the Hejaz stood in stark contrast to the ultraconservative Nejd in the country's centre, in which the Saudi-Wahhabi alliance originated. From 1926 until 1955, the Hejaz enjoyed a commercial legal domain largely beyond the purview of religious authorities. However, in the mid-1950s, religious jurists succeeded in gaining control of commercial adjudication in the region until a decade later, when the monarchy re-established secular oversight in the form of the Ministry of Commerce.[9] Within the ministry's commercial courts, three secular judges oversaw the adjudication of business disputes. By the late 1960s, Wahhabi clerics had reasserted institutional control, putting in place two religious judges and one secular regulator in each judicial panel.[10] Al Rajhi Bank's origins in the Hejazi city of Jeddah date to this period of competition between royal technocrats and Wahhabi religious authorities during the kingdom's mid-twentieth-century era of modernization.

While the Al Rajhi family's parent holding firm, Al Rajhi Holding Group, was founded in 1936, the first modern Al Rajhi Bank began in the 1960s as a money-changing business in the traditional street market in Jeddah. Its founder, Sulaiman Al Rajhi, supplied paper cash to other money dealers in the city from a suitcase.[11] Unlike the cosmopolitan business class of the Hejaz, the Al Rajhi family traces its origins to the Nejd, in the conservative interior of the country. The Al Rajhi family enjoyed a close relationship with Ibn Saud, the modern state's founding monarch. This interpersonal relationship between the king and the Al Rajhi family was reinforced by land grants offered to the family and Al Rajhi's oversight of much of the king's personal business dealings.[12] This relationship between bank and monarchy was already in place by the time the Saudi economy began to grow the institutions necessary for modern economic development. Further, due to the personal ties between the royal family and the Al Rajhis, as well as the position of the latter within the financial sector later on, the monarchy has held little institutional leverage over the bank's alleged involvement in financing terrorism.

The tribal wars of the 1920s, in which the Wahhabi Ikhwan routinely raided commercial centres on the coast, left a mutual suspicion between the new Saudi state and the Hejazi merchants. Both Ibn Saud and his Wahhabi base of support were openly hostile both to the Hejazi moneychangers and the foreign banks around Mecca.[13] This hostility was rooted not only in the tribal conflict, which lingered in the kingdom's political memory, but also in the fact that many traditional money-changing houses and foreign banks engaged in *riba* (the charging of interest) and other business practices forbidden by Islamic law. Due to its traditional financial practices grounded in religious considerations, Ibn Saud favoured the Al Rajhi network.[14] Indeed, despite the centuries-old financial position of Hejazi commercial families, the wealthiest families of today's Gulf States do not originate on the Red Sea coast but in the conservative desert region of the Nejd.[15]

Distrust of foreign banks and a steadily increasing supply of foreign currency from the 1940s onward prompted Ibn Saud to search for alternatives to the Egyptian and British banking interests seeking to establish a greater presence in the kingdom. In the early 1950s, the kingdom's finance minister, Sheikh Abdallah Suleiman, turned to American financial experts to formulate a solution to the kingdom's currency convertibility crisis. This solution encompassed the creation of the kingdom's central bank, the Saudi Arabian Monetary Agency (SAMA), which opened its doors in 1952, a year before Ibn Saud's death.[16]

## AL RAJHI BANK AND THE SAUDI REGULATORY SYSTEM

Suleiman arranged the creation of the regulatory agency to avoid business practices based on interest, and article 3.7 of the Saudi Arabian Monetary Agency charter stipulates the prohibition of interest payments in the kingdom's financial sector.[17] The timing of SAMA's founding, and its initial institutional function, had implications for the royals' relationship with the Al Rajhi family, particularly as SAMA embodied potential competition for the Al Rajhi network in regard to the handling of the kingdom's royal funds.[18] Unlike Al Rajhi's traditional orientation, SAMA embodied technocratic modernity. Given that its revenues were based upon charging the state fees for its services, SAMA enjoyed considerable autonomy, operating beyond the purview of the Ministry of Finance and conducting its recruitment of personnel independently of the civil service.[19] Additionally, the agency in its early years assumed a certain professionalism via its personnel, which at that point consisted of careerist American and Lebanese financial experts and a board of governors subject to royal decree.[20]

Al Rajhi Bank, the largest Islamic bank in the world by the mid-2000s,[21] was founded first as a money-dealing operation in the traditional *souk* of Jeddah in 1957, and then recast as a modern, Sharia-compliant bank in 1987. The bank's growth from a street-based money-dealing operation to a multinational bank can only be understood by examining the organization's role in the Saudi economy. Unlike banks following a Western business model, traditional moneylenders in the Gulf remain tied to specific industries and often also participate directly in these same industries' non-banking operations.[22] Additionally, lending is often predicated upon the requirement that the debtor spend the loaned cash at businesses affiliated with the bank through family and personal ties.[23] As a moneychanger, Al Rajhi Bank enjoyed a comfortable position through its close social proximity to the royal family and by serving as the preferred financial institution for facilitating remittances for foreign workers in Saudi Arabia from across the Muslim world. Even as its financial status grew, the bank maintained traditional business practices to the point that individual cash couriers frequently travelled to Europe to exchange notes for gold and other currencies in order to replenish their individual Saudi branches.[24] Al Rajhi Bank's status as a Sharia-compliant financial institution eventually clashed with the kingdom's regulatory stance in the 1980s, but the bank's lobbying ability allowed it override SAMA's opposition to the religious nature of its business practices.

As noted above, the kingdom has historically walked a fine line, in terms of political economy, between governing its regulatory institutions according to modern technocratic expertise or religious considerations. While SAMA was prohibited from conducting business based upon interest, thereby avoiding violations of Islamic business practices, the agency itself largely opposed the promotion of Islamic banking in the kingdom and focused instead on regulating banks' levels of reserve capital and providing financial advice to the state.[25] Even as oil revenues flooded the kingdom with capital in the 1970s, the increased need for financial institutions was met through an increased presence of foreign banks, regulated by SAMA.[26] Traditional banking remained the domain of the informal sector, based in the street market.

The fact that Al Rajhi Bank managed to lobby the Saudi state to allow it to become a modern, Sharia-compliant bank is noteworthy for two reasons. First, SAMA's institutional status within the kingdom enabled Al Rajhi to lobby the royal family and overcome the central bank's opposition to its modernization. Unlike other countries in the Middle East, SAMA has kept an institutional distance between itself and the members of the royal family by never having royals on its board.[27] The second reason is the fact that SAMA also acts as the manager of the kingdom's sovereign wealth fund. Yet, despite SAMA's technocratic acumen and institutional distance, Al Rajhi managed to override the agency's opposition to its modernization. Al Rajhi's prominence in the kingdom has only increased with its modernization – a degree of prominence, moreover, that became the focus of a 2010 International Monetary Fund (IMF) assessment that remarked upon the kingdom's highly concentrated banking sector.[28] As of 2016, Al Rajhi alone held 16 per cent of the kingdom's banking industry market share.[29]

While the early 1970s and the aftermath of the Yom Kippur War catapulted capital into the Persian Gulf in the form of oil revenue, 1979 marked another geopolitical turning point for Sunni monarchies in the region, and for Saudi Arabia in particular. The Iranian Revolution brought to power a regime that was openly hostile to Riyadh, and which could rival Saudi Arabia's position as a geopolitical representative of Islam. That same year, meanwhile, the Soviet Union invaded Afghanistan. Domestically, the Saudis experienced their direst security threat since eradicating the Ikhwan decades earlier, when Mecca's Grand Mosque was seized by terrorists led by Juhayman al-Otaybi, the grandson of one of the original Ikhwan commanders. The need to harness Islamic legitimacy to maintain security at home and project power abroad to counter the Iranian and Soviet threats would impact the Saudi banking sector through the official introduction of Islamic banking.

The institutional changes brought about in response to the events of the 1970s cannot be overstated. As the Gulf was flooded with oil wealth, the technocratic elements within the Saudi bureaucracy began to lose ground to the religious-minded traditionalists. Further, the assassination of King Faisal in 1975 at the hands of his nephew, Faisal bin Musaid, led to a new era of caution on the part of the monarchy regarding religious elements in the kingdom. Many believe that Faisal's assassin sought revenge for the 1965 police killing of the traditionalist prince, Khalid bin Musaid, over his opposition to the modernization of Saudi life.[30] Following Faisal's murder, his successor, King Fahd, allowed concessions to Wahhabism in the form of allocating greater funds to religious schools and universities, despite declining state budgets through the early 1980s.[31] With the monarchy exercising greater caution regarding religious affairs and facing pushback from other ministries over the resolution of commercial disputes, SAMA, for its part, began to lose institutional predictability on the issues in its purview.[32]

In the early 1980s, the Al Rajhi family operated Saudi Arabia's largest money-dealing and remittance service. However, after one branch of the family's banking network nearly collapsed as the result of silver bullion speculation in 1982, SAMA stepped in to regulate the informal banking sector by mandating the registration and conversion of traditional moneylending operations into modern commercial banks.[33] Traditional money dealers were mandated to convert their institutions by the end of 1983 if they were to stay in business.

While Al Rajhi sought to morph into a commercial bank, its traditional religious mores stipulated that the bank would be Islamic in nature and follow Sharia-compliant business practices. SAMA was not only hostile to this notion but did not acquiesce to Al Rajhi's pleas until 1988.[34] SAMA's director at the time, Hamad Al-Sayari, proved a strict regulator, in keeping with the professionalism of the agency's institutional legacy; however, royal mandates determined final decisions regarding regulatory outcomes.[35] After an aggressive campaign to convince the state to allow it a banking licence, the Al Rajhi Banking and Investment Corporation came into being.[36] The bank was allowed to provide Islamic financial services provided that the word "Islamic" did not appear in the bank's name.[37] While SAMA's stance opposed the introduction of overt Islamic banking within the kingdom, Riyadh openly supported the spread of Islamic financial institutions elsewhere in the world.[38] In Saudi Arabia itself, Al Rajhi remains the only bank of a primarily Islamic orientation; other banks in the kingdom largely focus on conventional financial services.[39] As to why the state forbade

Al Rajhi from holding an overtly Islamic moniker, the proscription was a response to concerns that the existence of an outwardly "Islamic" bank might implicate other Saudi financial institutions as being somehow "un-Islamic" in their business practices.[40] As the bank grew, the Al Rajhi conglomerate expanded its non-banking activities into the fields of construction and philanthropy. This combination, one may suppose, placed it at the social nexus for working with Al-Qaeda over the course of the 1980s and 1990s. SAMA, one of the regulatory bodies tasked with thwarting money laundering and terrorist financing, began collecting suspicious activity reports (SARs) on Al Rajhi Bank in the 1970s, but its weakness in the face of Al Rajhi's influence in the kingdom would remain a persistent institutional condition.

As to how Al Rajhi survived its transition from a traditional money-dealing network into a modern bank, the bank itself operated as but one of many ventures overseen by the Al Rajhi family. These ventures extended from banking and construction to the poultry business and the non-profit sector. In 1978, these ventures were formally melded into the Al Rajhi Trading and Exchange Company.[41] Even with its full conversion to a modern joint-stock banking venture in 1987, the shareholder majority remained with the Al Rajhi family. As the bank and its affiliated businesses expanded, its connections with the Saudi state also expanded in the form of contracts for infrastructure projects.[42] Al Rajhi wealth was prominent enough to warrant mention in a 1996 US diplomatic cable, which noted that the family's wealth dwarfed that of most of the members of the Saudi royal family.[43]

At the time of its transition from traditional money dealer to modern bank, the Al Rajhi Company for Currency Exchange and Commerce was already worth $7 billion, while its founder, Sulaiman Abdul-Aziz Al Rajhi, was the richest man in the kingdom outside of the royal family.[44] Yet, despite its wealth, the Al Rajhi family's religious mores continued to guide their business. Unlike other burgeoning Saudi billionaires, who began travelling in private jets and buying holiday homes in Europe and elsewhere in the 1980s, the Al Rajhis maintained austere business premises and remained close to their traditional Bedouin roots.[45] Socially embedded within the religious segments of Saudi society, Al Rajhi Bank patronized numerous religious charitable causes in the kingdom. In a domestic environment in which an emboldened Wahhabism was accorded greater leeway by the Saudi state, some of Al Rajhi Bank's charitable clients were alleged to be financing terrorism.

## COUNTERTERRORIST FINANCING AND AL RAJHI BANK

If Saudi Arabia comprises a strong state, it also lacks institutional standardization. Laws and major bureaucratic decisions rest upon royal decree and the monarchy's negotiation of power dynamics between the *ulama* (Islamic religious scholars), factions within the royal family, and changes in the Middle Eastern geopolitical landscape. While monarchical mandate remains the ultimate arbiter of state decisions in the kingdom, the legal realm relies on traditional Sharia law. The ultraconservative Hanbali tradition of Islamic jurisprudence, from which Wahhabism derives, is the official juridical orientation of the kingdom. In order to understand the Saudi legal approaches to terrorism and terrorist financing, the tensions between royal decree and the Hanbali legal code must be taken into account. Additionally, while Western de jure notions of CTF regulation are relatively new and date to the early 2000s, Saudi surveillance of the financial system dates to the mid-1970s.

Certain characteristics of the Saudi legal system place the monarchy in a precarious position in relation to religious authorities of the ulama. The kingdom's legal system consists of Sharia, with the king serving as the final point of appeal for legal decisions. During the late 1980s and early 1990s, the same period in which Al Rajhi reinvented itself as a modern bank, religious authorities and business groups began advocating for a reassertion of Islamic religious mores in the kingdom.[46] Elements of this reassertion included King Fahd's issuance of decrees explicitly stating that royal authority drew legitimacy from the Quran and Prophetic tradition.[47] In the legal realm, judges were still to be appointed by royal fiat.[48] However, with the Sharia judicial system overseeing all aspects of both civil and criminal law, this would place any royal override of legal decisions potentially at odds with religious bases of power in the kingdom. Understanding this balancing act is key to comprehending how the Saudi state, which had been collecting SARs since the 1970s, might overlook suspicions of terrorism financing on the part of Al Rajhi Bank.

The reforms of the early 1990s enacted by Fahd's decrees culminated in the Basic Law of Saudi Arabia in 1992. While the king is considered above the kingdom's ostensibly separate legislative and judicial powers, article 67 of the Basic Law stipulates that the monarchy has regulatory purview in areas for which Sharia law has no specific answer.[49]

Despite the supposed urbanity of commerce, to which the royal prerogative is most applicable, the monarchy's actions are curtailed by theories originating in Sharia law.[50] Royal oversight of regulatory mandates is bound by the legal theory of the medieval scholar Ibn Taymiyyah, who stipulates that regulations issued cannot fly in the face of Sharia dictates.[51] In the case of Saudi Arabia, it is not inconsequential that Ibn Taymiyyah's theories outline the range of the monarchy's royal authority in the regulatory sphere. His interpretation of Sharia law is also the legal basis of justification drawn upon by Sunni terrorist groups such as the Islamic State and Al-Qaeda.

The intellectual founders of the Sunni jihadist groups – Ibn 'Abd al-Wahhab, Sayyid Qutb, and Ibn Taymiyyah – were all Hanbali juridical thinkers. For the Saudi monarchy, it is ironic that during the 1990s, Sunni jihadists would draw upon Ibn Taymiyyah's philosophy and juridical decisions to advocate for the overthrow of the royal family.[52] In the regulatory realm, thus, the kingdom is institutionally at an impasse with its own religious legitimacy. Within Saudi law, both terrorism and terrorist financing fall under the same category of crime, as designated by Sharia law: *hiraba*, or the "killing and terrorization of innocent people, spreading evil on the earth, theft, looting, and highway robbery."[53]

Regarding the prevention of terrorism and terrorist financing, both legal frameworks were present by the time the modern Al Rajhi bank is suspected to have begun serious involvement in funding groups such as Al-Qaeda. The presence of Sharia law since the kingdom's beginnings indicates that whatever action (or inaction) was taken by the Saudi state regarding terrorism enjoyed a legal basis to draw upon when it came to countering terrorism. In terms of banking supervision, SAMA began operating its surveillance system in the mid-1970s, as Saudi Arabia began mandating the collection of suspicious activity reports (SARs) in 1975.

SAMA was the primary agency concerned with collecting financial surveillance in the kingdom. SARs were to be collected by financial institutions and reported to law enforcement and the central bank. The original purpose of such financial intelligence collection was the crackdown on illegal remittance systems and underground banking overall.[54] Institutionally, in its original design, this surveillance regime was intended to monitor and sanction financial services precisely like Al Rajhi Bank prior to its reinvention as a modern Islamic bank in the 1980s. It must be noted that these regulatory arrangements began well before 1979 – the year of both the Soviet invasion of Afghanistan and the Iranian revolution – when the international situation motivated the kingdom to turn a blind eye to terrorist activity abroad. Rather, such surveillance was domestically motivated to help modernize the Saudi financial system and increase its efficiency. This surveillance commenced prior to the lobbying by Al Rajhi to pressure the kingdom into allowing it to become a modern bank. In other words, the Saudi regulatory apparatus for financial surveillance was already partly in place by the time Al Rajhi supposedly began supporting terrorism in the 1990s.

The beginnings of Saudi Arabia's system of financial surveillance in the 1970s coincided with a marked increase in the kingdom's efforts to leverage the "soft power" of religion to promote Sunni Islam around the world. One loophole in the Saudi financial intelligence system consists of limiting royal regulatory purview to legal areas in which Sharia law is uncertain. A second loophole relates to the kingdom's approach to regulating *zakat*, or Islamic charity. Unlike in the West, where taxes and charity are conceptually separate types of financial activity, Islamic thought holds little differentiation between the two. For Saudi citizens and enterprises, regulation of taxes and charity are inextricably linked, as zakat is levied on all Saudi interests and both taxes and charity are regulated (since 1950) by the Department of Zakat and Income Taxes (DZIT). In order to meet these requirements, Saudi entities often have special committees to facilitate paying such fees.[55] Despite regulatory attempts to increase transparency as to where such charity funds are destined, the chief regulator of SAMA lamented that many payments are sent abroad for unknown uses.[56] A primary function of Islamic banking institutions is the facilitation and oversight of zakat for their clients.[57] In the case of Al Rajhi Bank and other suspected terrorist financiers, it was through charitable foundations that funds supposedly moved from the bank to terrorism.

In the Western states, most governments began developing welfare institutions in the late nineteenth century. In these countries, private charity and government-backed social assistance are separate economic phenomena, both contributing to social causes. In Islamic economic thought, charity, whether provided by private actors or the state, is one and the same thing. Charitable foundations provide the lion's share of social welfare, and the state has historically supported such foundations in Islamic countries through zakat taxation. In the case of Saudi Arabia, it is such charitable organizations that have served as conduits for transmitting terrorist funds from backers to fighters.

Al Rajhi Bank was one of several banks that supposedly transmitted such funds. The 9/11 hijackers from the Al-Qaeda cell in Hamburg allegedly received money through Al Rajhi accounts held by Mahmoud Darkazanli and Abdul Fattah Zammar, who are suspected of having provided the cell with logistical support.[58] Mohammed Galeb Kalaje Zouaydi allegedly transferred funds directly from Al Rajhi Bank to terrorists involved with 9/11, the 2002 Bali bombing that killed 204 people, and the 2004 Madrid attack that killed 192.[59] In addition to holding an account of a premier Al-Qaeda financier, Al Rajhi Bank provided extensive financial support for the Al-Haramain Islamic Foundation and the SAAR Foundation;[60] each of these non-profit is suspected of having provided financial support to Al-Qaeda. In 1999, representatives from the US National Security Council and the Office of Foreign Asset Control went to Saudi Arabia to warn both Al Rajhi Bank and SAMA about the financial institution's ties to jihadist groups, and Al-Qaeda in particular.[61] Securing Riyadh's cooperation in counterterrorist financing efforts would prove a perennial struggle for the US, until the kingdom's own security interests began to align with those of Washington.

The Al-Haramain Islamic Foundation (AHIF) came into being in the late 1980s with the purpose of supporting Wahhabi social action around the world. In 1997, AHIF opened a branch office in Ashland, Oregon. At its height, AHIF had operations in fifty countries and disbursed between $30 and $80 million in its charitable work until its closure in 2004.[62] US intelligence sources discovered that AHIF had supported the Makhtab al-Khidamat (MAK), or Afghan Services Bureau – a mujahideen recruitment and fundraising organization that would later be absorbed into Al-Qaeda – and had even established a presence in Albania with the backing of Osama bin Laden.[63] During the 1980s and 1990s, Al-Qaeda's financial apparatus was closely intertwined with that of MAK, which recruited Al-Qaeda members, published propaganda, and boasted more than thirty offices in the United States alone.[64] A 2003 cable by then Secretary of State Colin Powell notes that AHIF's influence was so widespread that Al-Qaeda received support from some twenty of the NGO's branches, including those within Saudi Arabia.[65]

In 1999, AHIF's links with Al-Qaeda were shown to be even more direct. That year, an Al-Haramain representative deployed a

Bangladeshi terrorist to scout American consulates in India.[66] Upon his arrest by Indian authorities, where he was found to possess bomb-making materials, the terrorist confessed that the planning for the foiled attacks on US targets in India had been conducted on AHIF premises in Bangladesh.[67] AHIF also assisted Al-Qaeda in carrying out the attacks on US embassies in Kenya and Tanzania.[68]

The US had received advance warning of Al-Qaeda's presence in Kenya prior to the 1998 Nairobi attack. In 1997, Kenyan police raided the Nairobi home of Wadih el-Hage, a Lebanese American who served as Osama bin Laden's secretary.[69] Based on evidence yielded by the raid, Kenyan officials suspected that the banker Saleh Abdul Aziz Al-Rajhi had been supporting Al-Qaeda.[70] El-Hage's personal affiliation with bin Laden began in 1986, while working in a MAK office in Quetta, Pakistan.[71] In the early 1990s, el-Hage's tenure in Nairobi included involvement in the illicit diamond trade[72] and forging documents for Al-Qaeda members involved in the Nairobi attack.[73] In 2002, the US and Saudi Arabia jointly began designating AHIF branches as supporters of terrorism, while the UN listed the foundation itself as a terrorism supporter in 2004. El-Hage was tried in the US and sentenced to life without parole in 2001.

Juan Zarate, former Assistant Secretary of the Treasury for Terrorist Financing, notes that Al Rajhi's suspected involvement in Al-Qaeda surfaced again in 2002, when Bosnian officials raided an Al-Qaeda property in Sarajevo. Among the seized evidence were documents linking Al-Qaeda to another Saudi charity, the Benevolence International Foundation. After the FBI raided the charity's Chicago offices, the Department of the Treasury discovered a list of major backers who were allegedly involved in supporting Al-Qaeda; this list included the founder of Al Rajhi Bank, Sulaiman Al Rajhi.[74] According to a 2003 CIA report that became public knowledge in 2007, Sulaiman Al Rajhi was a member of a group of prominent financiers known as the "Golden Chain." Allegedly, Al-Rajhi was not only a financier but played an additional role in helping Al-Qaeda front charities disguise their financial activity and avoid arousing a regulatory crackdown by Riyadh.[75] Concurrent to the Bosnian raid, US authorities began Operation Green Quest, which focused first on the SAAR Foundation and later on the Safa Group that would replace SAAR. Both these entities were supposedly intertwined with Al Rajhi Bank.

One of the first US responses to 9/11 was to undertake renewed regulatory action against terrorist financing. Beginning in October

2001 and continuing through June 2003, a grouping of US intelligence and regulatory agencies conducted Operation Green Quest in order to uncover and rectify terrorist financing vulnerabilities in the American financial system. By the time of its completion, Green Quest had frozen $33 million and issued seventy indictments.[76] A key focus of the operation was the SAAR Foundation, an Al Rajhi-backed front for terrorist financing.

Yaqub Mirza founded the SAAR Foundation in 1984 with financial infusions from Sulaiman bin Abdulaziz Al Rajhi, after whom it was named.[77] From its base in Herndon, Virginia, the organization sought to expand Islam through the founding of over a hundred branch offices and non-profits.[78] While SAAR closed in December 2000, it was replaced by the Safa Group, which was operated by the same individuals. Although tasked with promoting Islam, the foundation actually did little to win converts and instead invested in Virginia real estate and agricultural businesses in the US and South America.[79] Virtually all of the organization's 130 subsidiary groups functioned out of the same address, at 555 Grove Street in Herndon, and managed to avoid outright intervention by the US government due to the close relationship that Sulaiman Al Rajhi enjoyed with the Saudi royal family.[80] Over the course of the late 1990s, it enjoyed significant donations, raking in $1.7 billion in 1998 alone.[81]

A 2002 investigative piece by the *Washington Post*, citing both American and European investigators, noted that SAAR transferred $20 million in funds to two individuals, Youssef Nada and Ahmed Idris Nasreddin.[82] Authorities raided the bank used by Nada – Al Taqwa Bank, based in Switzerland and the Bahamas – in 2001. Al Taqwa boasted shareholders that included two members of the bin Laden family, and counted Nada and Nasreddin on its board.[83] The bank was able to establish itself in Switzerland due to the presence on its board of directors of Albert F.A. Huber, an outspoken Nazi.[84] Al Taqwa Bank, Nada, and Huber were all designated as supporters of terrorism by the US Treasury Department in November 2001.[85] According to the *Washington Post* investigation, Nada and Sulaiman Al Rajhi met through their mutual involvement with the Muslim Brotherhood.[86] The FBI met with SAAR representatives multiple times prior to 2001.[87]

## BLOCKED ENFORCEMENT

While Al Rajhi came under massive scrutiny from a number of sources, from damning media reports and investigative journalism to the governmental agencies of several countries, the bank has enjoyed blocked regulatory enforcement by its home state. Indeed, this blockage has come in the form of Saudi-US diplomatic action and the shielding of the bank from civil lawsuits originating in American courts. Both are analyzed below. While the kingdom and Al Rajhi Bank have endeavoured to build regulatory capacity to counter terrorist financing, the bank has yet to face penalty for its alleged prior activities. Instead, Saudi Arabia included Al Rajhi in the process of developing an increased regulatory capacity and in its bureaucratic reshuffling of the banking and charitable sectors.

Shortly after 11 September 2001, the United States began pushing for greater Saudi action against terrorist financing in the kingdom. Suspicion about Saudi knowledge about and involvement in terrorist financing ran high in the US, and led to strained diplomatic ties between the two countries. However, due to the precarious situation of the Saudi monarchy in regard to the religious radicalism in its borders, the US opted for a cautious strategy in working with Riyadh to curtail terrorist financing. On 24 September 2001, President Bush, along with Secretary of State Colin Powell and Secretary of the Treasury Paul O'Neill, complimented the Saudis on their cooperation with US efforts to curtail terrorist financing.[88] Yet, according to current and former intelligence and foreign policy officials, the Saudis were mostly reluctant to cooperate too closely on security issues related to terrorism.[89]

In 2002, the Council on Foreign Relations singled out Saudi Arabia and its charities as conduits for terrorist funds. According the Council, not only was Saudi Arabia dragging its feet in cooperating with the US, but the Bush administration was defending Riyadh with praise despite its weak cooperation.[90] Additionally, the National Security Council advised the administration to push the Saudis with an ultimatum and set a three-month deadline to "punish" terrorist financiers, following which US would take unilateral action against the latter.[91] Prince Bandar, Saudi ambassador to the US at the time, noted that the kingdom would have to act carefully and slowly due to the religious conservatism of the Saudi population.[92] In other words, a poorly planned monarchy-led crackdown on the kingdom's socioreligious institutions, many of which relied on Al Rajhi Bank for financial support, could trigger a potentially destabilizing backlash as well as economic problems.

From 2001 through 2005, Saudi Arabia implemented changes in an effort to cleanse its financial system of terrorist funds. However, it was only because of discreet but continuous pressure on the part of the Americans and an increased terror threat level within the kingdom that these changes were allowed to take place. These measures, largely de jure in nature, included the kingdom's entering into greater involvement with the Financial Action Task Force, adopting UN resolutions, and developing domestic fortified finance capability. In October 2001, Saudi Arabia took initial action by adopting UN Security Council resolution 1373, which mandates the freezing and seizure of terrorist assets in the financial system.[93] Additionally, the kingdom established a full-fledged FIU in 2005. Al Rajhi Bank was present and involved in the development of the new domestic regulations.

In March 2002, an American delegation from the Department of the Treasury travelled to Saudi Arabia to secure the kingdom's cooperation against Al-Qaeda and its financial network. One of the goals of the meeting consisted of initiating joint action against the Al-Haramain Islamic Foundation, and the two countries jointly designated the organization as a financier of terrorism on 11 March 2002.[94] According to Juan Zarate, then Assistant Secretary of the Treasury for Terrorist Financing, the Saudis stepped up their crackdown on Al-Qaeda's financial network in May 2003 after an outbreak of several terrorist attacks in the kingdom.[95] This critical juncture for Saudi domestic security vis-à-vis Al-Qaeda may have brought Al Rajhi even closer to the monarchy and other organs of the Saudi state. However, despite increased cooperation, the financing of terrorism from within the kingdom yielded ongoing aggravation for the Saudis due to the reticence of captured Al-Qaeda members and skepticism within intelligence circles as to whether or not supposed wealthy donors, such as those of the "Golden Chain" mentioned above, were genuine contributors.[96] In total, the combined wealth of the individuals involved in the Golden Chain amounted to more than $85 billion, or 42 per cent of Saudi Arabia's gross national product.[97]

It must be noted that the relationship between the Saudi state and Al Rajhi Bank is neither simple nor necessarily simpatico. The Al Rajhi affiliation with the kingdom's conservative base, upon which the monarchy relies for its legitimacy, is what drives Saudi caution in dealing with issues related to terrorist financing. According to an investigative piece by the *Wall Street Journal*, American intelligence agencies contemplated implementing covert action to sabotage and infiltrate Al Rajhi Bank.[98] Another strategy would have been to pressure other countries to regulate Al Rajhi's activities more heavily within their own jurisdictions; however, the Bush administration opted for a plan of action centred on closely and quietly lobbying the Saudi government.[99] Indeed, were it not for SAMA's technocratic acumen and surveillance apparatus, the latter having been in place since 1975, the Saudi state may have proven incapable of curtailing Al Rajhi Bank's activities due to the bank's position in the kingdom's economy and society.

US diplomatic cables from 2004 indicate particular concern over Al Rajhi Bank's suspected involvement in funding terrorism. According to correspondence to the US Secretary of State, Zarate met with Ali Al Ghaïth, then director of banking inspection, insurance, and financial leasing at SAMA. In the meeting, Al Ghaïth argued that public suspicion of Al Rajhi Bank was unfounded and that the bank had received a clean bill of health following an August 2003 audit conducted by Ernst & Young. Zarate mentioned "particular accounts of concern" connected to Al Rajhi Bank, and indicated to Al Ghaïth that the institution's regulatory capacity warranted a review as well as an investigation of particular accounts. What is notable in the cable is that Al Ghaïth was "fed up" with American suspicion into Al Rajhi's purported terrorist financing.[100]

This regulatory and diplomatic tension extended into late 2004, when both American and Saudi officials conducted a joint onsite examination into Al Rajhi Bank's CTF capabilities. In a November 2004 diplomatic cable, Secretary of State Powell notes that the Saudi CTF regime was robust in its ability to prevent the kingdom's financial system from being used for terrorist financing. Pertaining to Al Rajhi Bank in particular, Powell mentions that the US provided Riyadh with evidence regarding a number of terrorist-affiliated accounts, and that "the US and Saudi governments have agreed to work together to meet a mutual goal of ensuring Al Rajhi Bank is fully equipped to monitor and note suspicious patterns and trends in account activity, so as to create a preventative system within the institution."[101] Powell notes that the reason for a joint review of the bank was so that Saudi and US authorities could "work collectively with Al Rajhi Bank" in implementing measures designed to prevent future malfeasance.[102] During the review, SAMA personnel would be present at "all meetings" with the bank's personnel; and the review would include meetings with specific managers who oversaw the relevant accounts.[103]

Although it is not publicly known if bank officials faced arrest or other penalties in Saudi Arabia, the bank's presumed relationship to terrorism is not one-dimensional. Not only did the bank keep accounts that were used by terrorists directly, the bank's founder and head supposedly contributed to terrorist groups through charitable foundations, which in turn allegedly supported terrorist groups logistically. The bank's relationship to the Saudi state would remain close, however, as Riyadh engaged in bureaucratic reshuffling later in the decade to better regulate charities and develop its FIU.

In the mid-to-late 2000s, the British bank HSBC came under increased scrutiny for nefarious financial practices ranging from aiding in tax evasion to laundering money for drug cartels and financing terrorism. Investigations into the bank across multiple countries exacted a number of penalties against the institution, including a 2012 fine for $1.92 billion, the largest financial penalty ever levied against a bank.[104] HSBC also had ties to Al Rajhi Bank. A 2012 report by the US Senate's Permanent Subcommittee on Investigations details a number of HSBC's internal emails debating the value of maintaining ties with Al Rajhi over the latter's financial relationships.[105]

US Senator Carl Levin notes that 2005 marked a year of confusion for HSBC regarding Al Rajhi, and that the British bank instructed its affiliated branches to cut all ties with Al Rajhi Bank outside of the Middle East over concerns related to terrorism. Yet, later that year, HSBC retracted its instructions to its affiliates and allowed each country branch to determine its own interactions with Al Rajhi. That next year, following threats by Al Rajhi Bank, HSBC relinquished and supplied the Saudi bank with US$1 billion.[106] HSBC's confusion regarding Al Rajhi thus was due not simply to general mismanagement on its part but also to the regulatory grey area resulting from the bank's close relations with Riyadh and the US in developing the kingdom's financial surveillance apparatus.

HSBC's confusion is noteworthy, as 2005 marked a turning point in US-Saudi relations with President Bush and Crown Prince Abdullah meeting that April to rebuild ties. Facing ongoing threats from Al-Qaeda within its own borders, the Saudi state began to take a more overt stance against terrorism, alongside the US.[107] While the heads of state schmoozed diplomatically, the two countries were involved in further developing the kingdom's fortified finance regime.

From 2005 to 2006, the kingdom was developing its FIU system in order to secure membership in the Egmont Group, an international organization of FIUs from various states. With the establishment of the kingdom's FIU, the Egmont Group officially recognized Saudi compliance, despite the fact that SAMA's practice of SAR collection dated to the 1970s.[108] The Saudi FIU was only officially admitted, however, in May 2009. For its part, Al Rajhi Bank's position in the late 2000s was something of a gray area, yet it continued nonetheless to enjoy a comfortable relationship with its home state.

The Saudi FIU began operations the day before the fourth anniversary of 9/11, on 10 September 2005, thanks to assistance from the United States and with the involvement of Al Rajhi Bank. Indeed, between 9/11 and 2005, the Saudis froze forty-one bank accounts for a total of $5,697,400 – a paltry 4 per cent of estimated global terrorist funds at the time.[109] Diplomatic cables from 2006 describe meetings in Riyadh between US Treasury officials, Saudi representatives from SAMA and its FIU, and representatives from Al Rajhi Bank to help facilitate the kingdom's entry into the Egmont Group as a full member.[110] While the Saudis made institutional improvements in the areas of reporting and regulating charities, the cable describes bank officials as reluctant to discuss their relationships with the Saudi FIU or to talk about their monitoring practices.[111]

A diplomatic cable disseminated through the American intelligence community in 2009 describes US efforts to assist Saudi Arabia in developing its fortified finance regime. In mid-May 2009, coinciding with the official date of the kingdom's Egmont Group admission, the Treasury Department's Deputy Assistant Secretary Daniel Glaser travelled to Riyadh to enhance American cooperation with Saudi Arabia in the area of threat finance.[112] The meeting described in the cable is noteworthy for its attendees. Aside from Glaser, the Saudi attendees included governmental officials and the heads of two banks: Riyad Bank's chairman Rashed Al Rashed and Al Rajhi Bank CEO Sulaiman Al Rajhi. Notably, Al Rajhi Bank was the sole private bank in attendance (Riyad Bank being state-owned), highlighting the singular relationship between the Saudi government and Al Rajhi.

During the meeting, which covered CTF issues and financial strategies to isolate Iran over its nuclear program, Sulaiman Al Rajhi discussed his bank's efforts to increase CTF reporting: "Things are better now as the Kingdom of Saudi Arabia had suffered from terrorism so institutions know that these systems are for the good."[113] Al Rajhi noted that his bank had augmented compliance training and reporting of suspicious activity. As for charities, Al Rajhi described how Saudi banks were barred from transferring charitable funds unless the charity in question held the requisite state licence. When certain charities endeavoured to circumvent the ban, Al Rajhi worked with SAMA to track or curtail the transfer of funds.[114] However, uncertainty over the legality of the bank's dealings and its standing was strong enough to cause confusion among its commercial partners, such as HSBC.

While Al Rajhi Bank enjoyed the privilege of assisting its own government and the US in regulating its own activities, US officials assisted the bank by helping to shield it from lawsuits and investigations originating in the United States. Throughout the 2000s, survivors of the 9/11 attacks sought to bring lawsuits, under the 1992 Anti-Terrorism Act, against entities suspected of supporting Al-Qaeda. Defendants attacked in the suits included Saudi royals and banking interests, including Al Rajhi Bank, which in turn accused the US of seeking to "extort Saudi money" and "meddle in the region."[115] However, the 9/11 survivors' legal efforts were stymied thanks to the diplomatic connection between Saudi Arabia and the US. Repeated attempts to sue Al Rajhi Bank by survivors, insurance companies, and others have been summarily dismissed in US courts. In September 2020, however, the US courts shifted position, as the US magistrate for the Southern District of New York, Sarah Netburn, ordered Saudi Prince Bandar bin Sultan to testify in regard to the 9/11 attacks.[116]

ANALYSIS

While it cannot fully be known if Al Rajhi Bank knowingly and actively supported terrorism, the bank's relationship to the Saudi state is certain. The Al Rajhi banking family developed in the same sociopolitical circles as the Saudi royal family, with both families originating in the Nejd, the Arabian Peninsula's hyper-conservative Wahhabi interior. Indeed, during the founding period of the Saudi monarchy, the royal family had relied on the Al Rajhi network for assistance in managing its financial affairs. Owing to the split between the new Nejdi rulers and the established Hejazi banks at the time, the affinity between Al Rajhi Bank and the monarchy has persisted into the contemporary era, strained though the relationship may be due to diverging interests.

It is highly possible that Al Rajhi Bank financed terrorist activity, particularly given its position as the only institution in the country operating openly as an Islamic bank. The particularities of the Saudi tax system – with both the state and private corporations contributing, through zakat, to a deep institutional network of Islamic charities – have provided ample potential sources of logistical and economic support for Al-Qaeda and other jihadist groups that rely on donations from within the kingdom.

Data indicate that Al Rajhi Bank maintained multiple ties to charitable organizations suspected of links to Al-Qaeda, beginning shortly after the bank's evolution into a modern commercial bank in the 1980s. This period, in which the Saudis were engaged on two fronts – against Soviet encroachment and the revolutionary Iranian regime – provided an additional motive for promoting Sunni jihadist groups such as Al-Qaeda. Furthermore, the likelihood of the bank being ignorant of the activities of its account holders is small. Not only was the Saudi state capable of knowing what financial dealings were taking place within its territory through its central bank, SAMA, but Al Rajhi was suspected of having ties to extremist groups, at multiple levels that coincided with its close social proximity to the Saudi state. These levels included the personal charitable work of its founder Sulaiman Al Rajhi, charities it helped to establish, and multiple accounts held by individual terrorists and terror-connected banking affiliates.

While the proximity and importance of Al Rajhi Bank to the Saudi monarchy is fairly straightforward, what is less certain is the motivation behind the bank's suspected activities. It can easily be argued that the bank held greater loyalty to the monarchy than to causes such as those of Al-Qaeda. The bank came under intense scrutiny from the US: in the court system, in the media, and by American law enforcement and intelligence agencies. Additionally, the bank appears to have been intimately and elaborately connected to financial networks linked to jihadist groups. However, the blockage of enforcement against the bank, and how this occurred, raises several possibilities as to the bank's close relationship to the state. The first is that the bank was simply too important politically for the Saudi state to crack down on its activities directly. A more likely possibility is that the bank's activities were guided by a notion of supporting Wahhabi terrorist groups under the assumption that it was *helping* the monarchy's interests. Promoting the bank's religious agenda through its charitable activities dovetails with both motivations.

Regardless, Al Rajhi Bank's close involvement in building Saudi Arabia's regulatory capacity after 9/11 indicates that the bank has enjoyed, and continues to enjoy, a privileged position in Saudi politics. The bank was present at multiple meetings between US financial officials and those of Saudi Arabia; indeed, it was often the only private banking institution to be significantly involved. Furthermore, while it is unclear whether the monarchy turned to Al Rajhi Bank for help in developing its financial surveillance capability, or if involving the bank was a practical example of the adage about keeping friends close but enemies closer, the bank's involvement in developing the apparatus that would police its own activities has been thoroughly documented.

The most striking aspect of the Al Rajhi Bank case is the nature in which it was included in its own enforcement efforts. As the US investigated Saudi financial networks and their ties to terrorism via charitable organizations, it actively assisted both the Saudi state and Al Rajhi Bank, despite the role that the latter purportedly played in financing terrorism. And although the bank was involved in Saudi Arabia's regulatory reshuffle, it has also neither been successfully sued nor faced fines for its activities. On a deeper, theoretical level, the case of Al Rajhi Bank illustrates that security interests supersede goals related to regulatory harmonization or elegance. Indeed, regulations designed to fortify finance are the product of states seeking to ensure their own security, and therefore any efforts to build regulatory capacity in this arena will derive from such a goal.

# 4

# Halk Bank of Turkey

INTRODUCTION

In the mid-2000s, Halk Bank, one of Turkey's last remaining state-owned banks, came under international scrutiny for assisting Iran in circumventing economic sanctions in one of the largest money laundering and terrorist financing schemes in history. The scandal over the bank's activities placed increased strain on Ankara's long relationship with the West and heralded a renewal of Turkish interest in influencing Middle Eastern geopolitics. This chapter first examines Halk Bank's history of development and ownership by the state in the wider Turkish political economy, and specifically the bank's role as an instrument of foreign policy and domestic political coalition binding. It also addresses Ankara's adoption of fortified finance regulations and the development of Turkey's secret laundering arrangements with Iran. Last, this chapter discusses the Turkish state's defence of Halk Bank and its lending regime under the leadership of the Justice and Development Party (AKP), after the bank came under enforcement pressure for violating international sanctions.

Turkish politics encompass a cluster of contradictions. Aside from serving as a bridge between Europe and the Middle East since ancient times, modern Turkey has oscillated between varying degrees of authoritarian and democratic rule. One near-constant characteristic of Turkey's political institutions is statism in its political economy, including a high concentration of state ownership in the country's financial sector. Since becoming a modern republic in 1923, the Turkish economy has retained this characteristic despite engaging in liberalization efforts during the 1980s in an effort to prepare for economic integration into Europe. State-owned banks, including Halk Bank, remain an integral institutional component of the Turkish political economy. This institutional binding, along with a tradition of tight managerial proximity to the government, places Turkey's state-owned banks at the service of both domestic economic policy and foreign policy initiatives. Altogether, this close proximity provides a ready environment for political corruption while positioning the state to actively insulate the bank from regulatory penalty.

## HALK BANK AND STATIST LEGACIES

The modern Turkish republic emerged out of the remnants of the Ottoman Empire in the aftermath of the First World War. Formed in 1923 after Turkish nationalists repelled European attempts at colonization, the early Turkish state was birthed amid regional and international environments rife with statist approaches to economic affairs. This environment, together with early ideological currents in the Turkish nationalist movement, formed the circumstances in which Halk Bank was founded in 1938.[1] In the spring of 1923, in the midst of the proto-republic's negotiations with European powers over Ottoman-era capitulations, foreign debts, and national boundaries, the 1923 Economic Congress at İzmir laid a nationalist groundwork for the modern Turkish economy.

Reminiscent of the sort of statist thinking found in Republican China and popular in European states at the time, Turkish nationalists placed economic prowess at the forefront of their efforts to secure political independence and national security. At the 1923 Economic Congress, Mustafa Kemal Atatürk stated that "national sovereignty should be supported by financial sovereignty."[2] The rest of the 1920s witnessed a holdover of Ottoman-era institutional arrangements characterized by the continued dominance of foreign capital in a number of industries in what remained a heavily agricultural political economy. However, after six years of laying institutional groundwork, the economic downturn of 1929 ironically pushed Turkey into the early stages of creating its own modern, national banking sector.

In 1926, the new republic adopted a number of legal institutions from Europe, including a mostly Swiss legal system in conjunction with a mixture of Italian and German commercial codes.[3] Due to a certain wariness resulting from late Ottoman-era economic privileges extended to European interests, the new republic sought ways to limit foreign competition in its financial sector. It is worth noting here that Turkey, neutral throughout the Second World War, imported institutional economic influences from Fascist Italy, Germany, and the Soviet Union throughout the 1920s and 1930s. Germany's banking industry under Nazi rule shifted abruptly between the early and late 1930s, with nationalization predominating in the earlier part of the decade and increased privatization later on.[4] Turkey's creation of Halk Bank in 1933 reflected the nationalized aspect of the German banking sector in the early 1930s.

The early 1930s saw the crystallization of statism as the basis of Turkey's economic orientation. In 1931, Atatürk formally declared: "Our people are certainly statist because they naturally demand that their needs be satisfied by the state. Considering that point, there is complete conformity between the program of our party and the nature of our people."[5] While such statist orientation was also designed to help withstand the effects of the Great Depression, it would also play a role in the establishment of state-owned banks. Halk Bank, with its specialty of financing small and medium-sized enterprises, was uniquely placed within Turkey's political economy. This focus on small and medium-sized enterprises would not only turn the bank into an elemental force for helping Turkish political parties maintain their constituencies, it also created political liabilities in the event that serious privatization was ever considered. Functioning as a state bank devoted to small businesses and the Turkish middle class, the bank's domestic positioning would serve as a pillar for regime binding and political clientelism. Additionally, Halk Bank's focus on small and medium-sized enterprises, as opposed to a specific industry, placed it in a durable position in Turkey's political economy.

In 1933, Halk Bank was incorporated with the specific focus of fostering "favorable conditions to tradesmen, artisans and small business owners and triggering capital accumulation; for both long-lasting economic development and for preserving social equilibrium."[6] Unlike the Soviet Union, Turkey's Kemalist-era state-owned banks were not solely focused on state-owned enterprises. Rather, Ankara opened state-owned banks with the purpose of supporting critical sectors of the capitalist economy and to support Turkish nationalism.[7] Indeed, Atatürk emphasized and condoned individual entrepreneurship and profit seeking when it came to Halk Bank's client base: "You artisans, when the day comes that I witness great factories being built in the place of your small shops, I'll be elated to the highest degree."[8]

After it began open operations in 1938, Halk Bank expanded over the next several decades by opening branches and serving as a conduit of state funds to its small business client base. From 1938 until 1950, Halk Bank provided capital to small and medium-sized enterprises through public funds transferred directly from the state. In 1950, this "People's Fund" took on bureaucratic and institutional characteristics more reminiscent of a conventional bank in its own right, as it opened branches and made loans to small businesses.[9] Coming to power in 1950, Turkey's Democratic Party broke with the hardline statist policy legacy of the Republican People's Party (CHP) and instituted a number of modest reforms to privatize state-owned enterprises. While Halk Bank remained state-owned, its operations were reformed, moving away from functioning as a direct organ of the state toward operations as a bank owned by the state. During this era, the bank remained part of Ankara's overall economic strategy to insulate the Turkish economy from external market forces and foreign competition. Until the 1980s, when Turkey undertook aggressive liberalization reforms, Halk Bank steadily expanded its presence throughout the country, opening additional branches and increasing its lending capacity. Yet although its organizational infrastructure matured and expanded, it remained a state-owned bank.

If Halk Bank's history could be summarized in a single characteristic, it would be its ongoing institutional linkage with the state despite phases of attempted liberalization of the Turkish economy. Under Democratic Party rule in the 1950s, Ankara relied on access to capital through the Marshall Plan in its attempt to liberalize trade and allow free capital flows while seeking to sell state-owned enterprises. These efforts were cut short due to inflationary pressures and a rising trade deficit.[10] Through periods of intermittent military and civilian rule, from the coup d'état of 1960 until the 1983 election of Turgut Özal, Turkey's economy remained introspectively oriented and reliant on import substitution and protectionism. Under Özal, Halk Bank avoided a planned "privatization" and thus remained a state-owned bank, and also morphed into its current incarnation.

## PARTIAL LIBERALIZATION AND DOMESTIC COALITION BINDING

The 1980s witnessed a move toward neoliberalism in economies around the world. Turkey, along with other countries with statist economic legacies, undertook structural reforms in order to check rising inflation and high unemployment resulting from increasing oil prices. As a political figure, Özal is notable in that his career spanned involvement in both military and civilian governments. Under military rule, Özal held the post of Deputy Prime Minister of Economic Affairs prior to his assuming power as prime minister in 1983. As a power broker, Özal was uniquely pedigreed, combining liberal, technocratic, economic institutional experience with Islamist credentials, plus he enjoyed a certain level of comfort among Turkey's authoritarian military elite.[11] Notably, in carrying out liberalization and privatization, he followed a trajectory of neoliberal populism that combined all these contradictory characteristics. Not only did neoliberal populism create the institutional environment that Halk Bank currently inhabits, it also links the economic orientation of Özal's legacy with that of the current authoritarian government under the Justice and Development Party (AKP).

Common under hybrid, semi-democratic regimes, neoliberal populism seeks to install policies designed to facilitate economic efficiency and disincentivize rent seeking in concert with intervention by the state.[12] Neoliberal populist policy is also often affiliated with a charismatic leader and a "shallow" democratic environment.[13] Despite Özal's admiration for Thatcherism and privatization, the process of privatizing state-owned banks and other enterprises that began in the mid-1980s was slow-moving and never fully matured.[14] Indeed, for many state-owned enterprises, Halk Bank included, the process was never completed.

In 1985, Özal initiated privatization policies aimed at liberalizing sectors of the Turkish economy. The two goals of state-owned bank privatization were to expand share ownership and increase state revenues through the sale of state shares.[15] Specifically, thirty-two state-owned companies were targeted for privatization through block sales, public sales, and direct sales of assets and subsidiaries.[16] In 1994, under Implementation of Privatization Law 4046, the Privatization High Council, in concert with the Privatization Administration, was charged with overseeing the privatization of state enterprises. The prime minister sits on the Privatization High Council and recommends entities for privatization, while also overseeing the Privatization Administration.[17] This legal positioning of the prime minister in the privatization process, combined with the failed privatization of Halk Bank, would position the bank in a situation uniquely conducive for kleptocracy and money laundering.

Turkey's domestic politics during the Özal era marked an ideological shift in Turkish politics that laid the foundations for later Islamist movements under later prime ministers Necmettin Erbakan and Recep Tayyip Erdoğan. Unlike the secularist military rulers that preceded his rise to power, Özal's ideological orientation combined aspects of Islamism and Turkish nationalism with a highly technocratic Western liberalism. Breaking from Turkey's staunchly secular Kemalist orientation, Özal drew domestic support from small business interests in the country's Anatolian interior, and from social and religious conservatives.[18] Despite his drives for economic liberalization, Özal's domestic orientation was a soft neo-Ottoman outlook. At his funeral, mourners even walked through Istanbul shouting Islamist slogans.[19] As noted at the beginning of this chapter, small businesses and the lower middle class served as Halk Bank's primary customer base, and it was to this same demographic that Özal appealed politically. Not coincidentally, later Islamists like Erbakan and Erdoğan would appeal for political support to this same constituency.

The number of Turkish state-owned banks and the scope of state ownership contracted under the privatization reforms of the 1990s. Özal's reform attempts remained incomplete, but privatization of the banking sector advanced under later prime ministers Tansu Çiller and Mesut Yılmaz in the late 1990s. Four state banks – Etibank, Sümerbank, Anadolubank, and DenizBank – were all fully privatized through the total block sale of the banks' shares to single buyers.[20] Halk Bank had not previously been a premier state-owned bank, but it took on greater importance given its continued ownership by the state in the face of the privatization of most other banks. Its capital increased as a result of private investment infusions through the sale of minority shares, even as it grew as a result of absorbing other banks. Through the 1990s, Halk Bank absorbed Töbank, a bank owned by Turkish schoolteachers, as well as Sümerbank and all assets and liabilities of Etibank.[21] In 2001, Halk Bank also absorbed the branches of the state-owned EmlakBank. All three of Turkey's remaining state-owned banks number among the country's top seven, ranked by total assets.[22]

Turkey's banking sector is not only highly concentrated in terms of ownership, but also politicized and prone to corruption. As mentioned above, thanks to its failed privatization through the sale of minority shares to private investors, Halk Bank's position in Turkey's political economy was reconfigured in a manner uniquely conducive to political cronyism and money laundering. It was this positioning that would make the bank serviceable for laundering Iranian money under sanction for terrorism.

As a result of the financial crises in 1994 and 2001, Turkey's banking sector reoriented itself in favour of state-owned banks. In 1994, a law was passed by decree that was designed to clarify previously incoherent and contradictory laws pertaining to the privatization of state-owned enterprises.[23] The new law, which allowed the government to pass privatization laws by fiat, was subsequently overturned by Turkey's Constitutional Court in the aftermath of the country's 1994 currency crisis. Turkish elites committed to the country's legacy of statism drove the effort to strike down the privatization law, which was replaced with Implementation of Privatization Law 4046.[24] This statist legacy, combined with the unique legal positioning of the prime minister in matters of privatization, contributed to the politicization of state-owned banks such as Halk Bank. A politically driven financial crisis in 2001 would further solidify the state-owned banks in an advantageous position vis-à-vis their private counterparts.

Within the Turkish economy, state-owned banks hold a number of institutional advantages over private banks. State bank operations are highly politicized and offer a means for political elites to distribute rents to important constituencies and allies.[25] This dynamic creates a moral hazard by which state banks can provision loans based on political connection rather than potential profitability or the debtor's ability to service the debt. Halk Bank, like Ankara's other banks, issues more loans than its private counterparts as a result. Indeed, the opacity of this politicized lending scheme leads to an inability to accurately gauge the state-owned banks' efficiency.[26] When this politicized lending dynamic is placed in the context of Turkey's legal structure for privatization, it becomes clearer why Halk Bank failed to fully privatize.

In its efforts to raise revenues and stabilize the financial system in the wake of the 1994 crisis, Turkey sold minority shares in its state banks. However, through consolidation, Halk Bank grew in size throughout the 2000s. Having absorbed EmlakBank in 2001, Halk Bank acquired Pamukbank in 2004. This period of growth occurred at a critical juncture in Halk Bank's history, as in November 2001, the state planned to sell the bank in its entirety under Law 4603 (concerning the privatization of state commercial banks). Article 16 of that law would have placed all of the bank's operations under the auspices of its general manager, a position appointed, in turn, by the prime minister. This structural arrangement was intended as temporary until privatization; however, the government scrapped the planned sale in 2006, and so the arrangement remained in place. This new arrangement effectively placed the bank's operations under the oversight of the prime minister via his appointee, the bank's general manager. As noted in figure 4.1, Halk Bank's politicized lending practices were enabled by this institutional arrangement, placing the bank in a position uniquely conducive to cycles of corruption and the financing of politically motivated activities.

While the Turkish government, under Recep Tayyip Erdoğan, cancelled plans to fully privatize Halk Bank in 2006, the government did offer the sale of minority shares in the late 2000s. In 2007, the bank offered 25 per cent of its shares in an IPO, followed some years later by a second offering of 23.92 per cent on 16 November 2012.[27] In sum, the Turkish state retains ownership in the bank of 51.1 per cent. As of 2016, Ankara owns Halk Bank through its sovereign wealth fund, the Turkey Wealth Fund.

Since the turn of the millennium, Turkish politics have followed an increasingly authoritarian trajectory under Erdoğan's AKP. As noted by Mahmut Cengiz and Mitchel P. Roth in their study of Turkey's underground economy, corruption has deepened within the Turkish state during the AKP's time in power.[28] Halk Bank's primary customer base of small enterprises, artisans, and other small borrowers overlaps significantly with the AKP's key constituency. Founded to serve entrepreneurial clients from Turkey's lower middle class and small businesses, the bank retained this orientation into the twenty-first century. Halk Bank's financial strategy remains focused explicitly upon Turkey's small-scale borrowers and artisans. In a 2014 prospectus memo aimed at luring limited private shareholders, the bank outlined a strategy calling for increasing and deepening the institution's penetration of the small and medium-sized enterprise market.[29] This focus upon local artisans, small business groups, and local unions of independent tradespeople remains the focus of Halk Bank's plans for long-term growth and profitability.[30] And again, this sector of Turkey's political economy also forms the bedrock of the AKP's voter base.

The 2002 Turkish election demarcated a profound shift in the country's political landscape in that more than half of the electorate voted for a different party than in 1999.[31] Attracted by the AKP's conservatism together with its economic performance at the local level, the party

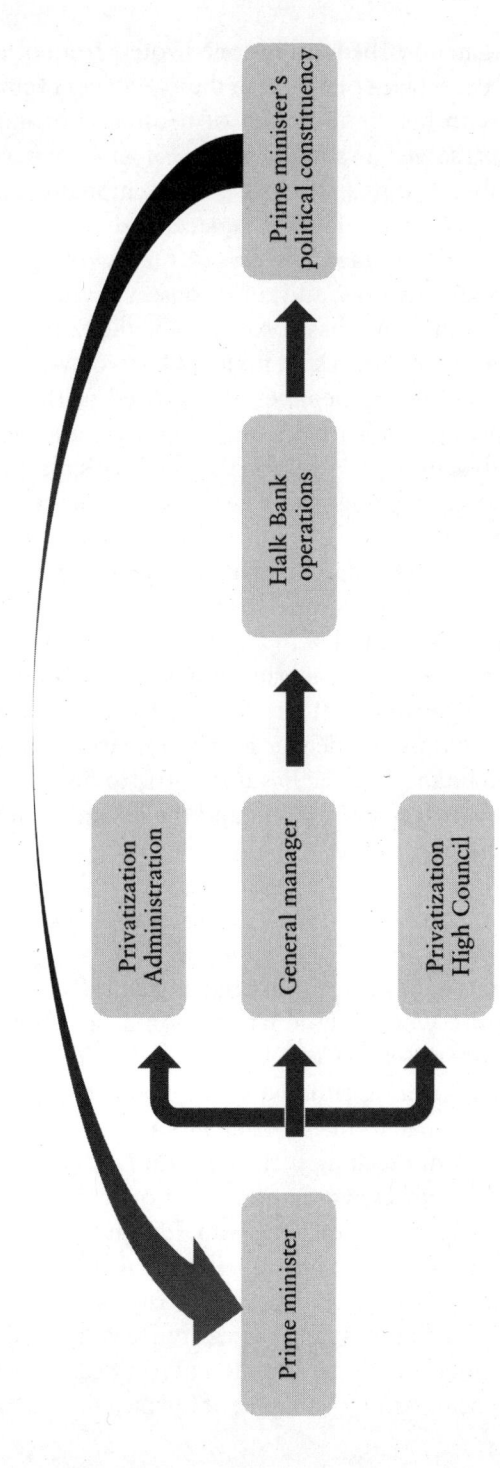

Figure 4.1 Halk Bank and the Turkish government.

founded by Erdoğan absorbed disillusioned voters from other parties. The Motherland Party (ANAP), which in the 1980s had brought Turgut Özal to power with his combination of neoliberal economics and Islamist sentiment, served as a major source of AKP's voters in 2002. Erdoğan's AKP absorbed half of ANAP's voters, along with nearly the whole of the Islamist Virtue Party.[32] Indeed, Özbudun notes that in 2002, the nascent AKP managed to recreate Özal's voting coalition of urban tradesmen and artisans, and rural conservatives.[33]

Halk Bank's key customer base proved to be the same base of support for Erdoğan's AKP. The AKP's middle-class voters, socially conservative and economically neoliberal, consisted of the "small and midrange enterprisers" of Turkey's cities, who were alienated from traditional Republicanism.[34] Additionally, the AKP's platform placed small and medium-sized enterprises at the centre of its strategy for Turkey's economic growth.[35] It is not coincidental that Halk Bank's long-term strategic plan for deepening its market penetration of small and medium-sized enterprises overlaps with that of the AKP; rather, the bank is in part a useful tool of the AKP for maintaining its electoral coalition. Furthermore, given the prime minister's position in overseeing Halk Bank's organizational structure, it becomes clear how the bank serves as a coalition binder for Erdoğan's party. Ankara's adoption of a fortified finance regime has done little to displace this institutional linkage between state, bank, and the ruling party's primary economic voter base.

### FORTIFIED FINANCE IN TURKEY

Turkey's perennial geopolitical goal has historically centred upon forming part of the West, despite its position as a regional Middle Eastern power. Since the early Cold War, the modern Turkish republic's unique geographic location situated it as a major player in Western security planning through its membership in NATO. In economic terms, Ankara has spent years seeking inclusion into Europe – since 1999, to be precise, when Turkey was named as a potential member of the European Union.[36] Economic melding with Europe has thus far proven elusive, however, in part due to the qualitative regulatory challenges posed by Turkey's financial system and corruption. Concerns over corruption and the banking system's integrity are issues which Ankara has sought to rectify through the adoption of fortified financial regulations. Yet despite being an early adopter of fortified finance regulations and institutions, none of these measures have managed to disrupt the connections between Halk Bank and the Turkish state, even as they have deepened over the same period.

As mentioned in the introduction, the internationalization of the fortified finance regime to counter money laundering and terrorist financing began with the establishment of the Financial Action Task Force (FATF) in 1989. Turkey joined the FATF in 1991, only a year after most Western states joined the organization when it began functioning in 1990. Indeed, Turkey's joining the AML/CTF regime coincided with Ankara's efforts to adopt general neoliberal reforms under the Özal administration. Domestically, Turkey outlawed money laundering in November 1996 with Law 4208, and established MASAK, its own financial intelligence unit (FIU), a few months later in February 1997. In 1998, Ankara joined the Egmont Group of FIUs.

Despite a long experience with terrorism, much of it related to Kurdish separatist organizations in the country's southeast, Turkey's terrorism laws originated in parallel with the beginning of its adoption of the AML/CTF regime. Turkey's 1991 anti-terrorism law (Law 3713) is profoundly broad and defines terrorism as any act undertaken "with the aim of changing the characteristics of the Republic," "seizing the authority of the state," or altering its sociopolitical order.[37] Notably, as Turkey's AML/CTF regime expanded, Ankara's anti-terrorism law was amended five times between 1995 and 2010. It was also in this period that Turkey began moving toward authoritarianism under the AKP, for whom the law would prove useful in neutralizing political opposition.

The central component of any country's regulatory apparatus to counter terrorist financing is the FIU. Turkey's FIU – Mali Suçları Araştırma Kurulu, or MASAK – was instituted in 1997 and placed under the supervision of the finance ministry. Under the Prevention of Laundering Proceeds of Crime Law 5549, enacted in 2006, MASAK is responsible for collecting suspicious activity reports (SARs) from banks and reporting suspected financial malfeasance to the public prosecutor for potential prosecution.[38] Article 2 of Law 5549 stipulates mandatory reporting of suspicious activities by banks, pension funds, jewellers, money dealers, and most businesses associated with high-end transactions.[39] Furthermore, article 19, chapter 4 mandates MASAK to track and collect data related to terrorist financing. Even prior to the 2006 law's implementation, in the early 2000s, the filing of SARs increased more than 300 per cent from the 1990s.[40]

Over the course of the 2000s, Turkey deepened its involvement in the international AML/CTF regime by joining treaties designed to counter corruption, terrorist financing, and organized crime. In December 2000, Turkey became a signatory to the United Nations Convention against Transnational Organized Crime, which it would ratify in 2006. Regarding terrorist financing, Turkey joined the UN International Convention on the Suppression of the Financing of Terrorism in September 2001. By 2006, Ankara had implemented its own law, the Prevention of Laundering Proceeds of Crime Law 5549, and signed the Council of Europe's Convention on Laundering, Search, Seizure, and Confiscation of the Proceeds from Crime and on the Financing of Terrorism in 2007.[41] Given Turkey's desire to join the European Union and the Eurozone, Ankara's regulatory adoptions amounted to more than simple juridical theatre; they formed part, indeed, of a greater, if haphazard, Turkish economic effort to join Europe during the 1990s and 2000s. Furthermore, this regulatory adoption of the fortified finance regime coincided with the overall Turkish effort to liberalize and privatize sectors of the country's economy. Notably, the growth of Turkey's CTF regulations happened in parallel with its terrorism laws.

The new millennium represented a turning point for Turkey in seeking to adhere to international standards of financial regulation. While Turkey had initiated its adoption of the fortified finance regime by joining the FATF in 1991 and establishing MASAK in 1997, it was the involvement of the EU and the IMF in the aftermath of Turkey's 2001 financial crisis that helped accelerate Ankara's regulatory adoption of international standards in the 2000s.[42] However, despite Turkey's formidable de jure adoption of threat finance laws and regulations, and its robust legal and regulatory capabilities, the FATF issued a number of reports of concern pertaining to actual enforcement.

In the mid-2000s, the FATF released a number of evaluations regarding Turkey's compliance with the organization's forty-one recommendations pertaining to countering money laundering and terrorist financing. In 2007, the FATF asserted that Turkey's banks served as the primary means of laundering and financing terrorism within the country's financial system.[43] Despite the small volume of SARs filed relative to the size of the Turkish financial sector, Turkey's banks provided steadily increasing numbers of reports.[44] However, in terms of funds linked to terrorism outside of Turkey, a number of FATF's recommendations remained unimplemented as of 2007. Nonetheless, throughout the decade, Turkey implemented significant improvements to its threat finance regime on issues related to terrorism.

The 2007 FATF report noted that Ankara was noncompliant or only partially compliant in areas of customer due diligence, politically exposed clients, transactions to and from high-risk jurisdictions, and mandates to file SARs related to terrorist financing. In 2014, the FATF recorded multiple improvements in the state's capacity to counter terrorist financing, including the Law to Combat Terrorist Financing 6415, enacted by the National Assembly in 2013, which effectively harmonized Turkey with the 1999 UN International Convention for the Suppression of the Financing of Terrorism. Notably, article 3 of this law defines terrorism in alignment with mainstream international standards: "acts intended to cause death or serious bodily injury for the purpose of intimidating or suppressing a population or compelling a government or an international organization to do or abstain from doing any act."[45] The law stipulates, in article 4, that terrorist financing includes the "collection of funds for a terrorist or terrorist organizations."

Turkey's de jure declaration of international cooperation also improved. Importantly, Law 6415 mandates that Turkey freeze the funds of organizations designated under UN Security Council resolutions 1267, 1988, and 1989 "without delay."[46] It also mandates that Turkey strive to comply with asset seizure requests made by foreign states under a principle of reciprocity,[47] and stipulates that such foreign powers direct requests either to the foreign ministry, to MASAK, or directly to the Ministry of Justice.[48] In the case that a foreign country makes a request for Turkey to freeze or seize criminal or terrorist assets, the ultimate decision to follow through falls under the authority of the Council of Ministers.[49] The Council of Ministers, being Turkey's cabinet, is filled with presidential appointees under the guidance of the prime minister.

A Financial Action Task Force follow-up evaluation of Turkey's CTF regime conducted in 2014 noted multiple improvements in terms of Ankara's compliance with international standards. However, the FATF recorded a lack of compliance in some key areas: politically exposed clients, dealings with risky jurisdictions, and incomplete vetting of "unusual large transactions."[50] Additionally, the FATF discovered that Turkey lacked a cohesive mechanism for seizing and freezing terrorist funds.[51] All of these key areas of concern were highlighted in Halk Bank's gold-based scheme for laundering money for Iran and in Ankara assisting Tehran in avoiding sanctions. Furthermore, corruption provides one of the only explanations that can reconcile Turkey's deepening financial regulations with its haphazard performance in combatting financial crime.

The international CTF regime takes into account the potential risks that politically exposed persons (PEPs) and risky jurisdictions pose in regard to money laundering. The FATF defines PEPs as individuals, either foreign or domestic, who are "entrusted with prominent public functions."[52] The primary fear concerning PEPs in relation to money laundering and terrorist financing is that such individuals – in cases of foreign PEPs – may enjoy diplomatic immunity that can enable them to avoid prosecution.[53] Similarly, key figures of domestic political stature may enjoy the ability to circumvent prosecution or arrest due to the abuse of their positions. Indeed, a key FATF concern regarding PEPs is that such individuals may "capture" financial institutions through shareholding, management, or other means, and thereby become able to launder money or finance terrorism.[54] The FATF's concern is that capture of financial institutions effectively enables politically powerful persons to manipulate those organizations to benefit corrupt or criminal enterprises. Not surprisingly, once Halk Bank came under international scrutiny for its accused laundering of terrorist funds for Iran, attention centred on key personalities within the Turkish and Iranian governments.

A number of countries around the world are deemed by the FATF and other major economic organizations as problematic jurisdictions for money laundering and terrorist financing. The FATF considers only two states, Iran and North Korea, as being wholly non-compliant and extremely high-risk jurisdictions.[55] Other jurisdictions are considered potential risks as war zones or failed states. The FATF's assessment of high-risk jurisdictions relies upon a number of criteria or sources, ranging from countries listed under international sanctions by organizations such as the UN, to a lack or low level of involvement in AML/CTF institutions, to other information provided by FATF member states.

Given that it is a neighbour to Iran and thus serves as a logical transit country between Iran and many of its potential export destinations, it would naturally be difficult for Turkey to attain full compliance with FATF's threat finance mandates. As to Halk Bank's suspected laundering of terrorist funds for Iran throughout the 2000s, the ensuing banking scandal touched on all three of Turkey's compliance deficiencies: politically exposed persons, business involving high-risk jurisdictions, and large, suspicious sums. Combined, these weak links in Ankara's fortified finance regime would facilitate one of the largest money laundering operations in history. Halk Bank's unique institutional linkage with the state would also assist in helping the bank escape regulatory enforcement. Not only was the state the majority shareholder in the bank at the time of the alleged laundering, but the prime minister himself constituted a politically exposed person charged with oversight at the time of the regulatory escape.

## HALK BANK, IRAN, AND BLOCKED ENFORCEMENT

The end of the Cold War substantially expanded Turkey's geopolitical influence. The expansion of the European Union and the Eurozone brought with it the enticing prospect of Ankara's affiliation as a member state. To the east and south, the Middle East and Central Asia offered new possibilities for Turkish interests. The former Soviet republics in Central Asia presented Turkey with a chance to expand its influence among Turkic peoples across Eurasia. Economically, the collapse of the Soviet Union also afforded Ankara the possibility of accessing the region's lucrative natural gas and oil deposits, and leveraging its geographic location as a transit country between Central Asia's energy sources and European markets.

Domestically, Turkey has evolved into an increasingly authoritarian regime since the election of the Justice and Development Party (AKP) in 2002. Coincidentally, over the same period, Halk Bank underwent partial privatization while Ankara progressively adopted more elements of the international fortified finance regime. In 2012, allegations emerged that Halk Bank had assisted Iran in laundering $20 billion in oil and natural gas revenues for an equivalent amount in gold.[56] Institutionally, the linkage of Halk Bank to the Turkish state and the situation of the prime minister in a position of oversight created a perfect storm in which the bank's ownership and management by the state effectively insulated it from regulatory enforcement.

Turkey's relationship with Iran must be understood in light of the two countries' centuries-old legacy of competition, rather than a simple situation of amicability or animosity. While the Middle East reeled at the implications and aftermath of the 1979 Iranian revolution, Turkey avoided an outright alliance with Sunni states against Tehran. Indeed, Turkey was one of the first states to recognize the post-revolution Iranian government.[57] After the transition to civilian rule, the Turkish government under Turgut Özal opted for a stance of "positive neutrality" toward both Baghdad and Tehran during the Iran-Iraq War.[58] Özal's strategy was diplomatically successful, as evidenced by the two warring countries using Ankara as an intermediary. Aside from direct security concerns, Özal leveraged Turkey's position for purposes of economic statecraft.

Structurally, Özal consolidated his foreign policymaking power at the expense of the foreign ministry by tasking foreign trade relations away from the ministry and placing such functions directly under the prime minister.[59] Özal sought to move beyond Turkey's Kemalist legacy in foreign policy and rekindle relations with the Middle East. Prior to taking office, Özal stated that Turkey's neighbours afforded potential "natural trading partners" and that Turkey should resume its historical "proper place" as the link between the Middle East and Europe.[60] Indeed, it was Turkey that initiated the creation, together with Iran and Pakistan, of the Economic Cooperation Organization in 1988.[61]

Özal pursued a path of liberalization and privatization throughout the 1980s in order to make Turkey more competitive. However, he also pursued an economic foreign policy of seeking to increase Iraqi and Iranian dependence on Turkey.[62] As Iran was surrounded geographically by mostly hostile Arab states, Ankara found itself in the advantageous position of being able to offer Tehran an outlet to the wider economic world. Turkey would emerge in the 1980s as a key market for Iranian exports.[63] In the area of oil and gas, Turkey's long time fear of Russian encroachment in the Middle East made Iran an attractive source of energy. Given the international sanctions against Iran, Turkey serves as one of Tehran's only outlets for exporting its oil and gas – an advantageous situation for Turkey, which remains dependent on energy imports.[64]

Despite its proximity to the energy riches of the Middle East and Eurasia, Turkey is naturally impoverished in terms of domestic energy sources. Additionally, Turkey has little capacity for storing the natural gas it requires and therefore depends upon a constant flow of imported energy.[65] Given that a reduction in energy imports from Iran would increase Ankara's reliance upon Russian oil and gas, and that this in turn would jeopardize Turkey's position among the Central Asian republics, a stable flow of Iranian energy is a paramount security and economic concern. Indeed, more than 90 per cent of Iranian gas exports are destined for Turkey.[66] Iran's unique relationship with

Turkey brought Tehran roughly $10.5 million per day from natural gas alone.[67] With Tehran under sanctions for issues pertaining to both terrorism and its nuclear program, much of the energy revenue passing from Turkey to Iran requires some form of laundering.

With Turkey's dependence on Iranian energy, and Turkey offering Iran an export market, a symbiosis developed under Özal that would also characterize foreign economic policy between the two states under future administrations. Turkey's strategy of economically leveraging Iran would continue in the 1990s and mature in the 2000s as increasing Islamism in Turkey's political landscape warmed relations between the two countries amid an otherwise turbulent region. Halk Bank's laundering of Iranian funds thus follows a longstanding Turkish strategy of using economic statecraft for purposes of resource acquisition and securing influence with its Persian neighbour.

Since the Iranian revolution in 1979, Tehran has pursued a path toward becoming a regional power. Religiously Shia and ideologically revisionist with regard to areas of the Middle East with significant Shia populations, post-revolution Iran holds longstanding animosity toward secular Arab regimes, Israel, and the conservative Sunni monarchies of the Persian Gulf. Iran's pursuit of regional influence has long included support for Shia militias, terrorist groups, and rebel proxies in the Middle East and beyond. Since 1979, Iran's support for terrorism and the pursuit of its nuclear program have led to the imposition of multiple sanctions against Tehran. It was precisely when Iran was at its most isolated, due to mobilized threat finance regulations, that Ankara was laundering money on its behalf.

Iranian financial support for terrorism in the Middle East and elsewhere comprises a longstanding facet of Tehran's geopolitical strategy. In 1982, at the height of both the Iran-Iraq War and the Lebanese Civil War, a contingent of 1,500 soldiers from Iran's Islamic Revolutionary Guard Corps set up training camps in Lebanon's Beqaa Valley with the stated purpose of exporting the Iranian revolution across the Arab world.[68] Three years later, Hezbollah articulated its ideological platform, which effectively placed it directly under Iran's guidance and recognized the Tehran government as "the vanguard and new nucleus of the leading Islamic State in the world."[69] Logistically, the Shia group required that all its members undergo training in the Iranians' Beqaa Valley camps. Hezbollah also enjoys, by some accounts, between $200 and $350 million per year in Iranian largesse.[70] Iran maintains a permanent contingent in Lebanon of some five hundred personnel for purposes of training Hezbollah members and provides funding for Hezbollah-affiliated social services.[71] It is worth mentioning that no organizational separation exists between Hezbollah's social services wing and its terrorist activity. In 2000, Hezbollah's deputy secretary-general, Naim Qassem, noted that the organization's secretary-general oversees both sides of the group's operations.[72] While Hezbollah's self-funding activities have matured since the 1980s, the group continues to receive Iranian support estimated at about $100 million per year.[73]

Iranian support for Hezbollah is not limited to the Middle East, nor do the group's operations avoid civilian targets. After its 1983 attacks on the US embassy and Marine Corps barracks in Beirut, Hezbollah expanded its reach and scope with Iranian support. In 1994, Hezbollah bombed the Argentine Israelite Mutual Association, a Jewish community centre in Buenos Aires, leaving eighty-five dead and hundreds injured. Iran's embassy in Argentina provided a base of support for the attack as well as for an earlier bombing at the Israeli embassy in Buenos Aires in 1992.[74] In 2003, an Argentine judge issued arrest warrants for four Iranian officials for assisting in the attack. Prosecutors also recommended twelve warrants for prominent Iranian officials, including the country's supreme leader Ayatollah Ali Khamenei[75] and Ali Fallahian, formerly minister of security and intelligence.[76]

Tehran's support for terrorism includes using Hezbollah for assassinations of Iranian dissidents abroad, setting up foreign banking operations to support Islamist recruitment, and establishing local businesses as money laundering fronts in multiple countries. Throughout the 1990s, Iran assisted proxies around the world in establishing a presence for purposes of advancing Tehran's interests. In 1997, Iran established bank branches in Albania as a means of promoting militant networks in Europe.[77] In expanding its influence in Europe, the Central Bank of Iran's governor, Mohsen Nurbakan, oversaw investment operations in the region to promote Iranian-backed Islamist groups in the Balkans.[78] In 2013, Bulgaria's interior minister, Tsvetan Tsvetanov, attributed a bus bombing to Hezbollah which took place a year earlier in the coastal city of Burgas, killing seven and wounding thirty-two.[79]

Iranian support for the group also extends to Africa, where Tehran actively supports Islamist militant activity on the continent. In seeking to compete with more successful Saudi-backed Sunni networks, Iran established a number of mosques and schools in sub-Saharan Africa aimed at expanding the number of Shia adherents beyond the region's Lebanese expatriate communities.[80] Financed through its embassies in the region, Iran has also established a number of cultural centres to recruit for Hezbollah-affiliated efforts to gather intelligence for potential attacks on Western targets.[81]

At varying levels of intensity, tensions between Tehran and the West have remained a constant factor in Middle East politics since 1979. US-led international sanctions against Iran parallel Tehran's support of terrorism and its pursuit of nuclear weapons. With the US as the epicentre of these efforts, the sanctions have touched all aspects of the Iranian economy. By the late 2000s, Iran's economy was nearly strangled through the sanctions' combined focus on key members of the Iranian government and on the country's energy sector and currency. While Tehran has also experienced multiple sanctions by the UN and the European Union, and remains on the FATF's blacklist, the multilateral economic efforts to curtail Iran's terrorist activity and nuclear program originated in the United States.

In the mid-1980s, US-led sanctions on Iran focused on curtailing Tehran's ability to access arms from abroad. In 1984, Iran was designated a state sponsor of terrorism, which economically severed the country from most of the American economy. In 1987, the US outlawed the import of Iranian goods. The Clinton administration expanded the sanctions regime and increased its multilateral reach by using diplomatic and economic leverage against Iran such as blocking bank loans and penalizing companies doing business with the Iranian energy sector.[82] The 1996 Iran and Libya Sanctions Act not only limited investment in Iranian oil resources but effectively placed companies from US allies on notice for potential sanction should they do business with Tehran.[83]

Even prior to the post-9/11 expansion of the international fortified finance regime, US pressure was successful in curtailing international lending to Tehran. The US effectively thwarted loans to the Iranian government from both the International Monetary Fund and the World Bank over the course of the 1990s.[84] In the 2000s, American economic statecraft nearly crippled the Iranian economy through entirely financial means.

In the 2000s, as Turkey progressively and haphazardly adopted the fortified finance regime into its domestic political economy, Iran came under increasing economic pressure over its support for terrorism and its nuclear weapons program. In 2005, the Bush administration banned Iranian banks from the American financial system, effectively cutting Iran off from most of the world's financial markets.[85] By penalizing third parties doing business with Iran, most Iranian financial assets were essentially frozen.[86] In 2010, the US Senate passed the Comprehensive Iran Sanctions, Accountability, and Divestment Act, which mandated the sanction of any foreign bank that conducted transactions with Iran.[87] In 2012, the US pressured Iran further by threatening to deny foreign banks the ability to conduct dollar transactions if they conducted business with the Central Bank of Iran.[88]

Shortly after 9/11, US Secretary of the Treasury Paul O'Neill and General Counsel to the Treasury David Aufhauser travelled to Brussels to pressure the Belgian-based Society for Worldwide Interbank Financial Telecommunication (SWIFT) for access to financial intelligence.[89] Overseen by the National Bank of Belgium and governed by top executives from the world's major banks, SWIFT serves as the international clearinghouse for all formal high finance transactions.[90] While the US-SWIFT intelligence relationship was uneasy after 9/11, it offered Washington an alternative mechanism – aside from pure intelligence collection – to pressure Iran. In early 2012, the US effectively prodded SWIFT into excluding Iran from conducting dollar transactions. Furthermore, American pressure succeeded in dissuading SWIFT from allowing Iran to conduct transactions related to its energy sector.[91]

With the US dollar serving as the premier reserve currency around the world, the US threat to bar banks from conducting any business involving Iranian currency decisively lowered its value. As a result, bank runs ensued in Iran as the value of the rial fell by 40 per cent and consumer prices nearly doubled.[92] Lacking the ability to access hard currency, Iran needed a way to launder revenues from its oil and gas exports and thereby convert hydrocarbons into cash. Turkey's Halk Bank assisted in providing this service.

As mentioned in the introduction, money laundering at its core comprises the "transfer of value" from one asset to another.[93] To obfuscate the laundered money from its nefarious origins or destination, the transfer of value must occur in a way that evades detection by interested authorities. Gold, given its accepted value worldwide, provides an optimal vehicle for transferring value. Halk Bank and Iran would exploit this golden loophole, exchanging gas for gold so that Iran could then access hard currencies in exchange.

In December 2013, Turkish police stormed apartments across Istanbul as part of a crackdown on suspected financial corruption. Halk Bank's general manager, Süleyman Aslan, was arrested along with Iranian businessman Reza Zarrab, a former associate of then Iranian president Mahmoud Ahmadinejad. In Aslan's home, police discovered $4.5 million stashed in shoeboxes.[94] Also arrested were the sons of Turkey's economy, urban development, and interior ministers, and an AKP-affiliated mayor.[95] Aslan began his financial career at Ziraat Bank, Turkey's oldest state-owned bank, in the early 1990s, and became general manager of Halk Bank in 2011.[96] As the scandal unfolded, Halk Bank emerged as the centrepiece in a massive money laundering scheme between Iran and Turkey.

Concerns had emerged regarding Halk Bank's role in Iranian business dealings as early as 2008. On 28 January of that year, the US Treasury undersecretary, Stuart Levey, met with representatives of the Turkish foreign ministry and finance ministry, and officials from Halk Bank, to address international concerns over the bank's dealings with Iran.[97] Halk Bank's general manager at the time, Halil Celik, along with the bank's chief compliance officer, declared that their institution closely followed the best practices of the fortified finance regime, such as monitoring transactions and maintaining close client familiarity.[98] In regard to their Iranian clients, the bank officials noted that their institution held "long-dormant correspondent accounts" acquired via the merger of Pamukbank into Halk Bank in 2004.[99]

Halk Bank's own compliance unit issued an official statement regarding the bank's commitment to implementing fortified finance practices within the institution. Halk Bank declared that its internal policies reflected not only Turkish counterterrorism legislation, but also FATF recommendations through the latter's cooperation with MASAK and Turkey's Banking Regulation and Supervision Agency (BRSA).[100] Notably, the bank also stated that it mandated anti-money-laundering, anti-terrorist-financing, and know-your-customer training for all of its employees in compliance with FATF best practices and US-led sanctions.[101] As mentioned earlier, Turkey became a FATF member in 1991.

According to Wikileaks, in 2009 the US Treasury's Assistant Secretary for Terrorist Financing and Financial Crimes, David Cohen, met with representatives from Halk Bank and Turkey's BRSA. In this meeting, the BRSA assured Cohen that the agency collected all relevant financial intelligence from Turkey's banks. Halk Bank declared that "no deals are financed on a cash-for-goods basis" in the bank's dealings with Iran.[102] Despite this assertion, however, such deals are precisely the business that Halk Bank appears to have conducted.

As mentioned above, upon arresting Halk Bank's general manager and other suspects, police discovered stashes of cash valued in the millions in the various suspects' Istanbul apartments. The cash functioned as part of a laundering plan developed by Reza Zarrab in which Turkish lira would be converted to gold, shipped to Dubai, and then sent to Iran as payment for Turkish imports of Iranian oil and gas. The laundering was massive, amounting to thirty-six metric tonnes of gold shipped from Turkey to Iran in August 2012 alone.[103] Zarrab, the Iranian middleman – whom the *Atlantic* described as a "swashbuckling gold trader"[104] – allegedly paid millions of dollars to Halk Bank's general manager, along with payments to Turkey's economic minister.[105] From 2012 to 2013, as Iran struggled due to sanctions to obtain hard currencies, Turkey sent approximately $13 billion in gold to Tehran; this gold exportation dropped to nothing by January 2014, following the arrest of Halk Bank's general manager.[106]

State ownership of Halk Bank, along with the AKP affiliations of the Istanbul mayor and the ministers whose sons were arrested in the raid, brought political as well as economic scandal to Ankara. Shortly after the arrests, as Halk Bank's stock prices fell under the shadow of the Iranian gold dealings, Prime Minister Erdoğan and the Turkish government quickly enacted countermeasures to protect the bank. Using a combination of diplomatic pressure, domestic political intimidation, and bureaucratic reshuffling, the government seems to have shielded the bank from penalty.

Within days of the Istanbul raid, police officers connected to the laundering investigation were either reassigned or fired from the force outright. Hüseyin Çapkin, Istanbul's chief of police, resigned on 19 December, only two days after the raid.[107] Amid this purge of more than thirty senior police officials from Istanbul's police force was the firing and reassignment of 350 police officers in Ankara the following month over what Prime Minister Erdoğan called a "dirty plot" on the part of Turkey's judiciary in consort with the police.[108] As the purges took place, Erdoğan declared in a speech that the police force was "tainted" and simultaneously assured a zero-tolerance approach to corruption.[109] As for Halk Bank, Erdoğan decried the scandal as part and parcel of a "plot by Turkey's enemies" such as his exiled political archrival Fethullah Gülen.[110]

In early 2014, the AKP government implemented a law aimed at curtailing the powers of Turkey's judiciary. During open debate prior to the law's implementation, physical fighting erupted in the National Assembly. The new law mandated that the justice ministry would dictate judicial appointments, as opposed to the independent, arm's-length High Council of Judges and Prosecutors.[111] Judicial officials involved with the Halk Bank case were summarily dismissed or reassigned as part of a massive shuffle of nearly 120 judges and prosecutors.[112] Since the beginning of the scandal with the arrests a month prior, thousands of police had been reassigned or dismissed.[113] Murat Arslan, the head of YARSAV, Turkey's association of prosecutors and judges, declared the bureaucratic shuffle to be politically motivated in its entirety and that Erdoğan was seeking to insulate himself and other AKP affiliates.[114] As for Turkey's banking authority, the BRSA, Erdoğan stated in an interview with Al Jazeera that the regulatory body had conducted a full audit of Halk Bank and its general manager's affairs. According to the prime minister and the banking authority, there was "no trouble" to be found.[115]

Reza Zarrab, the Iranian businessman at the centre of the laundering scandal, enjoyed special protections provided by Erdoğan, who advocated for Zarrab's integrity and described him as a charitable figure.[116] Zarrab's charitable activity included multiple donations to the Social Development Center for Education and Social Solidarity, a charity founded by Ermine Erdoğan, the prime minister's wife.[117] Zarrab had also provided gifts to Halk Bank general manager Süleyman Aslan, including a $37,000 piano, a luxury watch valued at $350,000, and millions of dollars in currency.[118]

The AKP's countermeasures effectively insulated the bank and its general manager, along with others suspected of laundering money for Iran. In October 2014, prosecutors in Istanbul opted to drop all charges. Ekrem Aydıner, Istanbul's only prosecutor for anti-terrorism and organized crime remaining with the case, announced that the case could not advance due to a lack of grounds and insufficient evidence to prove a conspiracy.[119] On 17 October, the primary investigation against Aslan was dropped.[120]

The Turkish state effectively deflected any threat finance enforcement at the domestic level. If anything, Ankara's domestic enforcement blockage had the effect of deepening both the ruling AKP's grip on political power and the country's general level of authoritarianism. However, the case would revive in the United States with the arrest of

Mehmet Hakan Atilla, Halk Bank's deputy general manager. Reza Zarrab, the Iranian financier, would also resurface in the United States, and the Turkish government would once again seek to protect its bank. One police official involved in the investigation, who was purged in the wake of Ankara's police and judicial reshuffle, fled Turkey for the United States, whereupon he passed evidence, in the form of recordings and documents, to American authorities.[121]

Halk Bank's Iranian middleman, Zarrab, was arrested in Miami on 19 March 2016 while attempting a vacation trip.[122] Halk Bank official Mehmet Hakan Atilla was also arrested, on charges of sanctions evasion, while travelling to New York on business.[123] The US indictments against Zarrab and Atilla included charges of fraud, money laundering, and conspiracy. While the charges largely focused on sanctions evasion pertaining to Iranian state entities assisted by Halk Bank, it also included allegations that the Turkish bank had facilitated transactions for Mahan Air, a commercial airline.[124] The US Office of Foreign Assets Control blacklisted Mahan Air in October 2011 for supporting the Iranian Islamic Revolutionary Guard Corps' Quds Force (IRGC-QF),[125] the arm of the Iranian military that helped form and provides support for Hezbollah.[126] Mahan Air supported the IRGC-QF by offering "covert travel" for personnel, weapons, and cash.[127] Shortly after Mahan Air was designated as an entity supporting terrorism, Reza Zarrab wrote to the governor of the Central Bank of Iran offering his services for "economic jihad."[128]

At the time of the arrests, Halk Bank issued a statement in 2016 that highlighted its purported compliance with the international fortified finance regime. It stated that the bank not only followed all AML/CTF regulations through its cooperation with Turkey's regulatory body, but also in "jurisdictions where the foreign branch is located."[129] Moreover, it specifically claimed that it complied with all sanctions, including those stated by the US Treasury's Office of Foreign Assets Control.[130]

Notably, Zarrab became the primary witness against Atilla after striking a deal with prosecutors and agreeing to testify as to the bank's involvement in laundering. After testifying that Prime Minister Erdoğan had overseen Halk Bank's channelling of funds to Iran, Turkey seized all assets in the country of Zarrab and his family.[131] Despite Zarrab's testimony, Atilla was acquitted of money laundering but convicted of conspiracy and fraud.[132]

Shortly after Atilla's conviction, the Turkish state indicated its willingness to defend its bank should the US seek to penalize the institution. Turkey's deputy prime minister, Mehmet Şimşek, declared that Ankara would do "whatever is necessary" to assist banks threatened as a result of Atilla's trial.[133] Şimşek's verbal rebuttal at the New York trial also contained a telling contradiction, as he stated that Halk Bank itself, not the Turkish government, would pay any levied fines.[134] Halk Bank's status as a state-owned bank was sufficient to warrant the government's negation of any such fine, either through bailout or subsidy. The Turkish foreign ministry similarly stood firm in dismissing the US conviction as not having "any legal value."[135] After American prosecutors requested a sentence of prison time for Atilla, Halk Bank's shares paradoxically rose rather than fell.[136] As to whether or not Halk Bank will suffer major financial punishment from the US, either in the form of fines, blacklisting, or being severed from dollar transactions, the bank has yet to face any.

In October 2019, the US pursued charges against Halk Bank for violating AML/CTF laws, later seeking to pursue "escalating fines" against the bank for noncooperation.[137] After efforts to force the recusal of judges from the case, Halk Bank emphasized its status as an extension of the Turkish state by asserting "sovereign immunity." In 2020, Halk Bank based its defence on the Foreign Sovereign Immunities Act, which prohibits "criminal prosecutions of state-owned entities."[138] By way of retort, American prosecutors claimed that "sovereign immunity cannot overcome the sovereign right of the United States to set the rules to use the US financial system."[139] What is notable about the lagging legal efforts to hold Halk Bank to account is that both the Turkish and American parties to the case acknowledge, explicitly or tacitly, that the dispute is geopolitical rather than purely legal. Unlike a private bank, Halk Bank is an extension of the Turkish state, and Ankara has been defending it from penalty. In the event that it did ultimately face monetary punishment for its actions, the bank's structural connection to the Turkish state allows it to absorb any damage.

## ANALYSIS

The Halk Bank case clearly illustrates a financial firm with deep institutional linkage to its state escaping enforcement for laundering money for terrorism. This Turkish case is unique in that it involves a state sponsor of terrorism as opposed to simply a terrorist group using the financial system of another country. Furthermore, the case involves overlapping sanctions against the state sponsor of terrorism for other issues than terrorism alone. In their various manifestations, the sanctions against Iran address concerns regarding Tehran's nuclear program and engagement in interstate war, along with its support for groups such as Hezbollah. Regarding the fortified finance regime, what is less explicable is how Ankara's state-owned bank knowingly assisted Tehran in circumventing these sanctions even as Turkey simultaneously deepened its adoption of AML/CTF regulations. The only feasible explanation is that states will defend banks when those banks are extensions of the state.

Halk Bank matches the independent variable of institutional linkage to its home state. Aside from long state majority ownership and failed privatization, the bank's governance remains linked to the Turkish executive through its managerial structure. Furthermore, the bank's primary client base places the bank in a unique position as a coalition binder for the political party in power. Indeed, Halk Bank's main client base coincides closely with the primary voting demographic for Turkey's Islamists under the AKP.

Critics of the case may point out that significant international disagreement over sanctions against Iran make the case an American one, and that, rather than breach the international fortified finance regime, Ankara simply disregarded US interests. However, Ankara opted into the fortified finance regime through its entry into the FATF in 1991, long before any sanctions against Iran in regard to its nuclear ambitions. Similarly, while the FATF had concerns over Turkey's implementation of AML/CTF regulations, Ankara progressively adopted more international standards throughout the 2000s. Turkey adopted financial regulations, and the capacity to follow through on them, implementing know-your-customer rules and the monitoring of suspicious activity. Indeed, these measures were effective, as evidenced by the government's attempted crackdown in December 2013, when multiple arrests took place in Istanbul. Had these financial regulations not been in place, no such enforcement attempt would have occurred. Turkey's judicial and law enforcement authorities did not fail to act but were thwarted by the state itself through bureaucratic reshuffling and political intimidation.

As for the regulations and legal changes that Turkey adopted to achieve de jure compliance, none of these measures were sufficient to displace either Turkey's statist legacy or its structural relationship to its bank. Pre-existing institutional arrangements between the Turkish state and Halk Bank remained intact despite the state's deepening involvement with the fortified finance regime. Furthermore, Turkey's fortified finance regime did not disrupt its economic reliance upon Iranian energy imports.

Halk Bank has thus far escaped regulatory enforcement. Domestically, the AKP under Erdoğan has restructured Turkey's judicial and law enforcement apparatus through bureaucratic reshuffling in combination with political intimidation. The layoff and reassignment of hundreds of judges, police, and prosecutors effectively thwarted any domestic charges against Halk Bank officials and others associated with the laundering. Internationally, the conviction of Mehmet Hakan Atilla comprises the sole punishment faced by the bank or any of its personnel. US prosecutors have tried other individuals in absentia, but only Atilla was arrested and convicted.

Institutionally, Halk Bank remains free from penalty. Should the US levy fines against the bank, as was done against certain European banks engaged in similar activity, Ankara's statements indicate clearly that the state will negate any such penalty. A massive American fine against Halk Bank, or action to sever it from dollar transactions or SWIFT access, would deliver a massive blow to Turkey's economy while straining Ankara's position in NATO and its involvement in Syria. Should a fine be levied, Halk Bank's state ownership will place Ankara's government as well as its financial sector in the crosshairs of American economic statecraft. Out of pure necessity, the Turkish government would be forced to thwart any further enforcement against its bank.

Halk Bank's figure at the centre of the case, Mehmet Hakan Atilla, received a sentence of thirty-two months in prison rather than the twenty-year sentence sought by prosecutors.[140] The presiding judge, Richard M. Berman, declared that Atilla served as the "cog in the wheel" rather than the "mastermind" at the centre of the operation.[141] Atilla, Judge Berman stated, was only "following orders" from Halk Bank's general manager, Süleyman Aslan.[142] Institutionally, the Turkish state has moved to protect its bank through high-level diplomacy and economic statecraft. Halk Bank officials, as well as Turkey's economy minister and foreign minister, have taken part in defending the bank. The country's foreign minister, Mevlüt Çavuşoğlu, declared in a statement to the *Financial Times* that Turkey was working with the US to resolve the issue. Furthermore, the Turkish state indicated that it would step in, if necessary, to financially negate any fallout from US regulatory fines.[143]

In the realm of economic statecraft, Ankara moved to defend both its bank and the Turkish lira from American action a month prior to the Atilla conviction. In April 2018, Ankara withdrew 28.6 tons of Turkish gold held at the US Federal Reserve and redeposited the holdings with the Bank of England and the Bank for International Settlements.[144] Domestically, Turkish banks also adjusted the composition of their reserves with Turkey's central bank, replacing foreign currency holdings with gold.[145] Turkey also drew down its holdings of US bonds beginning in November 2017.[146]

Given that the US and Turkey each form part of the international conflagration of powers currently involved militarily in Syria, any American economic action against Halk Bank could have kinetic consequences for the Syrian civil war and the Middle East as a whole. The Turkish state has indicated that it will defend its bank against regulatory attack and negate any damage to the institution – or even to the linkage between bank and government. Turkey's withdrawal from US assets and from exposure to unilateral American seizure of Turkish gold indicates little willingness on Ankara's part to surrender on behalf of its bank.

# 5

# Institutional Independence and Regulatory Enforcement

INTRODUCTION

The three positive cases of blocked enforcement discussed above all occurred where the institutional connections of banks to their home states placed them in positions of critical importance to those states' security and stability. In these instances, the home states came to the defence of their banks in order to deflect or defuse an enforcement attempt and protect the targeted institution's integrity. However, some banks do indeed succumb to enforcement measures without any meaningful protection from their home states. This chapter explores why and how enforcement succeeds in the absence of such bank-state linkages, and addresses differing explanations for enforcement outcomes such as regulatory presence, rule of law, and authoritarianism. To account for these rival explanations, and to examine why fortified financial regulations are sometimes weak in enforcement scenarios, I explore the cases of the Bank of Credit and Commerce International (BCCI) and Jordan's Arab Bank.

Both BCCI and Arab Bank enjoyed institutional independence from their home states. BCCI operated out of the offshore tax havens of Luxembourg and the Cayman Islands. Contrary to popular conceptions of offshore tax havens as rogue jurisdictions that actively promote and attract illicit funds and protect them in the face of international pressure, each of these havens took an active role in shutting down BCCI's operations once it came under regulatory scrutiny for financing terrorism and other nefarious business activities. Thus, in the early 1990s, BCCI was forced by multilateral law enforcement and regulatory action to close its doors.

Arab Bank, which came under regulatory penalty in the form of administrative fines and civil suits in the US courts, paid its fines without benefitting from any blockage on the part of the Jordanian government. A financial institution lauded for its survival through multiple wars, decolonization, and population shifts, Arab Bank pursues an American business model and draws on financial structural models from the United States. When both it and BCCI came under regulatory scrutiny for financing terrorism, a lack of institution-state linkage left them exposed to regulatory crackdown.

## ENFORCEMENT AGAINST THE BANK OF COMMERCE AND CREDIT INTERNATIONAL (BCCI)

The history of the fortified finance regime is marked by a number of spectacular cases involving high-profile arrests, asset seizures, and publicized lawsuits. BCCI met a rapid regulatory demise in the early 1990s, following multilateral investigations into the laundering of proceeds from numerous crimes including financing terrorism. Although BCCI enjoyed a notable presence around the world, it was dually based in the tax havens of Luxembourg and the Cayman Islands. Ironically, its legal grounding in offshore political economies did little to protect it from regulatory enforcement.

BCCI was founded in the context of bank nationalization in Pakistan and the desire of its founder, Agha Hasan Abedi, to avoid state interference in financial affairs. Founded in 1972, the bank was established as a legal entity in Luxembourg in the aim of avoiding significant financial regulation, and with the purpose of becoming a multinational bank devoted to the developing world.[1] Abedi said that he envisioned the bank as a "world bank, a global bank for the Third World."[2]

In seeking to avoid regulatory scrutiny, BCCI developed a two-pronged strategy of establishing its legal presence in the two offshore tax havens while basing its operational headquarters in London. Its founding in Luxembourg in 1972 was followed by legal registration in the Cayman Islands in 1975. Additionally, the Cayman Islands office was registered as an offshore subsidiary of the Luxembourg entity, BCCI Holdings SA.[3] BCCI's founding structure was designed to preclude state meddling in the form of aggressive regulation or bank nationalization. Sensing Islamabad's intent to nationalize Pakistan's banking sector, which indeed took place in 1974, Abedi organized the new bank specifically to inhibit regulatory oversight and state linkage.

Prior to BCCI, Abedi had founded a bank in Pakistan, United Bank Limited, in 1959. However, Prime Minister Zulfikar Ali Bhutto's suspicion of United Bank for its association with the Pakistani military led his regime to place Abedi under house arrest prior to the planned bank sector nationalization.[4] Thus nationalized as a result, United Bank eventually reprivatized in 2002, and Abedi drew upon this experience in designing BCCI's structure as a private bank beyond the reach of state authorities. Notably, however, the cultural connection between BCCI and Pakistan would remain close. The Islamabad government of Muhammad Zia-ul-Haq would provide political support for BCCI's political activities despite the private bank's registration in offshore havens.

BCCI's legal homes in Luxembourg and the Cayman Islands provided a jurisdictional grounding to help prevent any home state interference. This institutional separation between bank and state assisted the bank in facilitating a number of money-laundering crimes and financing terrorism, but it also enfeebled the bank's position within the political economies in which it was embedded. Although tax havens provide the allure of corporate freedom beyond the reach of regular states, such havens also stand to lose little should a bank or other company registered in their territory face closure. Not only did the Cayman Islands and Luxembourg eventually assist American and European authorities in shutting down BCCI, both were also early entrants into the emerging fortified finance regime. Additionally, the closure of BCCI coincided with the founding of the Financial Action Task Force.

Popular depictions of tax havens conjure images of shadowy businesspeople from the ranks of the world's wealthy engaging in tax evasion, drug dealing, and other activities. Such activity exists; however, tax havens are not entirely independent of the powerful states that seek access to their financial systems. Many tax havens maintain affiliations with old established states through colonial legacies. Similarly, despite the BCCI founder's purposeful bank structure design, the truly "global" corporate entity simply does not exist. To operate, every bank and corporation must be institutionally based in some country's legal framework.[5] In seeking insulation from state linkages, BCCI paradoxically left itself more vulnerable to regulatory attack.

Through its London office and its Cayman Islands base, the bulk of BCCI's operations and legal presence resided within Britain's financial arena. Although the UK had been one of the early promoters of counterterrorist finance regulation, the City of London (as the central financial district of the larger London metropolis is known) lay at the centre of its own offshore financial network, which included the Caymans and other British-aligned pseudo-colonial holdings. BCCI appeared to have a "global" structure, but behind this façade, the bank depended in fact upon Britain's strategic legacy of competing with the United States as a financial centre. The idea behind offshore havens such as the Caymans – and, indeed, the City of London – was to offer a veneer of light, laissez-faire regulation.

BCCI's first legal home – Luxembourg – emerged as a proto-tax haven as early as 1929, with the introduction of holding company laws that allowed non-residents to enjoy a special tax-exempt status.[6] In the 1970s, the city-state became a major tax haven in parallel with the reorientation of the international financial system to monetarism. In 1981, as an element of its competition with Switzerland, Luxembourg augmented its laws to increase bank secrecy.[7] Not coincidentally, BCCI's growth coincided with Luxembourg's legal changes.

The Cayman Islands' status as a tax haven derives from their legacy as an otherwise innocuous holding of the British Empire. Nicholas Shaxson notes that the City of London forms the centre of a financial empire that encompasses many otherwise unimportant island jurisdictions around the world. Britain's island pseudo-colonies include several "Crown Dependencies" near the UK itself and fourteen other jurisdictions worldwide with a combined population of just 250,000 people, which offer a home to much of the world's hidden financial wealth.[8] Contrary to BCCI's calculations, however, these tax havens only project the *appearance* of statelessness. In reality, the UK has organized the City of London, the Caymans, and its other offshores as a lightly regulated arena in which the financial sector may operate while Britannia looms in the background.

BCCI's founding in the 1970s coincided both with the international monetary system's shift toward monetarism and the emergence of offshore finance havens. In 1962, the Bank of England began allowing the issuance of securities denominated in foreign currencies, thereby bolstering the embryonic Eurodollar market in an effort to reclaim the City's position as a major financial centre.[9] As noted by Eric Helleiner, the Euromarket effectively created an arena that was "offshore" and ostensibly "separate" from the rest of the British financial sector.[10] As Britain's chief regulatory body at the time, the Bank of England actively promoted this arena of light regulation.[11] As noted by Gary Burn, the City of London's Euromarket "punctured a hole" in the regulatory system of the banking industry.[12] This British regulatory reorganization also coincided with an approach to decolonization through the means of financial statecraft. The City created itself as the epicentre of a system of offshore finance – a system that also extended to the UK's dependencies and pseudo-colonies around the world.

The 1960s witnessed a surge of independence movements that virtually eliminated what remained of European colonialism. However, not all colonies proved sufficiently determined, or able, to free themselves from colonial rule. In the Caribbean, the Bahamas under British rule attracted the financial dealings of the American Mafia. In 1961, the Mafia's financial networks under Meyer Lansky began serious operations in the islands, having bribed the British colony's finance minister.[13] The Bahamas' burgeoning illicit finance contributed to the election of independence-minded populists in 1967 and eventual independence in 1973. As a result, the Bahamas' offshore finance institutions moved to the Caymans.[14]

The Caymans' independence and implementation as an offshore tax haven was the joint result of the islands' commercial aristocracy's efforts to retain the territory's dependence upon Britain on the one hand, and Britain's state bureaucracies battling over how closely to regulate and revamp the island on the other. When Jamaica achieved independence in 1962, the Caymans opted instead for continued association with the UK as a colonial holding. The UK thus remains responsible for its Caymanian holding's executive functions.

As offshore funds already stashed in the Caribbean flowed into the Caymans, London's bureaucracies stood divided over the emerging tax haven. From 1966 to 1979, the Caymans established a number of legal changes to attract financial clients seeking less regulation and to exploit regulatory regimes elsewhere in the world. Notably, these laws coincided with the introduction, in the United States, of the 1970 Bank Secrecy Act, which would later evolve into the AML/CTF regime. These legal changes served to flush more capital from the United States into the emerging offshore haven. In 1976, the Caymans implemented legal privacy coverage for offshore corporations and funds emplaced on its shores via the Confidential Relationships Law.[15] Enforcement of this law is overseen by the Caymans Protection Board, which not only oversees privacy but also controls Caymanian citizenship and visa processes.[16]

British bureaucracies clashed over the Caymans' emergence as a tax haven, with the Bank of England and the Overseas Development Ministry supporting its development, and the Treasury and the Foreign Office opposing it.[17] Tellingly, the Bank of England expressed little unease about the influx of illicit funds, but did have concerns over maintaining the sterling area. Palan notes that in a 1969 letter, the Bank of England declared "no objection to providing bolt holes for nonresidents," but expressed concern regarding the possibility of the Caymans becoming a haven for sterling.[18] In 1972, London restricted the sterling area to the British Isles, while the Caymans adopted their own currency, pegged to the dollar to attract illicit financial holdings from the US and Latin America.[19]

Despite ongoing protests from other organs of the British state, the Bank of England's fostering of the Caymans as a Caribbean tax haven continued.[20] Tellingly, the bank's regulatory authority over illicit finance regulation was shifted over to the Financial Services Authority in 2000.[21] The British bureaucracy primarily responsible for overseeing the fortified finance regime that would later emerge during this era was the Treasury, which had opposed the Bank of England's attempts to develop the Caymans as an offshore tax haven.[22] Far from unsupervised, the main stage of BCCI's activities was a deliberately created arena in which the state was not so much absent as willfully aloof, while acting nonetheless in a regulatory capacity. As shown below, not only did the Bank of England have knowledge of BCCI's activities, it assisted in obfuscating them.

The Caymans proved central to BCCI's activities and housed a virtual "bank within a bank" that cleared nefarious transactions and housed dubious accounts.[23] The Caymans' Confidential Relationship Law of 1976 afforded companies the ability to establish subsidiaries to keep much of their activities ostensibly secret. BCCI established such a subsidiary, ICIC Overseas, in the Caymans in 1976. In an incestuous shareholding scheme, ICIC owned 41 per cent of BCCI's legal home entity in Luxembourg.[24] BCCI's Caymanian presence allowed it to keep its transactions in the tax haven on the books, even if the actual funds were not housed there. Furthermore, BCCI's reluctance to digitize its operations, and its stubborn insistence upon maintaining handwritten ledgers and memos in Urdu, effectively placed much of the bank's $20 billion in assets inside a black box.[25] As early as 1978, alarm bells began to sound among banking circles over BCCI's activities.

The bank's original backing came from the newly oil-rich monarchies of the Persian Gulf. Sheikh Zayed bin Sultan Al Nahyan, the emir of Abu Dhabi, proved a perennial political and financial backer, despite – or perhaps because of – the bank's offshore situation and London headquarters. Notably, Al Nahyan came to power via a coup backed by British intelligence services.[26] It was also Al Nahyan to whom the Bank of England turned in an effort to forestall BCCI's collapse. In addition to its Gulf connection, BCCI sought and secured the support of Bank of America to increase its profile and legitimacy. Bank of America even became a significant shareholder. Together with BCCI, Bank of America jointly founded and invested in the National Bank of Oman to increase its access to the Gulf.[27] Although Bank of America's support was initially significant, it was also the first party to cast doubt upon BCCI's legality and long-term health.

As early as 1977, concerns arose at Bank of America about BCCI's viability due to the offshore bank's lending practices. These included the issuing of unsecured loans, lending to major shareholders, and lending over 10 per cent of the bank's capital to a single borrower.[28] Indeed, Bank of America documents outlining concerns about BCCI focus on the offshore bank's loans to "insiders."[29] A number of high-end loans on BCCI's balance sheet were for real estate purchases in the Persian Gulf – loans often made to political figures who offered no security, and that went mostly unpaid. Such borrowers included Saudi Arabia's intelligence chief at the time, Kamal Adham, who not only took out loans for purchases of unvalued real estate, but also borrowed from BCCI in order to reinvest the loan money back into the same bank.[30] In 1978, Bank of America issued a press release announcing the planned selloff of all of its BCCI shares by 1980.[31]

Across the Atlantic, the Bank of England took measures to curtail the bank's rapid growth in the UK, but did nothing to regulate its activities. In 1978, the Bank of England limited the number of BCCI branches permitted in the country to forty-five, and a year later refused to issue the bank a licence as a "recognized bank."[32] The Banking Act, enacted in 1979, delineated two allowable forms for British financial institutions: a bank must function either as a "recognized bank" or a "licensed deposit taker," the latter enjoying less status than the former. The Bank of England relegated BCCI to the latter status.[33] Despite concerns and knowledge regarding BCCI's lending activities and its involvement in terrorism and money laundering, the Bank of England did nothing to rein in the institution until 1991.

While BCCI lacked institutional linkages with what could be considered its home states – the Caymans or Luxembourg – it did everything it could to immerse itself in political affairs and foster relationships with political figures. From arms financing to laundering drug money and financing terrorism, BCCI's long list of high-profile political allies and acquaintances offers an idea as to how it managed to operate for more than a decade after concerns over its practices emerged. BCCI's catalogue of political friends and relations traces the geographical outlines of a shadow world comprising the darker aspects of international crime and statecraft.

Shortly after Jimmy Carter's departure from the White House, BCCI founder Agha Hasan Abedi met the former president and cultivated a relationship predicated on the bank's support for Carter's presidential library and humanitarian work.[34] One of BCCI's major account holders, a Saudi arms dealer named Adnan Khashoggi, helped fundraise for the library.[35] Through the bank's relationship with Carter, BCCI established political relationships in the West that included former British prime ministers James Callaghan and Margaret Thatcher.[36] Along with its Gulf connections, BCCI held several high-profile political figures either as allies or clients. BCCI provided financial assistance to Manuel Noriega's regime in Panama, financed both sides of Nicaragua's civil war, laundered Colombian drug proceeds, and provided banking services to a range of intelligence agencies.[37] In Zimbabwe, BCCI was initially the only bank allowed into the country, in 1980, due to its long-time support for Robert Mugabe.[38] In Pakistan in the late 1980s, BCCI's charitable activities included the funnelling of money through its BCC Foundation to the Ghulam Ishaq Khan Institute of Engineering Sciences and Technology. The institute's director at the time, Abdul Qadeer Khan, was the mastermind behind Pakistan's nuclear weapons program.[39] In the Middle East and Afghanistan, BCCI's activities would include the financing of terrorism and would even provide the initial financial rubric for Al-Qaeda.

In the mid-1980s, BCCI's primary Gulf backer, Sheikh Zayed, began financing the Palestinian Abu Nidal terrorist organization as a means of placating the group and preventing it from attacking Gulf interests.[40] Following the bank's closure, regulators discovered that BCCI's London headquarters had served as an intermittent office for Abu Nidal, where the terrorist organization also held an account.[41] In return for BCCI's services, Abu Nidal occasionally assisted in coercing specific clients on behalf of the bank.[42] The attacks carried out by Abu Nidal's organization included bombings, assassinations, and kidnappings of citizens and officials from multiple countries.

The Palestine Liberation Organization (PLO), one terrorist group that practiced astute long-term financial planning, used BCCI extensively to finance its investments. In 1981, the PLO lent the Nicaraguan government $12 million via BCCI and used funds in BCCI accounts to purchase holdings in airline companies and access to duty-free airport space across the developing world.[43] Iran-backed Hezbollah oversaw the activities of its Europe-based fighters through BCCI's London infrastructure.[44] Other terrorist groups who used BCCI's services included Peru's Shining Path, which used the bank to institutionalize routine payment mechanisms for cartels seeking access to drug shipments.[45]

The CIA, which itself used BCCI's services to channel funds to anti-Soviet fighters in Afghanistan, claimed to have begun looking into the bank's financing of terrorism as early as 1983 and that it informed other intelligence and law enforcement agencies about the bank's activities; however, other organs of the US intelligence community denied ever receiving such information.[46] In the regulatory aftermath of BCCI's closure, it was found that Ghassan Qassem, the bank's primary London manager, worked as a paid informant for American and British intelligence services and provided them with information related to some of the bank's dealings with terrorist organizations.[47]

The 1980s witnessed a multinational increase in outside support for Afghan fighters against the Soviet Union. The US and Saudi Arabia worked with Pakistan under Muhammad Zia-ul-Haq to provide the Afghan mujahideen with the needed materiel, financing, and training. BCCI's longstanding relationship to the Sunni Gulf monarchies and the Pakistani government placed it in a unique position for assisting in this cause, while its hyper-cloaked legal home bases offered an easy means for intelligence services to channel money toward the war effort. Al-Qaeda, one of the terrorist groups to emerge from the Soviet-Afghan war, used BCCI as a model for money laundering and financial secrecy, and likely relied upon the bank's former employees to establish its financial networks in the 1990s.[48]

Following BCCI's closure, one area of the bank's operations that proved difficult for the Senate Committee on Foreign Relations to penetrate was its relationship to the CIA. Bureaucratically, an image emerged that pitted the Federal Reserve against the intelligence community over the central bank's attempts to discover the CIA-BCCI relationship. The Fed, which had worked closely with the Manhattan District Attorney to crack down on the bank, received pushback not only from Langley but also from the Bank of England. Both countries, the UK and the US, were amply aware of the bank's activities and tried to obfuscate relevant investigations prior to its collapse.

New York congressman Chuck Schumer noted that as early as 1983, the federal government had extensive knowledge of BCCI's activities.[49] In 1984, Senator Paula Hawkins met with Zia-ul-Haq as part of a congressional delegation in which she queried him over a "Pakistani bank's" involvement in money laundering through the Cayman Islands.[50] Indeed, former CIA deputy director Richard Kerr claimed that the agency began reporting on BCCI's activities that same year.[51] However, the agency had in fact begun reporting to the Department of the Treasury, the Federal Reserve, the FBI, and certain other intelligence agencies about the bank's money laundering activities beginning in 1983.[52] Despite such reporting, the CIA pled ignorance about much of BCCI's activity in relation to intelligence operations financed by the bank, and that of many of the bank's shareholders. In particular, the CIA feigned ignorance regarding the bank's secret control of First American Bank, its activities pertaining to the Iran-Contra affair, and its use by other intelligence services.[53] The bank would finally suffer a regulatory coup de grâce in 1991 at the hands of the Fed and the Manhattan District Attorney. The Financial Crimes Enforcement Network (FinCEN) – the US Treasury's FIU – came into being just a year earlier, in 1990.

Across the Atlantic, the British government also had longstanding knowledge of the bank's activities, specifically in London and the Caymans. However, London only opted to take action following intense American regulatory pressure. What becomes clear about the Bank of England's defence of BCCI is that the UK was seeking not to defend the bank so much as safeguard the reputation of its central bank and integrity of its offshore financial arena.

Findings from Senator John Kerry's report to the Committee on Foreign Relations claimed that the Bank of England had only partial regulatory oversight over BCCI's operations due to the bank's offshoring in Luxembourg and the Caymans.[54] But although the Bank of England considered those jurisdictions to be BCCI's "lead regulators," Kerry's report overlooked the fact that the Cayman Islands were not a separate jurisdiction from the UK. As noted earlier, the Bank of

England actively cultivated the islands as an offshore tax haven following their decision to remain a British colony. The Caymans not only provide a playground for secretive financial dealings but also serve as a hub of British intelligence activity, with MI6 enjoying a major presence there.[55]

For its part, Luxembourg also knew about BCCI's activities and in 1985 sought to have the bank relocate its legal home to the UK, with the Bank of England as its lead regulator. The Bank of England refused.[56] Luxembourg attempted to spread around the regulatory liability posed by BCCI by pushing for the formulation of a College of Regulators under a 1983 Basel Committee agreement that offered such a mechanism as a means of regulating renegade banks.[57] Luxembourg complained that only 2 per cent of BCCI's activities occurred within its jurisdiction, thus warranting such collaboration.[58] Eventually, such a regulatory college did meet in 1988; however, despite multiple audits outlining malfeasance, the regulators recommended no specific action.[59]

In the late 1980s, the Bank of England sought to conceal audits of BCCI, to the extent of seeking to broker a deal with Abu Dhabi to cover up the exposure of British depositors to the bank's malfeasance. In 1987, the Bank of England undertook a half-baked audit of BCCI's ledgers using the latter's own auditors, who found nothing amiss with the bank's dealings.[60]

After conducting a proper audit of the bank in 1990, the accounting firm Price Waterhouse described the magnitude of BCCI's nefarious affairs and bad balance sheets to the Bank of England. Thereupon, the British central bank began to lobby Abu Dhabi for assistance in letting Sheikh Zayed move the bank to the emirate from London.[61] Britain was hesitant to close the bank, concerned about the financial scandal that would surely ensue due to anticipated losses on the part of the bank's 120,000 British depositors.[62] Individual depositors stood to lose nearly $404 million, while municipal government depositors stood to lose nearly $160 million.[63] The Bank of England's governor, Robin Pemberton, flew to Abu Dhabi in an effort to lobby Sheikh Zayed for cash infusions into the bank and for the possibility of moving the bank's base of operations to the emirate.[64] The Abu Dhabi government agreed to the move, flushing the bank with $1.2 billion and promising London that it would cover the bank's losses.[65]

In his testimony before the House of Commons Treasury and Civil Service Committee, Pemberton defended the move and declared that "it was a matter of realism that we do have occasions of fraud in banks, but that if we close down a bank every time we find an individual act or two of fraud we would have rather fewer banks than we do at the moment."[66] From Pemberton's statement, it becomes clear that Britain's motive in defending BCCI was securing the integrity of its financial sector and diffusing blame across multiple jurisdictions – a very different kind of move from defending a bank in which the London held an institutional linkage.

The British parliamentary record in the aftermath of BCCI's closure indicates that the Bank of England feigned ignorance of BCCI's attempts to avoid having a jurisdictional base. British MPs described the Bank of England as having created a "culture of the 1980s, when a nod and a wink were given in the direction of regulation," even as it otherwise exhibited a laissez-faire attitude toward how most British banking was carried out.[67] In the 1992 parliamentary debates, it was noted that BCCI was the only bank to have ever faced attempted regulation via a "college of regulators."[68]

On both sides of the Atlantic, it was widely assumed that BCCI was structured much as its founder Abedi had originally intended – as a "global" bank without a state. However, the bank was not so much a stateless entity as one for which no state wished to bear ultimate responsibility. The scope of BCCI's criminality may never fully be known, but what is apparent is its involvement in a wide array of political circles that included current and former heads of state, revolutionaries, drug cartels, terrorists, and multiple intelligence services. However, any ostensive "statelessness" the bank hoped to obtain by locating itself in two tax havens was a veneer at best. While Luxembourg's comprehension of the bank's activities may have been limited, the UK's was not. The Caymans were actively cultivated as an offshore tax haven by the UK, and the Bank of England in particular acted as a bureaucratic driving force in this regard. Eventually, the Bank of England faced a financial monster that was the product of the regulatory environment it had created and about which it had prior knowledge.

In 1990, as the British authorities worked with Abu Dhabi to remove BCCI, and the financial liability it represented, through Gulf-backed bailouts and physical relocation of its headquarters, regulatory pressures were building across the Atlantic. In the US, Jack Blum, a lawyer working for the Senate Subcommittee on Narcotics, Terrorism and International Operations, reported BCCI's activities to the Manhattan District Attorney, Robert Morgenthau. After relating to the prosecutor his knowledge of BCCI's array of criminal and terrorist activities, the New York DA began applying pressure.[69] After bureaucratic resistance from Price Waterhouse and government agencies in the US and the UK, Manhattan prosecutors secured the audit results they needed. After obtaining this information from Morgenthau's office, the Federal Reserve began pressuring the Bank of England to take action.[70]

The following year saw a multinational crackdown on BCCI's operations. On 5 July 1991, British police raided the bank's UK offices, while the Bank of England contacted regulatory authorities in more than sixty countries to request their cooperation in closing the bank.[71] The British governor of the Caymans placed the bank's three divisions in the country under receivership and froze the assets of eight corporations linked to the bank. Luxembourg and other European jurisdictions followed suit.[72] Later that year in the US, the State Department confirmed BCCI's involvement with the Abu Nidal Organization, among other terrorist groups, and the symbiosis that existed between terrorist financing and drug dealing.[73] By the end of July, BCCI's offices were closed in forty-four separate states.[74]

In the end, BCCI was not institutionally linked to any particular state. No state in which BCCI was legally rooted held an ownership stake in the bank. Certainly, the history of the bank's activities illustrates a financial institution instrumental to the shadowy dealings of a number of actors, state and non-state alike. However, the bank was not a going concern of any specific state so much as one that provided a variety of services to state clients engaged in covert activity. The Caymans and Luxembourg, however, continue to function as offshore tax havens. So long as they continue to service those who must conduct business dealings beyond the view of their constituencies, banks such as BCCI have the potential to resurface.

Contrary to Abedi's vision, BCCI was not a bank without a home state, though it was one without state linkage. In its home jurisdictions of the Cayman Islands and Luxembourg, the banking world remained well within the purview of state power. The Cayman Islands were actively cultivated to serve as an offshore haven by its UK colonial masters, contrary to the recommendations of a number of British government bureaucracies. Even geographically minute Luxembourg demanded in 1990 that BCCI relocate outside the city-state within a year.[75] The two places that might have proven durable state backers of BCCI, Abu Dhabi and Pakistan, were not BCCI's home jurisdictions. Both the emirate under Abu Zayed and Pakistan under Zia-ul-Haq provided political and financial backing to the criminal bank, but neither proved capable of safeguarding BCCI from its multilateral closure in its primary jurisdictions. Abedi had established the bank offshore to avoid the fate of a state takeover, such as the one suffered by his previous bank in Pakistan, United Bank Limited. As for Abu Dhabi, the UK actively sought the emirate's support in an effort to forestall the deterioration of the bank's balance sheets. Had BCCI been linked to a home state, the very situation it sought to avoid, the bank might have enjoyed protections in the face of regulatory crackdown. During the ill-fated attempt by the ad hoc "college of regulators" to restructure the bank, the Bank of England, Luxembourg, and the Caymans sought to have BCCI relocate to Abu Dhabi, which held a stake in it.[76] In the end, however, the emirate was given no advanced notification when regulators around the world commenced closing BCCI.

Concurrent with the BCCI's collapse was the emergence of the international lynchpin of the fortified finance regime. In 1989, the Financial Action Task Force was created by the G7. The United States in 1990 created the Financial Crimes Enforcement Network, the prototypical financial intelligence unit, under the umbrella of the Department of the Treasury. The same year, Congress passed the Anti-Terrorism Act, exposing terrorist financiers to civil litigation. While the UK's fortified finance apparatus would continue to evolve, the Bank of England eventually lost its premier status as the country's financial regulator.

Contrary to notions that the UK could not regulate an otherwise "global" bank, the UK actively chose to regulate BCCI selectively. The British government facilitated the creation of the Caymans as a financial colonial holding designed to attract banks like BCCI. Furthermore, had the Bank of England been truly incapable of regulating the bank, Britain would not have been able to limit BCCI's growth in the country in 1978 and relegate it to second-tier status in 1979. Rather than regulate the bank in the face of multiple audits in the 1980s, the Bank of England engaged in financial geopolitical diplomacy in an attempt to shift the problem abroad.

## ENFORCEMENT AGAINST THE ARAB BANK OF JORDAN

Some banks demonstrate a remarkable ability to operate and survive in regions characterized by profound political turmoil. In the

Middle East, Arab Bank of Jordan is one such financial survivalist. Headquartered in Amman, the bank has survived decolonization, shifting borders, and multiple wars between the Arab states and Israel. However, despite its adeptness at surviving Middle East turmoil, the bank came under regulatory penalty for financing terrorism in 2005, when it faced a $24 million fine for its ties to Hamas. Over the ensuing years, Arab Bank faced multiple civil lawsuits in US courts for violations of the 1990 Anti-Terrorism Act. Unlike many longstanding banks in the Middle East, Arab Bank was founded as a private bank on an American model. Additionally, the era of the bank's founding and growth precluded any attachment to a burgeoning state.

Outside of Egypt, localized modern banking in the Arab Middle East did not take root until the 1930s. Many banks that developed locally in the region faced a number of institutional hurdles in modernizing traditional lending and bookkeeping practices. Additionally, heightened political uncertainty – the result of the remnants of older Ottoman institutions intermingling with the new European administrations and nascent nationalist movements – hindered overall economic growth.

Arab Bank, then the largest indigenous Middle East bank not based in the Gulf, was founded in Jerusalem in 1930 following American banking models. Its founder, Abdul Hameed Shoman, drew upon his experience with Wall Street banking during the 1920s.[77] Arab Bank would emerge as closely intertwined with Palestinians in the following decades, while remaining at arm's length from the Jordanian monarchy and other state governments in the region.

Palestinian businessman Abdul Hameed Shoman came to the US in 1911, whereupon he commenced a successful career in textile manufacturing and sales. Driven by an admiration for the manner in which American banks worked with their clients, as well as Arab nationalism and a rabid antisemitism, Shoman desired to create a bank that could serve the political motivation of decreasing Arabs' reliance on European banks, and banks run by Jews. In his memoirs, Shoman argued that the Arabs "must gather strength by creating their own national institutions, for they would be their best buttress against the encroaching power of Zionism, the Mandate and colonialism."[78] Notably, one primary aspect of Shoman's desire to create Arab Bank was his antisemitism. He declared in his memoirs that, "all business dealings with the Jews – buying, selling or banking transactions – are damaging to our country's self-interests," and that there was "no need to fear any other group."[79]

Arab Bank opened in Jerusalem in 1930 and, from the beginning, Shoman went out of his way to secure private deposit holders and clients. Initially going "door to door" himself, Shoman actively engaged local shopkeepers and merchants among the Arab population of British Mandate Palestine.[80] As he gathered clients, Shoman argued for the benefits that such a modern bank could provide and even developed interest-free savings accounts to secure clients sensitive of the Islamic prohibition of interest.[81] Within British Mandate Palestine and beyond, Arab nationalism emerged as a constant theme in Shoman's business motivations and those of the bank he founded. This motivation animated the bank's efforts to open branches elsewhere in the Levant, North Africa, and the Gulf.

While statism was the primary feature of a number of banks that opened during this era, particularly those in areas seeking independence, Arab Bank's ownership structure was private in nature and, paradoxically, tied to Arab Nationalism. In describing the bank's logo, Shoman emphasized that the bank was not intended to be a national bank. Arab Bank, he declared, was not "backed by any government or central bank."[82] Describing his bank's solvency in times of crisis, Shoman affirmed that "God is our only refuge."[83]

As Arab Bank expanded its capital by increasing its issuance of shares, the bank's board discussed the importance of issuing ownership throughout the Arab world rather than just in one state. The board decided on "a new issue of shares which Arab nationals of any part of the Arab World served by the Arab Bank shall be permitted to purchase."[84] While the bank was founded, and for a time headquartered in British Mandate Palestine, Arab Bank deliberately sought to keep itself from becoming simply a Palestinian bank. Shoman himself declared that the bank "is not a Shoman property" and that it "does not belong simply to the people of Jerusalem, nor even to the people of Palestine but to the entire Arab nation."[85]

At the time of its founding, and through much of the twentieth century, Arab Bank's competition has largely been with national banks. In 1934, as Arab Bank opened its Jordanian branch in Amman, Ottoman Bank conducted most banking in the immediate region. Founded in 1856, Ottoman Bank was a joint venture between the Ottoman Empire and European imperial interests in the Middle East.[86] While Ottoman Bank's original purpose was to help safeguard British and French financial interests in the Ottoman Empire and ensure the security of long-term Turkish debt, in Transjordan after the First World War, the bank became the purview of the British administration. Banking in Transjordan under British administration was dominated by a combination of foreign banks with "little interest" in providing financial services to local businesses.[87] These local Arab merchants, however, were precisely the customer base that Shoman was seeking for his expansion of Arab Bank.

As Arab Bank expanded across what would become multiple countries after decolonization, Transjordan remained overly reliant upon British-subsidized aid, and most Mandate spending focused on the administrative infrastructure rather than the local economy.[88] With Arab Bank's drive to secure clients among local small businesses, and given Shoman's lack of a particular affection for any specific area of the Arab world, the Jordanian monarchy agreed to allow the bank to open a presence in Amman. Both in 1934, when Arab Bank was established in Transjordan, and 1944, when it expanded its shares, the British administration and Jordan's monarchy were suspicious of its intent. For their part, British authorities were skeptical of potential competition with Ottoman Bank's position in the country, while Jordan's Prince Abdullah was concerned with rumours circulating at the time regarding the bank's potential to disrupt political stability.[89] In a 1944 meeting, Shoman assured Prince Abdallah that "none of the bank's people will interfere in any activity of a political nature."[90]

The late 1940s and early 1950s proved pivotal for Arab Bank's standing in the political economy of the region, as well as for its situation throughout the remainder of the twentieth century and into the present. In 1948, with the Israeli war for independence, Arab Bank relocated its headquarters to its Amman branch.[91] The founding of Israel, in combination with the rise of Arab socialism, led to a number of branch losses for the bank that undermined its position in the Middle East and North Africa. Between 1948 and 1970, Arab Bank lost thirty-four branches entirely due to political risk, either from the wars between the Arab states and Israel, or from nationalization under dictatorships in Yemen, Libya, Iraq, Syria, Egypt, and elsewhere.[92] Tellingly, Arab Bank opened branches in Switzerland in 1961, and a Swiss subsidiary in 1962.[93]

Unlike the bureaucratic, authoritarian dictatorships of Jordan's Arab neighbours, the Hashemite kingdom remained a steadfast Western ally throughout the Cold War and into the twenty-first century. Additionally,

Jordan managed to sidestep the internal tumult that characterizes much of modern Middle East history. In contrast to other Arab states in the region, Jordan's relationship with Israel displayed a certain nuance, as a result of which Amman sometimes played an intermediary role between otherwise hostile states. Similarly, Jordan's affiliation with the UK and the US remained a constant factor in its foreign policy, while other states in the region engaged in decades of hostility with the West under the sway of Gamal Abdel Nasser's socialism or Ba'athism in Syria. Similarly, Jordan has thus far remained a stable state despite multiple jihadist and Palestinian groups operating in the kingdom and against the Jordanian government. Such diplomatic and domestic political acumen on the part of Jordan's monarchy also impacts the kingdom's political economy, in the context of which Arab Bank has never been threatened with nationalization and has been allowed to function as the American-style bank its founder envisioned.

Jordan's fortunate record of political stability is not coincidental. Over the course of the twentieth century and into the twenty-first, the country became a safe haven for multiple waves of refugees and political migrants from the surrounding states. Shortly after its independence in 1946, Jordan faced its first major geopolitical crisis in the context of Israel's 1948 war for independence. After reluctantly entering into the war against Israel, Jordan came to occupy and eventually annex one-fifth of what had been British Mandate Palestine.[94] Between its annexation of East Jerusalem and the West Bank, and the Palestinian refugees flooding into the kingdom, much of Jordan's population is of Palestinian origin. This influx of Palestinian refugees permanently altered the kingdom's demographics and political economy in a way that was conducive to Arab Bank's expansion. At the same time, Jordan's conservatism prevented the full political enfranchisement its Palestinian population, while its Western alignment served to keep banks privatized.

The influx of Palestinian refugees into Jordan created a unique problem in the kingdom's political economy. On the one hand, the new Palestinian population created a bourgeoisie in the kingdom due to its wealth and high calibre of human capital relative to the native Transjordanians. Indeed, the influx of Palestinian wealth significantly increased the kingdom's money supply, while the Palestinians' business activity came to form the core of Jordan's skilled middle class.[95] On the other hand, the new Palestinian population created an imbalance of economic power in relation to the kingdom's native subjects. To safeguard political power, the kingdom restricted Palestinian political activity and sought to empower the Jordanian Bedouins and the rural areas deemed more loyal to the monarchy.[96]

While other Middle East states experimented with nationalizing banks and certain industries, Jordan's political economy embarked upon private sector development. As early as 1949, Jordan implemented Law No. 41, which established the legal basis for the country's Chamber of Commerce.[97] The structure of Jordan's private sector deepened its autonomy vis-à-vis the state over the course of ensuing decades, with the formation of Jordan's Chamber of Industry in 1964 and the Association of Bankers in 1978.[98] The Association of Bankers, together with the other business organizations, effectively acts as a legal interest group that can lobby the state on behalf of its members.[99] The Association's general assembly represents not only Jordanian banks but also foreign banks operating in the country.[100] Arab Bank is the oldest bank in the organization. Aside from state funding for government-backed projects in the agricultural and housing sectors, Amman's liberal banking sector remains devoted to commercial lending, remittances, and the financial activity of private actors.[101] For its part, the state's direct involvement in specific industries is restricted to such areas as phosphate mining, oil, fertilizer, and cement.[102] Banking in Jordan is a private sector affair.

The Shoman family that founded the bank remains the predominant governing element in its shareholding and on its corporate board. When Arab Bank came under regulatory scrutiny for suspected terrorist financing, the Shoman family alone controlled 35 per cent of the bank, while other prominent shareholders included the government of Saudi Arabia (17 per cent), the former Lebanese prime minister Rafic Hariri, influential Palestinian-Jordanian families, and the Jordanian Social Security Corporation.[103] Along with the Shoman family presence on Arab Bank's board of directors, all members but the one representing the Hariri family supported the Shomans' leadership.[104]

While the Jordanian state exerts influence on Arab Bank through the involvement of the Jordanian Social Security Corporation in the bank's affairs, the bank's majority shareholders are private. Additionally, the majority of its board members are either private economic actors or politically connected to states other than Jordan. Indeed, when Hariri sought to increase his ownership share, Jordan's King Abdullah intervened to secure the Shoman family's control.[105] In this instance, the Jordanian state sought to preserve the bank's integrity as a private financial concern legally based within its borders.

Due to its absorption of Palestinians in 1948, roughly 40 per cent of Jordan's population is of Palestinian origin.[106] The kingdom's political economy and political system place its Palestinian population in a nebulous position. Jordan's Palestinian demographic is held at a distance in the country's political system, with occasional tensions arising with the state as a result. Amman's challenges with regard to the kingdom's Muslim Brotherhood and Hamas organizations relate to these sociopolitical tensions. Jordan's Palestinians – those who live outside of the refugee camps – are not economically disadvantaged. Palestinians dominate the top echelons of the kingdom's private sector, while indigenous Jordanians of old Bedouin extraction dominate state bureaucracies.[107]

The Palestinian dominance in the country's private sector is profound, with 60 per cent of Jordan's top five hundred companies owned by Palestinians and Palestinian capital, comprising 87 per cent of the kingdom's GNP.[108] Palestinian dominance of Jordan's banking sector is even stronger, with Palestinian-owned banks accounting for 92 per cent of its market capitalization.[109] Arab Bank dwarfs its rivals, alone encompassing 62 per cent of Jordan's bank-sector market capitalization.[110] On the question of how a bank's size in its home state influences enforcement outcomes for terrorist financing, it is worth noting that Arab Bank's behemoth presence in Jordan did not preclude enforcement from occurring. Additionally, the political divide between the Jordanian state and the Palestinians may in part explain why no institutional linkage developed between it and Arab Bank.

Despite Palestinian business dominance, Jordan's political system diminishes the influence of the Palestinian demographic while magnifying the political power of the kingdom's rural Bedouin base and other indigenous segments of the population. This divide has grown in recent decades with political reforms in Jordan's bureaucracies and increased opposition activity on the part of segments of the Palestinian population.

Since the late 1940s, Jordan's population has divided along a cleavage of native Jordanians on the one hand and those of Palestinian extraction on the other. While Palestinians would come to dominate the kingdom's private sector, the Jordanian state remained dominated by indigenous Jordanians based along old rural and tribal lines. As the Jordanian state expanded, the monarchy considered the indigenous population to hold greater loyalty to the crown than the incoming Palestinians, and drew from the kingdom's tribal structure to fill the ranks of the military and state agencies.[111] Indeed, "Jordanian" identity in the kingdom is often affiliated with employment in the public sector.[112]

Politically, Palestinians in Jordan have always remained partially disenfranchised from the state, despite their economic prowess. This virtual lockout from a meaningful presence in the state apparatus, in combination with the concentration of power and influence in the monarchy and tribal affiliations, placed the Palestinians in a position of active involvement in the kingdom's political opposition. Participation in the opposition by segments of the Palestinian population placed the Palestinians in a unique position when groups such the Muslim Brotherhood and Hamas began operations in Jordan.

The security of the Jordanian state has long interlocked with Western security interests in the Middle East, and this interlocking has involved the thwarting of domestic opposition to the monarchy. Jordan is situated in the midst of the Israeli-Palestinian conflict and yet has managed to maintain continuous rule despite being surrounded by Arab nationalist dictatorships, jihadist movements, and state collapse in neighbouring countries. The 1967 war with Israel brought an end to Jordanian control of the West Bank and introduced a second wave of Palestinians into the kingdom. The resulting yearlong Jordanian civil war wrought a permanent rift between Palestinian political organizations in the country and the monarchy. The secular nationalist Palestine Liberation Organization (PLO) proved the loser in its short conflict against Jordanian troops, and was driven out of the country.[113] On the macropolitical scale, the civil war crystalized "Jordanian" (as opposed to Palestinian) identity, while religious Palestinian groups grew in the ensuing years. Hamas, the terrorist group involved with Arab Bank's laundering scandal, was one such group.

Although Hamas' origins date to 1987, the group's roots in Jordan trace back to the Muslim Brotherhood. Unlike secular Palestinian nationalists, Jordan did not initially consider religious groups as potentially threatening to the state. Indeed, in the 1950s, the Muslim Brotherhood in Jordan cooperated with the monarchy against the secular nationalist groups.[114] When the Muslim Brotherhood helped create Hamas, the new organization's structure included a formidable apparatus consisting of administration, charity, public relations, and political activities alongside its paramilitary operations.[115] In Jordan, Hamas not only sought no linkage with the state but actively supported political liberalization and democratization movements in the country.[116]

The 1980s catalyzed Jordan's experimenting with political liberalization, which would culminate with the monarchy's expulsion of Hamas from the country in 1999. As the oil boom subsided in the 1980s and the country's economy entered a downturn, Jordan experienced an exodus of Palestinian capital from its private sector.[117] As the monarchy detached itself from claims to the West Bank in 1989, the state introduced political reforms as a means of increasing the throne's legitimacy.[118] Such reforms included the holding of full parliamentary elections, the legalization of political parties, an easing of press censorship, and the end of martial law in 1991.[119] The reforms favoured indigenous Jordanians and the social loci of the monarchy's historical power base: the Transjordanian-dominated bureaucracies, the Bedouin tribal groups, and the military.[120] Jordan's political liberalization coincided with economic adjustments that bolstered segments of the opposition. In the 1989 election, the Muslim Brotherhood won the largest share of parliamentary seats.[121]

In the 1990s, relations between Jordan and Israel brought Amman's tolerance of Hamas to a breaking point. A serious Hamas presence in Jordan formed in 1990, only a year after the Muslim Brotherhood's influential entry into the kingdom's limited system of representation. Khaled Mashal, the Hamas leader who became the chair of the group's political wing in 1996, relocated to Jordan in 1990 after his expulsion from Kuwait.[122] In 1997, Israel's botched attempt to poison Mashal in Jordan opened a rift between Amman and Jerusalem that emboldened the group within the country.[123] While Jordanian diplomatic pressure helped secure the antidote to Mashal's poisoning, Hamas operations designed to undermine Middle East peace negotiations drew attention to its presence in the kingdom. Hamas interpreted Amman's response to the Israeli assassination attempt as the monarchy offering full political backing to its activities;[124] but in 1999, Jordanian security forces closed Hamas offices in the capital and charged Mashal and other Hamas figures with possession of illegal weapons, fraud, and "raising funds for a non-authorized association."[125]

Jordan severed ties with Hamas in 1999, despite the surging of Islamist influence in other countries in the Middle East in early 2000s. Unlike the Muslim Brotherhood, which enjoys genuinely Transjordanian roots in the country, where it was founded in 1942 prior to the arrival of the Palestinians,[126] Hamas is a primarily Palestinian and urban phenomenon.[127] Overall, the Brotherhood in Jordan has also enjoyed an easier relationship with the monarchy through its provision of social services alongside royal-run charities and its close ties with the business community.[128] However, the late 1990s rift between the monarchy and pro-liberalization opposition movements led the Brotherhood to abstain from the 1997 Jordanian elections.[129]

When Jordan banned Hamas activity in 1999, the prime minister, Abdelraouf al-Rawabdeh, deemed the organization a threat to the country's stability.[130] Indeed, Jordanian intelligence officials uncovered a weapons smuggling and paramilitary training scheme that linked Hamas to Hezbollah in Syria, and included ongoing Hamas intelligence gathering operations on the Jordanian state.[131] The early 2000s marked a shift in Jordan's stance toward Hamas and its dealings with Arab Bank, whereby Amman's monitoring of the terrorist group would align with the increasing animosity the group faced from the secularist Fatah faction of the PLO. The acrimony Hamas faced from the secular Palestinian factions and Jordan coincided with increased Israeli scrutiny of Arab Bank's activities. In 2005, Arab Bank's lack of institutional linkage with Jordan left it exposed to administrative penalties and civil suits emanating from the United States.

The US designated Hamas as a terrorist group in 1997 and began designating entities as its financiers in the early 2000s.[132] In 2003, the US identified Hamas-affiliated charities in Europe as financiers of terrorism.[133] Through a network of charities in the West, money was funnelled from abroad to Hamas' local charities via Arab Bank.[134] The Palestinian Authority's security services noted as early as 2000 that Hamas routinely reallocated funds collected for social projects to the group's combatant arm, and often transferred monies raised in the Gulf states through Arab Bank.[135]

In 2004, during the height of the Second Intifada, the Israeli military raided Arab Bank's Ramallah offices on the suspicion that it was financing terrorism for Hamas, Islamic Jihad, and the al-Aqsa Martyrs' Brigades.[136] Later, in 2009, the Israelis declared the bank to be in the clear with regard to financing terrorism.[137] However, the early 2000s saw enforcement actions against the bank in the form of American fines in 2005, and civil suits in US courts beginning in 2004.

Juan Zarate notes that one year after the raid, on 17 August 2005, the US Office of the Comptroller of the Currency (OCC) and the Treasury Department's Financial Crimes Enforcement Network (FinCEN) levied a $24 million fine against Arab Bank for failure to comply with the Bank Secrecy Act.[138] The US accused the bank of conducting "willfully blind" business and facilitating suspicious transactions through its New York branch for purposes of terrorism financing.[139] The American regulatory order also reduced Arab Bank's New York branch to an "uninsured administrative office" without the ability to conduct transactions.[140] FinCEN also found that Arab Bank had conducted no monitoring of transactions through its New York office before June 2002.[141] American regulators discovered that Arab Bank also failed to submit adequate suspicious activity reports (SARs) on transactions through its New York branch even though most of these funds represented dealings with jurisdictions deemed to be high-risk for terrorism and terrorist financing.[142] These regulatory penalties served as the fortified finance regime's first salvo against Arab Bank. Shortly after the levying of regulatory fines, certain survivors of terrorism commenced pursuing further enforcement against the bank in the form of civil lawsuits.

Even as FinCEN's $24 million penalty against Arab Bank was levied in November 2005, the Jordanian government was in talks with US officials regarding penalizing the bank for financing terrorism. In February 2005, a US delegation that included Stuart A. Levey, the Treasury Department's Under Secretary for Terrorism and Financial Intelligence, travelled to Jordan to address concerns over Arab Bank's terrorist financing.[143] The US delegation met with representatives from the Central Bank of Jordan and the Jordanian finance ministry, as well as Arab Bank's CEO, Abdul Hameed Shoman.[144] In 2000, Shoman contributed to terrorism personally, while his staff contributed 5 per cent of their personal salaries to terrorist operations during the Second Intifada.[145]

Although Jordanian officials stressed Arab Bank's importance to the country in meetings with American regulators from the OCC, the Jordanian government declared that it would support regulatory penalty "as long as Arab Bank received due process."[146] Regarding Jordan's regulatory capacity, the American delegation lamented "significant systemic problems" with the country's fortified finance structure, while both American and Jordanian officials discussed the difficulty of effectively policing terrorist financing due to the lack of any significant regulatory capacity within Arab Bank or the neighbouring Palestinian Authority.[147] Jordan indicated that it was seeking Cypriot or Lebanese sponsorship for entry into the Egmont Group, and that planning was already underway for developing its own enforcement body under the auspices of the Central Bank.[148] Jordan's prime minister, Faisal Al-Fayez, agreed with Under Secretary Levey on the need for the kingdom to adopt its own fortified finance regime.[149]

The meeting between US officials and Arab Bank in Jordan illustrate the bank's earliest attempts at defending itself. Arab Bank administrators declared that if the OCC had given them better prior warning, the bank would have acted upon any noncompliant branch with the "wrath of God," but that the bank had been permitted "no time" to respond to the regulatory charges.[150] The Arab Bank representatives affirmed to the US officials that the bank intended to end all individual account transactions through New York and instead focus on "corporate credit and finance," ostensibly in an effort to decrease the risk of money laundering and terrorist financing.[151] Despite the repeated expression of concerns by Arab Bank and various organs of the Jordanian state about the effect that a scandal would have on the country's financial system, Amman made no attempt to block American regulatory action against the bank.

In 2004, meanwhile, lawyers representing victims of terrorism during the Second Intifada began bringing suits against the bank in the District Court for New York's Eastern District for knowingly financing Hamas and other Palestinian terrorist groups between 1995 and 2004 (see table 5.1). However, the civil case was stalled due to Arab Bank's refusal to produce court-ordered documents during the discovery process of the trial. Arab Bank refused to produce the relevant documents on the grounds that doing so would violate multiple laws and regulations pertaining to bank secrecy in Europe and the Middle East.[152] On 13 December 2006, Judge Nina Gershon of the Eastern District of New York ordered Arab Bank to produce the documents it had earlier proffered to FinCEN and the OCC.[153] In 2010, the court initiated sanctions against the bank for its continued failure to produce discovery documents on the grounds of violating bank secrecy laws.[154] In its attempt to stall, the bank sought to obfuscate its previous activities, even as Jordanian authorities worked with American officials to bring greater regulatory policing to both Arab Bank and the Jordanian banking sector as a whole.

During the period in which Arab Bank was being pressed by US courts to produce evidence pertaining to discovery, the bank was taking action to clean up its account records and obfuscate its involvement in terrorist financing. In February 2005, the US Treasury

Table 5.1
Sample of Hamas members and Arab Bank accounts

| Hamas member | Role | Account number(s) | Amount | Dates | Arab Bank branch |
|---|---|---|---|---|---|
| Ghazi Ahmed Hamad | Spokesman, Hamas, 2006–07 Editor, *Al-Watan*, *Al-Risala* | 1170465510 706785 | $152,986 | July 2000– January 2002 | Gaza |
| Jamal Salim | Senior leader, Hamas, West Bank | 4033906500 | $13,500 | December 2000– March 2001 | Nablus |
| Ismail Abu Shanab | Commander, Qassam Brigades; deputy to Sheikh Yassin | 236519510 | $173,172 | August 2000– August 2001 | Gaza |
| Ismail Haniyeh | Party leader, Hamas | 63517500 | $409,400 | July 2000– September 2001 | Gaza |
| Muhammad Hasan Shama'a | Co-founder, Hamas | 513636510 | $144,000 | January 2001– December 2001 | Gaza |
| Jamal and Muna Mansur | Jamal Mansur: founder, Hamas Research Institute, West Bank; spokesman, Hamas Muna Mansur: member (for Hamas), Palestinian Legislative Council | 4064788500 | $85,000 | December 2000– September 2001 | Nablus |
| Salah al-Din Darwazah | Commander, Qassam Brigades Hamas leader in Nablus | 4286871510 | $302,000 | July 2000– July 2001 | Nablus |
| Sheikh Ahmed Yassin | Founder and spiritual figurehead, Hamas | 36444 | $60,000 | 5 May 2001 (single payment) | Gaza |

*Source*: "Payments to Hamas Leaders," Osen LLC (Hackensack, NJ), accessed 10 May 2018, https://www.osenlaw.com/content/payments-hamas-leaders.

undersecretary met with Israel's counterterrorism director, General Dani Arditi, to discuss terrorist financing and Arab Bank in particular.[155] In briefing the US Treasury officials, the Israelis informed them that although Arab Bank had ceased financing terrorism after the filing of the civil suits, the bank was "playing with evidence, cleaning the records, and deleting accounts."[156] Even as the bank purportedly took measures to destroy incriminating evidence, Jordanian officials were working with US regulators in an effort to foster and strengthen the kingdom's fortified finance regime.

Throughout 2005, diplomatic meetings between the US and Jordan indicated that the kingdom's efforts in relation to countering terrorist financing were hampered by the immaturity of the regulatory regime and not by any effort on the part of the home state to protect Arab Bank. In July 2005, US Treasury officials met again with Jordan's central bank governor and finance minister to call on the kingdom to institute AML/CTF regulations for its banking system.[157] The central bank governor, Umayya Toukan, noted that the fortified finance regulations related to customer due diligence were already being practiced by banks in Jordan, other than Arab Bank.[158] Two months later, in meetings between US and Jordanian officials on implementing counterterrorist financing controls, the Central Bank of Jordan's deputy governor noted that the Amman government was "pressing the bank hard to comply fully and expeditiously with all US regulatory requirements."[159] Jordanian officials expressed the belief that their intermediate regulatory efforts should have prevented Arab Bank's terrorist financing activity.[160] Previous Jordanian efforts to counter terrorist financing depended heavily upon the country's intelligence services.[161]

Indeed, the kingdom had begun implementing aspects of its fortified finance regime as early as 2000. Article 93 of Jordan's Banking Law, enacted in 2000, mandated that banks report suspicious activities to the Central Bank if such activities were suspected of being linked to a crime.[162] Jordan's Central Bank Regulation No. 10, implemented in 2001, specifies money laundering as a primary concern.[163] Regulation No. 10 was implemented in conjunction with the kingdom's more generic Banking Law No. 28, which compels banks to report suspicious activity to the Central Bank, and frees the reporting banks from any potential legal liabilities pertaining to violation of privacy.[164] Regarding Hamas in particular, the Central Bank of Jordan mandated in 2003 that all banks in the kingdom "freeze any dealings" with Hamas and its charity affiliates.[165] Building upon its Penal Code

No. 16, implemented in 1960, Jordan enacted a number of laws designed to counter terrorism and terrorist financing in the years prior to the arrival in 2005 of the US regulators.[166] Amman's assurances about implementing terrorist financing and money laundering regulations came to full fruition in 2007 with Law No. 46, which established the country's financial intelligence unit within the central bank.

The numerous civil cases against Arab Bank yielded mixed results in terms of penalties. In one case, *Linde v. Arab Bank*, a jury found the bank liable for financing terrorism in 2014. While the verdict was vacated on a technicality, an undisclosed settlement was reached between the plaintiffs and the bank in 2015.[167] The bank stated in 2016 that it had earmarked $1 billion to cover settlement obligations.[168] The undisclosed settlement covered all of the case's more-than-five-hundred plaintiffs.[169] Notably, the bank stated in its annual report for 2015 that the settlement was "in the best interest of the Bank, and it has been entered into upon acceptable and satisfactory terms and without admission of liability of any wrongdoing by the Bank."[170] Additionally, the bank noted that it had "sufficient provisions to cover the expected financial obligations under this agreement."[171] Litigation brought against the bank by nearly six thousand foreign nationals under the Alien Torts Statute (ATS) of 1789 was dismissed in 2018.[172]

In the course of the civil suits against Arab Bank, Jordan did protest what it viewed as excessive efforts at penalization. In August 2017, Jordan filed an amicus curia brief arguing for the dismissal of the civil suits that had been sought under the Alien Torts Statute. An eighteenth-century law allowing non-US nationals to sue in American courts, the ATS provided a legal basis for thousands of plaintiffs to seek damages. Unlike *Linde v. Arab Bank*, in which the plaintiffs were American and smaller in number, payment of civil penalties for some six thousand foreign nationals under the ATS raised the possibility of undermining the very integrity of Arab Bank and destabilizing the Middle East. The Jordanians argued that aside from the ATS action comprising an infringement on Jordan's sovereignty, Arab Bank was the financial institution through which US aid to the kingdom was processed.[173] Additionally, Jordan argued that since Arab Bank alone constitutes between 20 and 33 per cent of the value of the country's stock exchange, a massive shock in civil penalties would potentially lead to the kingdom's economic collapse.[174] On average, Jordan receives more than $1 billion in American aid each year, with $6.375 billion pledged for 2018–22.[175] With the Middle East facing anemic reconstruction in Iraq, growing tensions between the Gulf states, Israel, and Iran, and potential state failure in Syria, Jordan's stability represented a lynchpin of US interest in the region, and Arab Bank an important conduit for maintaining this stability.

Although the civil suits filed under the ATS were dismissed in 2018, Arab Bank did face regulatory enforcement for violating the fortified finance regime. The first penalty came in 2005 as a $24 million fine from the OCC and FinCEN, while the second, arising from *Linde v. Arab Bank*, was settled out of court for up to $1 billion a decade later in 2015. Throughout the enforcement period, the Jordanian state did not act to block enforcement efforts by the United States; rather, Amman continued to work with American officials to implement its own fortified finance regime within its banking system, while building upon its earlier, unilateral financial regulation efforts.

## ANALYSIS

The cases of BCCI and Arab Bank illustrate banks being penalized for financing terrorism. In each case, the institution involved operated as a private bank without a linkage to the government of its home state. Furthermore, the arrangements between the banks and their home states were characterized by the banks' reluctance to have the government in a position of significant control or stakeholdership. In terms of the enforcement measures that befell the banks, such measures occurred either in the absence of the fortified finance regime or as the regime was deepened and integrated into the home state's domestic political economy.

A common stereotype relating to terrorist financing and money laundering is that such activities are a natural by-product of jurisdictions with bank secrecy and tax havens. Certainly, terrorist groups, fraudsters, and criminals launder money through such countries. However, to appreciate why such jurisdictions exist, they must be understood as the products of the states that create them. BCCI's structure was designed to avoid significant state oversight through its legal basing in tax havens in an effort to avoid truly having a home state. In their establishment and as they expanded, both BCCI and Arab Bank sought institutional arrangements that allowed them to avoid politics. Agha Hasan Abedi's situating of BCCI in tax havens, and Shoman's promise to the Jordanian monarchy to avoid meddling in political affairs, illustrate this fact.

Based on Abedi's experience in Pakistan, where his previous bank had been nationalized, he established BCCI's legal groundwork in the Cayman Islands and Luxembourg. While Luxembourg was not indifferent to the bank's activities, most of its transactions were based out of the Cayman Islands. The Caymans were cultivated as an offshore tax haven in the 1960s after they chose to remain a British domain. Promoted as a haven by the Bank of England, the Cayman Islands offered the appearance of a regulation-free domain in which innumerable financial dealings of questionable legality could take place. This state-created laissez-faire environment allowed BCCI to engage with numerous high-profile political leaders, terrorist groups, intelligence agencies, and drug cartels around the world. Despite doing business with such politically powerful actors – including states – the bank did not enjoy protection from its largest backers. Had BCCI been based in Abu Dhabi, whither the UK endeavoured to have it relocate, it might have enjoyed protection and backing from the state that provided its greatest largesse. However, BCCI succeeded only in precluding any state linkage that would have protected it from enforcement.

Thanks to its headquartering in Jordan, Arab Bank managed to avoid the formation of a significant institutional linkage with its home state. Much of this political economic luck was purely circumstantial: in its earliest years, there was almost no independent state in the Arab world to which the bank might have formed such a linkage. In 1930, Egypt was the only fully independent Arab state in the region. Indeed, in establishing Arab Bank in British Mandate Palestine, the bank's founder avoided such a linkage with the Cairo government. Similarly – and unlike Al Rajhi Bank in Saudi Arabia, where tribal and familial connections tied the bank to the monarchy – Arab Bank's modern orientation and Western structure at the time of its founding and early development precluded any pre-independence linkages between it and any ruling family.

The bank's expansion, throughout the 1930s and 1940s, across what would soon become multiple, independent Arab states, similarly kept the bank from forming a linkage with a single state. As such, Arab Bank remained private and independent. Certainly, multiple wars and bank nationalization programs across the region dealt Arab Bank a number of geopolitical blows; but Jordan, where Arab Bank has been legally based since 1948, refrained from nationalizing it or instituting majority state ownership. Thus, as other Arab states began nationalizing Arab Bank's branches, the institution's early multinational expansion afforded it the flexibility to maintain operation as a private bank.

When Arab Bank faced enforcement in the form of US civil suits, Jordan applied pressure to help safeguard the bank's survival. Having paid administrative fines levied by the US in 2005 and negotiated a settlement with plaintiffs from the first wave of civil suits against it under the Anti-Terrorism Act, the bank subsequently faced potential collapse under the weight of potential penalties under the Alien Torts Statute. When Jordan sought to have this third wave of enforcement dismissed, Amman pointed to the fact that its Social Security Corporation owned approximately 15 per cent of Arab Bank.[176] Nonetheless, the bank has remained a privately owned concern throughout its existence. Geopolitically, the Arab Bank case illustrates Jordan's precarious position vis-à-vis this bank, as it processes critical US aid for the kingdom while also serving as the premier financial organ for the country's political economy. Yet, despite such importance, Arab Bank remains much as it was established – a private bank based on an American business model.

A key factor in both the BCCI and Arab Bank cases is what they indicate as to the efficacy of the fortified finance regime. In both cases, enforcement occurred either in the near-absence of AML/CTF regulations or as such a system matured within the bank's home state. BCCI faced simultaneous crackdown in jurisdictions around the world in 1991 over its operations – a crackdown long predating the establishment of the Financial Action Task Force. Indeed, the global shutdown of BCCI in the fortified finance regime's earliest phases, as it was becoming truly international, begs the question as to whether or not the regime is effective at all. Certainly, BCCI's structure of apparent "statelessness" and its lack of state linkage offered it no means of political protection when the crackdown commenced. Additionally, its unique structure provided no pre-existing relationship between bank and state that would need to be broken up by the fortified finance regime. When enforcement commenced in 1991, the bank had no such linkage to call upon for political assistance.

In the case of Arab Bank, the fortified finance regime was already present when American regulators initiated the first wave of enforcement. However, Jordan's domestic laws were not yet fully developed. As early as 2000, the kingdom began implementing the legal groundwork for criminalizing money laundering. Meanwhile, its domestic legal framework grew over the course of the early 2000s, culminating in 2007 with the establishment of a financial intelligence unit. Notably, when US regulators arrived in 2005 to discuss the kingdom's adoption of the fortified finance regime and Arab Bank's financing of terrorism, the Jordanian state did not attempt to block enforcement. Even when faced with civil penalties under the US Anti-Terrorism Act, Jordan did not block enforcement efforts; instead, the bank defended itself through negotiated settlements with the American plaintiffs. Only when confronted with the prospect of the bank's collapse under the weight of payouts to six thousand plaintiffs did the Jordanian state step in to pressure the US courts diplomatically to safeguard the bank's existence. In other words, the Jordanian state allowed the bank to be punished but also took steps to ensure its survival.

Given that BCCI had no home state stakeholder to call upon for assistance when faced with enforcement, the obvious question arises as to how the bank managed to conduct so many illegal financial activities in a British domain. Certainly, London had designed the Caymans to provide a venue for bank secrecy and tax evasion. However, with BCCI's primary base of operations located in London, and its legal home in the Caymans, the question arises as to how the UK, with its sophisticated, centuries-old banking sector, allowed the bank's money laundering and terrorist financing to take place.

The cases of BCCI and Arab Bank illustrate enforcement against banks for financing terrorism despite massive disparities between the banks' home states in terms of GDP, regulatory presence, and corruption. Notably, given Jordan's authoritarian monarchy and the UK's parliamentary democracy, the fact that both these cases demonstrate enforcement outcomes for banks financing terrorism is counterintuitive. In both cases, enforcement actions were carried out despite their unpleasantness for the London and Amman authorities. The similar enforcement outcomes indicate that a country's regulatory capacity and political system may be irrelevant to ascertain whether or not enforcement will occur against banks that finance terrorism. Rather, these cases indicate that a bank's relationship to the government of its home state plays the causal role in determining enforcement outcomes, while the state's regime type and the bank's regulatory environment play only marginal, secondary roles.

# Conclusion

REVIEW OF RESEARCH DESIGN AND FINDINGS

The central theoretical and normative concern in literature on the fortified finance regime is whether or not AML/CTF regulations work. Financial regulations meant to combat money laundering and terrorist financing have proliferated and deepened in states around the world since the passing, in the United States, of the Bank Secrecy Act in 1970. However, the effectiveness of these regulations remains suspect. This book helps answer this question by addressing trajectories of enforcement and under what circumstances enforcement leads to penalties against a bank or is blocked.

The guiding theory of this research is that if a bank is institutionally linked to the state in which it based, then enforcement will be blocked by the home state. This book tests this theory by hypothesizing that institutional linkage is sufficient to thwart attempted enforcement. Using comparative cases to control for the possibility of rival causes, this book tests this hypothesis by tracing the history of banks suspected of financing terrorism and assessing their relationships to the states in which they are embedded.

This theory posits that when a bank enjoys a structural institutional linkage to its home state, then that state will come to its defence at home and abroad. At first glance, this phenomenon would seem confined entirely to state-owned banks; however, state linkages are not limited to such majority state-owned enterprises. A state's relationship to the banks within it is determined by the unique institutional characteristics of the political economy of that country's financial sector.

Furthermore, the relationship between a state and the banks within it may be rooted in deep institutional legacies that the fortified finance regime will not succeed in displacing.

Using comparative case studies, I tested how the independent variable of a state-bank linkage affects enforcement outcomes for banks facing penalty for financing terrorism. First, I demonstrated the institutional linkages of each bank to its home state, and how each evolved alongside the state in which it developed until the attempted enforcement took place. I also accounted for the presence of the fortified finance regime within the state in question, and how its presence impacted the bank that financed terrorism. Using qualitative data in the form of court and governmental documents, journalistic accounts, and communiqués from Wikileaks, I established the bank's plausible financing of terrorism whenever possible using account numbers gleaned from the data. Then, using the same documentary data, I traced how enforcement was either blocked or allowed to proceed. Contrary to popular belief, this shadowy world of threat finance is not obfuscated due to a lack of data.

The Bank of China and Turkey's Halk Bank both fit the classic model of state-owned enterprises. In both cases, the banks were established to be of service to the state and help financially safeguard national interests under the lingering threat of foreign financial dependence. The Bank of China survived multiple upheavals as China moved through various forms of authoritarian government and multiple wars. Throughout the tumult, the bank operated as an extension of Beijing's governments, as each came and went, without any structural severance between the bank and that government. Similar to the Bank of China, Halk Bank formed during the earliest phases of Turkey's modern development as a state-assisted means for fostering the growth of a Turkish middle class. Unlike the Bank of China, Halk Bank underwent genuine efforts at partial privatization; however, the state's majority ownership remained a constant throughout its history.

Unlike the total state ownership of the Bank of China, Halk Bank's role in Turkish politics was one of semi-democratic coalition binding. The bank's specific focus on small and medium-sized enterprises helped create a durable socioeconomic political coalition for emerging Islamist parties based in the working and middle classes. Domestic coalition binding aside, Halk Bank also served as an instrument of

Turkey's foreign policy of re-engaging with the Middle East and exercising leverage over Iran, its historical competitor.

Unlike Halk Bank and the Bank of China, Al Rajhi Bank was never a state-owned concern. The private bank originated as a family business in the pre-modern Arabian economy and developed into a modern bank in parallel with the development of the modern Saudi state. Due to the bank's involvement with the Saudi ulama and its support of religious institutions, the bank's operations became vital to the Saudi monarchy. Like European monarchies of the distant past, Saudi Arabia's monarchy relies heavily upon religious legitimacy, as well as economic dynamism, for its survival. Because of Al Rajhi's linkages to the royal family and to the religious pillar of the country's historic ruling elite, any capitulation on the part of the state to enforcing the fortified finance regime places the state's integrity at risk.

While the fortified finance regime has spread around the world, it remains questionable as to whether or not such regulations have displaced pre-existing relationships between banks and the states in which they are based. In the cases of blocked enforcement, each state in question exhibited, at some stage of development, a fortified finance regime at the time the enforcement efforts ensued. It is also worth noting that financial regulations imported from abroad pertaining to terrorism were layered onto existing domestic regulatory efforts.

This book controls for potential rival causes, such as authoritarianism and state capacity. Every state in which enforcement was blocked comprises an example of a strong state with more than enough capacity to control and surveil its financial system. Additionally, every state that blocked enforcement was at least partly authoritarian, and the linkage of each bank to its home state virtually ensured that the home state exercised some oversight of the bank's affairs. The fact that Arab Bank in Jordan, a monarchy, suffered penalties for financing terrorism indicates that authoritarianism is not sufficient, in and of itself, to block enforcement.

Both China and Turkey had formidable surveillance and enforcement capacities in place at the time enforcement was attempted against their banks. China's financial system surveillance apparatus and its adoption of the fortified finance regime predates the enforcement attempts against the Bank of China for financing Hamas and Palestinian Islamic Jihad. The Turkish attempt at enforcement is unique in that the enforcement actions were attempted by the state's own bureaucracies and at the hands of the country's own police and judiciary. The manner in which enforcement was attempted in Turkey indicates that Ankara's fortified finance regime was indeed working at the time that enforcement was initiated, but was thereupon blocked by the government. While the Chinese case demonstrates a state using diplomatic pressure to protect its bank from punishment by a foreign state, Turkey's massive bureaucratic reshuffling and the firing of key judicial and police officials illustrates a regime enacting a veto against its own enforcement apparatus to protect the integrity of its bank.

The case of Saudi Arabia's Al Rajhi Bank demonstrates a functioning and capable surveillance apparatus within the kingdom's financial sector overseeing a bank that influences Saudi financial regulatory policy. The Saudi central bank, which regulates the kingdom's financial sector, was not only in place when Al Rajhi came under suspicion of financing terrorism, but even assisted the state in developing its fortified finance regime. The structural braiding of Al Rajhi Bank with the monarchy on the one hand, and with the ulama on the other, existed prior to the development of the Saudi financial surveillance system. Furthermore, this older system was not displaced as the newer one was deepened at US behest.

The Jordanian case of executed enforcement juxtaposes with that of Saudi Arabia. Both states are conservative Sunni tribal monarchies originating in the same geopolitical era and region, and both states' political economies share a number of similar characteristics. However, unlike Al Rajhi's coalition-binding function in Saudi Arabia, Arab Bank was founded as a Western-style bank with an arm's-length structural relationship to the state. In contrast to the familial ties linking the Al Rajhi banking family with the Saudi monarchy and the ulama, Arab Bank is embedded in the economy of Jordan's Palestinian middle class. Although the Palestinians and their political activities entail consequences for the Jordanian state, Amman developed policies aimed at binding the Hashemite monarchy to the kingdom's non-Palestinian Bedouin population. Indeed, the orientation of Jordan's political economy is focused heavily upon linking the state's bureaucracies and the kingdom's rural Transjordanian base, which pre-dates the later waves of Palestinian settlement. Unlike most of the monarchies of the modern Middle East, Jordan's financial system demonstrates a legacy of private banking without any significant royal largesse. This institutional distance, however, did not preclude Arab

Bank from suffering administrative fines and settlements from civil suits brought against it.

## IMPLICATIONS

In each case of blocked enforcement, the institutional structural relationship between state and bank remained intact despite the arrival and adoption of AML/CTF regulations. The implications of this study are multifarious for questions pertaining to the international financial system and how it relates to international affairs. For institutional theory, the findings should not be surprising: namely, deep institutional configurations within a country's political economy are not likely to be dislodged by the importation of institutional paradigms from the outside. Rather, it is likely that the institutional imports will simply overlay the pre-existing configurations. Furthermore, a state's adoption of institutions from outside is no indication that they will function correctly in their new environment. As noted by other scholars of terrorist financing, one of the drawbacks of the fortified finance regime is that it is ill-suited to many of the environments where it is needed the most. This second institutional finding is also not surprising, given that a moral hazard exists for states seeking to enforce CTF regulations upon banks to which they are linked.

The fortified finance regime emerged and matured in liberal Western political economies where banking is a regulated but private affair. Regulations designed to counter terrorist financing and money laundering complete with surveillance of bank customers and the banks themselves, effectively deputizing the banks to act as an extension of the state's security and intelligence apparatus. Designed for private commercial banks in developed economies, these regulations are ill-suited to monitor state-owned banks or for financial systems based upon pre-existing and often pre-modern relationships between state and bank. In such structural configurations, fortified finance regulations place the state in the morally hazardous situation of having to monitor its own affairs, and those of critical political allies, within the state's political economy. In these cases, it is not surprising that enforcement misfires due to diplomatic pushback, bureaucratic shuffling, intimidation, or some other manifestation of state power.

A second implication of this book pertains to power politics and should come as no surprise – namely, that states will defend their interests. The financial sector is not typically viewed as a strategic terrain in international relations, even though it is such. As actors, banks are involved in geopolitics and security whether they choose to be or not. Terrorists deposit their money in bank accounts, while bankers and regulators now act as spies. Despite states, bankers, regulators, terrorists, and intelligence agencies inhabiting the same political economic universe, this motley crew of actors is rarely theorized in political science as interacting within the same environment. Yet, even as these actors often interact out of the theoretical sight of scholars, they are intimately intertwined.

The implications are somewhat chilling. The use of banks by terrorists should come as no surprise: banks offer incredible efficiency and ease of use when compared to the alternatives, and terrorists must pay for gasoline and groceries as much as for bullets and publishing propaganda. The normatively disconcerting implication of these findings is that states are intimately aware of the malfeasance that takes place in bank branches and is recorded in ledgers worldwide. With the possible but doubtful exception of Jordan, every state in this study appears to have had knowledge of the terrorist financing taking place in banks within their territories. In cases of institutional linkage, banks that escape punishment remain in position and with the potential to finance terrorism with impunity.

Even in the cases where enforcement occurred, the banks' home states did not want to take enforcement action against the targeted banks. Rather, in the cases of both BCCI and Arab Bank, officials only moved against the banks due to pressure from the United States. While Jordan did not stand in the way of administrative penalties or the first salvo of lawsuits against Arab Bank, none of the data indicates that Amman was eager to penalize the bank. Instead, the state in this case allowed enforcement to proceed and only intervened to ensure the bank's survival.

The case of BCCI and the Bank of England is even more nefarious. Not only did the Bank of England cultivate an offshore financial realm in the Caymans in which BCCI was able to thrive, it also later sought to save the bank by assisting in its relocation to Abu Dhabi. BCCI did business with dictators, terrorist groups, and drug cartels, and even assisted Pakistan with the smuggling of nuclear materials. When BCCI's activities are taken into account, the Bank of England's treatment of the case moves beyond the realm of simple regulatory malfeasance to one with real kinetic consequences for both geopolitical stability and public safety. In light of the global crackdown on BCCI, the UK's actions indicate a desire to safeguard not merely a single bank which thrived within the offshore financial system it had created, but rather that system itself. In short, even though the UK did not own BCCI, it sought to preserve the environment in which it thrived for the sake of its own interests. While BCCI as a predatory entity no longer exists, the environment that created it remains.

Extrapolating from the fact that states possess so much knowledge about banks' activities related to money laundering and terrorist financing, a deeper possibility arises as to the implications of this study for how states and banks interact within their shared institutional universe. The implications of conscious regulatory failure extend far beyond issues of terrorism. Given that governments enjoy such deep awareness of what takes place in regard to threat finance, questions arise as to whether states might similarly surveil oncoming financial crises and the financial activities that catalyze them.

The fortified finance regime was well and widely implemented in major economies around the world by the time of the financial crisis of 2008. With such a surveillance apparatus in place inside banks around the world, a dark question arises as to how states could have missed the subprime mortgage crisis, the Eurozone crisis, and other economic crises surrounding what transpired in 2008. Contrary to urbane notions that banking and the financial system are somehow above political affairs, the world of threat finance indicates that ballots, bombs, and bankers are more interconnected than the subfields of mainstream political science may care to admit. Murky as it is, this area offers a number of sordidly fruitful avenues for future research.

The policy implications of this study are straightforward. While state-bank linkages are sufficient to thwart enforcement, the presence of fortified finance regulations in a given country do offer leverage for potential enforcers. Given the international scope of the banking system, banks seldom hold all their assets within the confines of their home jurisdiction. This multinational presence in regard to banks' assets allows for states seeking enforcement to target assets beyond the borders of the bank's home state. Additionally, instead of simply seeking to deepen the fortified finance regime, it may prove more effective for states to target specific banks through fines and disallow them from engaging in specific currency transactions. Such unit-specific targeting could provide ample disincentive for banks to contemplate financing terrorism.

If a bank financing terrorism is linked to its home state, it may prove more effective to target the home state itself rather than just the malicious bank. Currency prohibitions and sanctions against state officials or governmental entities may be more effective in curtailing banks from financing terrorism. Instead of targeting a bank linked to its home state, potential enforcers may enjoy greater success in curtailing terrorist financing by targeting the enabling state well beyond the political or economic profile of the bank in question. From the standpoint of economic statecraft, this expands the range of opportunity for states seeking to stop terrorists from using banks to finance their operations. If international finance constitutes a geopolitical chessboard, states should act accordingly and acknowledge the role that other states play in issues pertaining to crime and terrorism.

## AVENUES FOR FUTURE RESEARCH

Regarding terrorists, there is little scholarship on how they choose to finance their activities. While banks provide an efficient means for moving funds and integrating them into the financial system, not all banks are equal. Hypothetically, while most economic actors should entrust their money to the most efficient banks for transactions and investment, these same banks may not offer the requisite security that a terrorist group requires. Terrorist groups may seek to entrust their funds to state-linked banks, perhaps in the belief that in such cases, the state will assist in safeguarding their bank of choice from outsiders. While terrorist groups may prove similar to other economic actors insofar as they seek maximum efficiency, further research is needed to determine how terrorists choose their banks and other aspects of their financial operations.

At the banking level, further research is needed to answer questions regarding corporate governance and corruption, and why and how financial institutions choose to engage in illicit activity. Regulation assumes that a bank's financial intelligence unit will pass relevant information along to upper management within the bank, and to government officials. However, it may be that communication and cooperation within the bank itself do not function efficiently. Certain personnel in the bank may be the subjects of bribes or coercion, while other departments are unaware or negligent. Similarly, a bank's FIU may clash with the bank's sales department or other offices, whereupon higher management is placed in the position of choosing between following the law and following their business interests. At the bank level, greater research into the corporate governance of illicit activity is needed to answer these questions. Similarly, at the banking level, further research should explore the effect of deferred prosecution agreements on bank behaviour, as deferred prosecution is a standard feature of US regulatory action.

As this study illustrates, the unitary actor assumption pertaining to states must be relaxed in order to answer a number of questions related to threat finance. States are not monolithic entities with uniform interests. Different bureaucracies may have divergent interests and differing professional cultures that dictate how they approach affairs of this nature. Clearly, as illustrated in the cases of BCCI and Halk Bank, different organs within a state may come into conflict over issues related to terrorist financing and money laundering. In the BCCI case, the Bank of England was in clear conflict with other British government agencies over its transformation of the Cayman Islands into an offshore financial centre. Similarly, Turkey's judiciary and law enforcement apparatus attempted domestic enforcement against Halk Bank's activities, but were later thwarted by the government in power through mass firings and bureaucratic reshuffling. Further research is needed to explore how and when certain state bureaucracies and agencies conflict over areas of financial regulation and enforcement.

At the level of the international financial system, there is no research that explores the possibility that states may have foreknowledge of malfeasance in the banking system in areas aside from terrorism. If states know about how terrorism is financed through the mainstream financial system yet refrain from overt regulatory action, states may similarly know of other indecent practices such as risky lending, the laundering of criminal funds, political corruption, and other illicit economic activities detrimental to growth and geopolitical stability. In studies of financial regulation or political economy, it is often widely assumed that relationships between banks and states are formal and cordial. As shown in this study, however, interactions between banks and governments may be informal, messy, conflictual, and not intended for widespread public knowledge.

Another international aspect of this phenomenon is that of American hegemony. In some form, the US is present at some level in every case in this study. Certainly, the US was the state seeking enforcement against banks financing terrorism in the cases of BCCI, Arab Bank, Halk Bank, and Al Rajhi Bank. Furthermore, even when the US government is not the party directly seeking action, the American legal system is often the venue for private actors seeking restitution against banks financing terrorism. In a number of cases, private actors spearheaded enforcement efforts or were involved in additional enforcement moves in conjunction with administrative action by the US government. The fact that the American legal system is so prevalent in such enforcement attempts, even when the US government is not the primary actor, indicates a form of judicial hegemony in the financial realm. This prevalence of the American judicial system raises questions of judicial autonomy, geopolitical interference, and sovereignty.

In the negative cases of BCCI and Arab Bank, the American legal system impacted political economies far removed from the United States. Similarly, in the case of Halk Bank, American courts offered a secondary enforcement mechanism after domestic enforcement attempts within Turkey were thwarted by the AKP. In the case of the Bank of China, ongoing lawsuits were effectively stillborn due to the actions of outside states, with Israel and China both taking action to prevent requisite testimony from occurring. The fact that such geopolitical jockeying is occurring in the American legal system underscores an aspect of US hegemony not often discussed in political science, despite its significant impact.

American hegemony aside, the second decade of the twenty-first century, and the beginning of the third, have blossomed into a period of incredible flux within the international system. Relations between China and the US under the premiership of Xi Jinping and, until recently, the Trump administration have seen an increased use of economic statecraft in power politics. As of this writing, a number of institutions and regional dynamics lately thought to be stable are evolving in unpredictable ways. The longevity of the European Union appears to be in question amid multiple crises pertaining to populism, while long-time conflicts in the Middle East between Israel and certain Arab nations may be ending amid the normalization agreements taking place in the Persian Gulf. Indeed, warming relations in 2020 between Arab monarchies and Israel could have profound implications for countering terrorist financing should normalization be established. If banks in the Gulf become inhospitable to terrorist financiers due to greater cooperation between Israeli intelligence services and Arab authorities, the resulting geopolitical shifts could have a significant impact on terrorist financing in the Middle East.

The complexity of these phenomena necessarily brings together substantive focuses from the fields of security studies, comparative political economy, international law, and financial regulation. Because of this complexity and the resulting substantive disciplinary overlap, there is little theoretical development as to terrorist financing and money laundering in political science. Literature on regulatory development and expansion does not address studies of terrorist organizations, while studies about terrorist groups and financing do not connect with those on great power politics and the financial system. This study offers a first foray into the dark crevasse between the existing literatures.

# Notes

### INTRODUCTION

1. It should be noted here that certain states, such as rogue regimes in North Korea and elsewhere, are not considered in this trend.

### CHAPTER ONE

1. Susan Strange, *The Retreat of the State: The Diffusion of Power in the World Economy* (Cambridge: Cambridge University Press, 1996), 4.
2. Susan Strange, *Casino Capitalism* (Manchester: Manchester University Press, 1997), 171.
3. Benjamin Cohen, "Phoenix Risen: The Resurrection of Global Finance," *World Politics* 48, no. 2 (January 1996): 293.
4. Eric Helleiner, *States and the Reemergence of Global Finance: From Bretton Woods to the 1990s* (Ithaca, NY: Cornell University Press, 1996).
5. Ibid., 112–13.
6. Greta R. Krippner, *Capitalizing on Crisis* (Cambridge, MA: Harvard University Press, 2011), 116–19.
7. Helleiner, *States and the Reemergence*, 150.
8. Ibid., 151.
9. Ibid., 166.
10. Daniel W. Drezner, *All Politics Is Global: Explaining International Regulatory Regimes* (Princeton, NJ: Princeton University Press, 2007), 147.
11. Ibid., 5.
12. Paul N. Doremus, William W. Keller, Louis W. Pauly, and Simon Reich, *The Myth of the Global Corporation* (Princeton, NJ: Princeton University Press, 1998).

13 Herbert Feis, *Europe: The World's Banker, 1870–1914* (New Haven, CT: Yale University Press, 1930), xv–xvi.
14 Jacob Viner, "International Finance and Balance of Power Diplomacy, 1880–1914," *Southwestern Political and Social Science Quarterly* 9, no. 4 (March 1929): 447.
15 Ibid., 450.
16 Jonathan Kirshner, *Appeasing Bankers: Financial Caution on the Road to War* (Princeton, NJ: Princeton University Press, 2007), 1.
17 Maurice Obstfeld and Alan M. Taylor, "Globalization and Capital Markets," in *Globalization in Historical Perspective*, ed. Michael D. Bordo, Alan M. Taylor, and Jeffrey G. Williamson (Chicago: University of Chicago Press, 2003), 121–88.
18 Timothy Wittig, *Understanding Terrorist Finance* (London: Palgrave Macmillan, 2011), 9.
19 Ibid., 10.
20 Nikos Passas, "Terrorism Financing Mechanisms and Policy Dilemmas," in *Terrorism Financing and State Responses*, ed. Jeanne K. Giraldo and Harold A. Trinkunas (Stanford, CA: Stanford University Press, 2007), 21–38, 24–7.
21 Rachel Ehrenfeld, "Funding Evil: How Terrorism Is Financed and the Nexus of Terrorist and Criminal Organizations," in *Terrornomics*, ed. Sean S. Costigan and David Gold (Aldershot, UK: Ashgate Publishing, 2007), 27–48, 27–8.
22 Jacob N. Shapiro, *The Terrorist's Dilemma: Managing Violent Covert Organizations* (Princeton, NJ: Princeton University Press, 2013).
23 Jacob N. Shapiro and David A. Siegel, "Underfunding in Terrorist Organizations," *International Studies Quarterly* 51, no. 2 (June 2007): 405–29.
24 Jacob N. Shapiro, "Vulnerabilities and Inefficiencies," in Giraldo and Trinkunas, *Terrorism Financing*, 56–71, 61.
25 Rachel Ehrenfeld, "Funding Evil," 27–48, 30.
26 Ibid., 31. See also Samuel Pope, "Diversion: An Unrecognized Element of Intelligence?", *Defense Analysis* 3, no. 2 (1987): 133–51; and Viktor Suvarov, "Spetsnaz: The Soviet Union's Special Forces," *International Defense Review* 16, no. 9 (1983): 1209–16.
27 Nicholas Ryder, *Money Laundering – An Endless Cycle? A Comparative Analysis of the Anti-Money Laundering Policies in the United States of America, the United Kingdom, Australia and Canada* (New York: Routledge, 2012), 40.

28 Brigitte Unger, *The Scale and Impacts of Money Laundering* (Cheltanham, UK: Edward Elgar, 2007), 80. See also John Walker, "How Big Is Global Money Laundering?", *Journal of Money Laundering Control* 3, no. 1 (1999): 25–37.
29 Ryder, *Money Laundering*, 41.
30 Jason Campbell Sharman, *The Money Laundry: Regulating Criminal Finance in the Global Economy* (Ithaca, NY: Cornell University Press, 2011), 21.
31 Ryder, *Money Laundering*, 41–2.
32 Ibid., 42.
33 Sharman, *Money Laundry*, 23.
34 Ibid.
35 Ibid. See also: Barry A.K. Rider, "Law: The War on Terror and Crime and the Offshore Centres: The 'New' Perspective?", in *Global Financial Crime: Terrorism, Money Laundering and Offshore Centres*, ed. Donato Masciandro (Aldershot, UK: Ashgate Publishing, 2004), 61–95.
36 Jeanne K. Giraldo and Harold A. Trinkunas, "Explaining Government Responses," in Giraldo and Trinkunas, *Terrorist Financing*, 283–4.
37 Sharman, *Money Laundry*, 25.
38 Peter Reuter and Edwin M. Truman, *Chasing Dirty Money* (Washington, DC: Institute for International Economics, 2004), 79–80.
39 Ibid., 79.
40 Ibid., 80.
41 Ibid., 80–1. See also Basel Committee on Banking Supervision, "Prevention of Criminal Use of the Banking System for the Purpose of Money-Laundering, 28 December 1988, https://www.bis.org/publ/bcbsc137.pdf.
42 Sharman, *Money Laundry*, 27.
43 Rohan Gunaratna, *Inside Al Qaeda* (New York: Berkeley Books, 2003), 161–8.
44 Paul Gleason and Glenn Gottselig, eds., *Financial Intelligence Units: An Overview* (Washington, DC: International Monetary Fund, 2004), 9.
45 Ibid., 12.
46 Ibid., 13–16.
47 Egmont Group, "About," accessed 4 May 2017, https://www.egmontgroup.org/en/content/about.
48 Louise I. Shelley, *Dirty Entanglements: Corruption, Crime, and Terrorism* (Cambridge: Cambridge University Press, 2014), 177.
49 Ibid., 195–7.
50 Millard Burr and Robert O. Collins, *Alms for Jihad: Charity and Terrorism in the Islamic World* (Cambridge: Cambridge University Press, 2006).

51 Petrus C. van Duyne, Klaus von Lampe, and James L. Newell, *Criminal Finances and Organizing Crime in Europe* (Nijmegen, Netherlands: Wolf Legal Publishers, 2003), 9.
52 Anne L. Clunan, "The Fight against Terrorist Financing," *Political Science Quarterly* 121, no. 4 (2006): 570.
53 Giraldo and Trinkunas, "Explaining Government Responses," 283.
54 Ibid., 284.
55 David Cortright, George A. Lopez, Alistair Millar, and Linda Gerber-Stellingwerf, "Global Cooperation against Terrorism: Evaluating the United Nations' Counterterrorism Committee," in *Uniting Against Terror*, ed. David Cortright and George A. Lopez (Cambridge, MA: MIT Press, 2007), 23.
56 Anne L. Clunan, "US and International Responses to Terrorist Financing," in *Terrorist Financing and State Responses*, ed. Jeanne K. Giraldo and Harold A. Trinkunas (Stanford: Stanford University Press, 2007), 266.
57 Van Duyne, von Lampe, and Newell, *Criminal Finances*, 9. See also: Sharman, *Money Laundry*.
58 Ronen Palan, *The Offshore World: Sovereign Markets, Virtual Places, and Nomad Millionaires* (Ithaca, NY: Cornell University Press, 2003), 48–9.
59 Ronen Palan, Richard Murphy, and Christian Chavagneux, *Tax Havens: How Globalization Really Works* (Ithaca, NY: Cornell University Press, 2010), 206.
60 Ibrahim Warde, *The Price of Fear: The Truth behind the Financial War on Terror* (Berkeley: University of California Press, 2007).
61 Ibid., 174.
62 Ibid., 178. See also: Timothy Wittig, *Understanding Terrorist Finance* (London: Palgrave Macmillan, 2011).
63 See: Juan Zarate, *Treasury's War: The Unleashing of a New Era of Financial Warfare* (New York: PublicAffairs, 2013).
64 Jimmy Gurule, *Unfunding Terror: The Legal Response to the Financing of Global Terrorism* (Cheltenham, UK: Edward Elgar, 2008), 373–9.
65 Ibid., 379.
66 Sharman, *Money Laundry*, 113–17.
67 Ibid., 5.
68 See Sharman, *Money Laundry*; and Cortright et al., "Global Cooperation against Terrorism" (refer to appendix A for a list of states that have adopted the global CTF regime).
69 Palan, Murphy, and Chavagneux, *Tax Havens*, 206–8.
70 Karl Polanyi and Robert Morrison MacIver, *The Great Transformation* (Boston: Beacon Press, 1944).

71 Francis Fukuyama, *The End of History and the Last Man* (New York: Simon and Schuster, 2006).
72 John J. Mearsheimer, "The False Promise of International Institutions," *International Security* 19, no. 3 (Winter 1994–95), 7.
73 Warde, *The Price of Fear*, 178.
74 Sharman, *Money Laundry*, 1.
75 See Kozo Yamamura and Wolfgang Streeck, eds., *The End of Diversity? Prospects for German and Japanese Capitalism* (Ithaca, NY: Cornell University Press, 2003).
76 Ibid.
77 Suzanne Berger, introduction to *National Diversity and Global Capitalism*, ed. Suzanne Berger and Ronald Dore (Ithaca, NY: Cornell University Press, 1996), 1.
78 Ibid., 25.
79 See Viner, "International Finance"; and Feis, *Europe: The World's Banker*.
80 See Kirshner, *Appeasing Bankers*.
81 Warde, *The Price of Fear*.
82 Sharman, *Money Laundry*.
83 Andrei Shleifer and Robert W. Vishny, "Corruption," Working Paper No. 4372, National Bureau of Economic Research (1993), 3.
84 Jakob Svensson, "Eight Questions about Corruption," *Journal of Economic Perspectives* 19, no. 3 (2005): 20.
85 Louise Shelley, *Dirty Entanglements: Corruption, Crime, and Terrorism* (Cambridge: Cambridge University Press, 2014), 12.
86 See table 1.1 for the World Bank's rule-of-law rankings.
87 See Sharman, *Money Laundry*.

## CHAPTER TWO

1 Tom Farthing, "The Banker Top 1000 World Banks 2016 Ranking," *The Banker*, 29 June 2015, http://www.thebanker.com/Top-1000-World-Banks/The-Banker-Top-1000-World-Banks-2016-ranking-WORLD-Press-IMMEDIATE-RELEASE.
2 See Orville Schell and John Delury, *Wealth and Power: China's Long March to the Twenty-First Century* (New York: Random House, 2014).
3 James Stent, *China's Banking Transformation* (Oxford: Oxford University Press, 2017), 205–7.
4 Ibid., 207.
5 Schell and Delury, *Wealth and Power*, 47.

6 "The Republic of China and Bank of China: Keeping Pace with History (1912)," Bank of China, accessed 22 July 2017, http://www.boc.cn/en/aboutboc/ab7/200809/t20080926_1601882.html.
7 Ibid.
8 Stent, *China's Banking Transformation*, 208.
9 "The Republic of China and Bank of China."
10 Yuanyuan Peng, *The Chinese Banking Industry: Lessons from History for Today's Challenges* (New York: Routledge, 2007), 44. See also: William N. Goetzmann and Elisabeth Koll, "The History of Corporate Ownership in China: State Patronage, Company Legislation, and the Issue of Control," in *A History of Corporate Governance around the World: Family Business Groups to Professional Managers*, ed. Randall K. Morck (Chicago: University of Chicago Press, 2005).
11 Ibid., 45.
12 "The Republic of China and Bank of China."
13 Ibid.
14 Ibid.
15 Ibid.
16 Peng, *The Chinese Banking Industry*, 48.
17 Ibid., 44, 48–9.
18 Linsun Cheng, *Banking in Modern China* (Cambridge: Cambridge University Press, 2003), 55.
19 Ibid., 57.
20 Peng, *The Chinese Banking Industry*, 49.
21 Ibid.
22 Cheng, *Banking in Modern China*, 61.
23 Ibid., 65.
24 "An Important Turning Point for Bank of China – Restructured as an International Exchange Bank (1928)," Bank of China, accessed 1 August 2017, http://www.boc.cn/en/aboutboc/ab7/200809/t20080926_1601876.html.
25 Peng, *The Chinese Banking Industry*, 54.
26 Ibid.
27 Ibid., 60.
28 Cheng, *Banking in Modern China*, 96.
29 Ibid., 99.
30 Ibid., 100.
31 Peng, *The Chinese Banking Industry*, 60.
32 Jonathan Kirshner, *Appeasing Bankers: Financial Caution on the Road to War* (Princeton, NJ: Princeton University Press, 2007).

33 "Persistent Monetary Fight Against Financial Invasion by Japanese Puppet Regime (1939–1943)," Bank of China, accessed 1 August 2017, http://www.boc.cn/en/aboutboc/ab7/200809/t20080926_1601863.html.
34 See Stephen Bell and Hui Feng, *The Rise of the People's Bank of China* (Cambridge, MA: Harvard University Press, 2013), 56.
35 Ibid., 57.
36 Ibid., 58–9.
37 Peng, *The Chinese Banking Industry*, 51–3.
38 Shiping Zheng, *Party vs. State in Post-1949 China: The Institutional Dilemma* (Cambridge: Cambridge University Press, 1997), 42–3.
39 Leo Goodstadt, "Peking Keeps in Touch," *The Times* (London), 10 September 1971.
40 Ibid.
41 Y.C. Jao, *Banking and Currency in Hong Kong: A Study of Postwar Financing and Development* (London: Palgrave Macmillan, 1974), 39.
42 Ibid., 48.
43 Steven R. Stark, "An Analysis of the Foreign Trade Practices of the People's Republic of China, Including Comments on the Canadian Experience," *University of British Columbia Law Review* 5 (1970): 181.
44 Barry Naughton, *The Chinese Economy: Transitions and Growth* (Cambridge, MA: MIT Press, 2007), 80–1.
45 Ibid., 82.
46 Susan L. Shirk, *The Political Logic of Economic Reform in China* (Berkeley: University of California Press, 1993), 33.
47 Ibid., 42.
48 Ibid., 184.
49 Ibid.
50 Bell and Feng, *The Rise of the People's Bank*, 62.
51 Ibid.
52 Schell and Delury, *Wealth and Power*, 342. See also: Zhu Rongji, *Zhu Rongji Meets the Press* (Hong Kong: Oxford University Press, 2011), 248.
53 Bell and Feng, *The Rise of the People's Bank*, 63.
54 Ibid., 271.
55 Howard Davies and David Green, *Banking on the Future: The Fall and Rise of Central Banking* (Princeton, NJ: Princeton University Press, 2010), 220.
56 Bell and Feng, *The Rise of the People's Bank*, 275. See also: "About Us," Central Huijin Investment Ltd, accessed 1 August 2017, http://www.huijin-inv.cn/huijineng/About_Us/index.shtml.
57 Ibid.

58 Ibid. See also: "About Us," Central Huijin Investment Ltd, accessed 1 August 2017, http://www.huijin-inv.cn/huijineng/About_Us/index.shtml.
59 Bell and Feng, *The Rise of the People's Bank*, 279–80.
60 Ibid.
61 Ibid.
62 Financial Action Task Force, *First Mutual Evaluation Report on Anti-Money Laundering and Combating the Financing of Terrorism: People's Republic of China* (Paris: FATF Secretariat, 2007), 22–3.
63 Song Yang, "Money Laundering in China: A Policy Analysis," *Journal of Contemporary Criminal Justice* 18, no. 4 (November 2002): 377.
64 Ibid., 378.
65 Cai Yilian, "Performing Anti-Money Laundering Obligation and Promoting Anti-Corruption Work," Issue Paper (Workshop F), ABD/OECD Anti-Corruption Initiative for Asia and the Pacific, 5th Regional Anti-Corruption Conference, Beijing, 28–30 September 2005, 1.
66 Zhou Xiaochuan (governor, People's Bank of China), speech to the First Meeting of the Ministerial Joint Conference on Anti-Money Laundering, Beijing, 27 August 2004.
67 Nicole Schulte-Kulkmann, "How China Fights Money Laundering: Recent Developments in Regulation and Supervision," *China Analysis* 56 (Trier: Research Group on the Political Economy of China, University of Trier, 2007), 26.
68 Tang Xu, Shi Yongyan, and Cao Zuoyi, "The Effectiveness of China's Anti-Money Laundering Policies" (Beijing: Anti-Money Laundering Bureau, People's Bank of China, 2010), 8.
69 Ibid., 8.
70 Schulte-Kulkmann, "How China Fights," 28.
71 Ibid.
72 Ibid., 32–3.
73 Ibid., 33.
74 Yilian, "Performing Anti-Money Laundering Obligation," 3.
75 "The People's Bank of China Decree No. 1 (2006)," art. 7, People's Bank of China, 14 November 2006, http://www.pbc.gov.cn/english/130733/2897917/index.html.
76 Ibid.
77 Peter Van Ness, *Revolution and Chinese Foreign Policy: Peking's Support for Wars of National Liberation* (Berkeley: University of California Press, 1970), 30–3.
78 Ibid., 218–20.

79 Gordon Thomas, *Gideon's Spies: The Secret History of the Mossad* (New York: St Martin's Press, 2005), 248.
80 Ibid., 248.
81 W.A.C. Adie, "China, Russia, and the Third World," *China Quarterly* 11 (July–September 1962): 209.
82 Robert A. Scalapino, "Sino-Soviet Competition in Africa," *Foreign Affairs* 42, no. 4 (July 1964): 644.
83 Ibid., 391.
84 Ibid., 390–1.
85 Financial Action Task Force, *Trade-Based Money Laundering* (Paris: FATF Secretariat, 2006), 3.
86 See John A. Cassara, *Trade-Based Money Laundering: The Next Frontier in International Money Laundering Enforcement* (Hoboken, NJ: John Wiley and Sons, 2016).
87 *Wultz v. Bank of China Ltd*, 865 F Supp (2d) 425 (SDNY 2012).
88 *Wultz v. Bank of China Ltd*, 32 F Supp (3d) 486 (SDNY 2014). Respondents' Memorandum of Law in Opposition to the Petitioner's Motion to Quash, *Wultz et al. v. The State of Israel*, Misc. No. 13–1282 (RBW) at p. 8 (DC Dist Ct 2013), blogs.reuters.com/alison-frankel/files/2014/08/wultzvbankofchina-wultzquashopposbrief1.pdf.
89 Ibid.
90 Account nos: 4750401-0188-150882-6 and 4762307-0188-034456-6. Declaration of Shlomo Matalon, 16 May 2009, *Wultz v. The Islamic Republic of Iran*, Civ. No. 08-01460 (DC Dist Ct 2010), http://blogs.reuters.com/alison-frankel/files/2014/10/bankofchina-plaintiffsoncantor.pdf.
91 Respondents' Memorandum to Quash, *State of Israel*, 6–7.
92 Walter P. Loughlin, "Anti-Money Laundering, Anti-Terrorist Financing, and The Global Banking System: Three Anomalies," *Forum on Public Policy* 1 (2012): 7.
93 *Moriah v. Bank of China Limited*, 72 F Supp (3d) 437 (SDNY 2014). Subpoena on Eric Cantor, No. 12 Civ. 1594 (SAS) (GWG) (SDNY 2014), https://blogs.reuters.com/alison-frankel/files/2014/10/bankofchina-plaintiffsoncantor.pdf.
94 Respondents' Memorandum to Quash, *State of Israel*, 10.
95 Ibid., 10–11.
96 *Wultz v. Bank of China Ltd*, 910 F Supp (2d) 548 (SDNY 2012), 551.
97 Ibid., 552.
98 *Wultz v. Bank of China Ltd*, 979 F Supp (2d) 479 (SDNY 2013), 484.
99 *Wultz v. Bank of China Ltd*, 910 F Supp (2d) 548 (SDNY 2012), 556.

100 *Wultz v. Bank of China Ltd*, 979 F Supp (2d) 479 (SDNY 2013), 485.
101 Ibid.
102 Ibid.
103 Respondents' Memorandum, *State of Israel*, 23.
104 Ibid., 15.
105 *Wultz v. Bank of China Ltd*, 32 F Supp (3d) 486 (SDNY 2014), 490n19.
106 Respondents' Memorandum, *State of Israel*, 16.
107 Ibid.
108 Israel, Ministry of Foreign Affairs, "PM Netanyahu to China – May 2013," 5 May 2013, http://mfa.gov.il/MFA/PressRoom/2013/Pages/PM-Netanyahu-to-visit-China-May-2013.aspx.
109 Respondents' Memorandum, *State of Israel*.
110 Ibid., 17.

## CHAPTER THREE

1 Rachel Ehrenfeld, *Funding Evil* (Chicago: Bonus Books, 2003), 45. See also: "Written Testimony of Jean-Charles Brisard, International Expert on Terrorism Financing, Lead Investigator, 9/11 Lawsuit, before the Committee on Banking, Housing and Urban Affairs, United States Senate," 22 October 2003, 15–16, https://www.banking.senate.gov/imo/media/doc/brisard.pdf.
2 Al Goodman, "Spain arrests suspected al Qaeda member," CNN, 24 April 2002, http://www.cnn.com/2002/WORLD/europe/04/23/inv.spain.terror.arrest/index.html). See also: "Global Relief Foundation," US Department of the Treasury, accessed 15 September 2020, https://www.treasury.gov/resource-center/terrorist-illicit-finance/Pages/protecting-charities_execorder_13224-e.aspx.
3 Ehrenfeld, *Funding Evil*, 45.
4 Louis Gordon and Ian Oxnevad, *Middle East Politics for the New Millennium: A Constructivist Approach* (Lanham, MD: Lexington Books, 2016), 158.
5 Kristian Coates Ulrichsen, "Saudi Arabia," in *Power and Politics in the Persian Gulf Monarchies*, ed. Christopher Davidson (New York: Columbia University Press, 2011), 63–4.
6 Ibid., 64.
7 David Commins, *The Wahhabi Mission and Saudi Arabia* (New York: IB Tauris, 2006), 108–10.
8 Ibid., 117.
9 Ibid., 119–20.

10 Ibid., 120.
11 Rodney Wilson, *Banking and Finance in the Middle East* (New York: St Martin's Press, 1983), 12.
12 Ibid., 13.
13 Rodney Wilson, Abdullah Al-Salamah, Monica Malik, and Ahmed Al-Rajhi, *Economic Development in Saudi Arabia* (Abingdon, UK: Routledge, 2004), 57.
14 Wilson, *Banking and Finance*, 13.
15 Michael Field, *The Merchants: The Big Business Families of Saudi Arabia and the Gulf States* (Woodstock, NY: Overlook Press, 1985), 73.
16 Wilson et al., *Economic Development*, 58.
17 Ibid., 59.
18 David Holden and Richard Johns, *The House of Saud* (London: Pan Books, 1981), 166–7.
19 Steffen Hertog, *Princes, Brokers, and Bureaucrats: Oil and the State in Saudi Arabia* (Ithaca, NY: Cornell University Press, 2010), 57.
20 Ibid., 57.
21 Rodney Wilson, "Islam and Business," *Thunderbird International Business Review* 48, no. 1 (2006): 109–23. See also: "Top Islamic Financial Institutions," *The Banker*, November 2015.
22 Wilson, *Banking and Finance*, 16.
23 Ibid.
24 Ibid., 18.
25 Wilson et al., *Economic Development*, 59.
26 Ibid., 60.
27 Sara Bazoobandi, *The Political Economy of the Gulf Sovereign Wealth Funds* (Abingdon, UK: Routledge, 2013), 68.
28 Ahmed Banafe and Rory MacLeod, *The Saudi Arabian Monetary Agency: 1952–2016* (New York: Springer, 2017), 153.
29 Ibid., 268.
30 Commins, *Wahhabi Mission*, 110.
31 Hertog, *Princes, Brokers, and Bureaucrats*, 126.
32 Ibid., 127.
33 Wilson, *Banking and Finance*, 171.
34 Wilson et al., *Economic Development*, 61.
35 J. Millard Burr and Robert O. Collins, *Alms for Jihad* (Cambridge: Cambridge University Press, 2006), 56–7.
36 Wilson et al., *Economic Development*, 61.
37 Ibid.
38 Ibid., 61–2.

39 Rodney Wilson, "Islam and Business," 119.
40 Wilson et al., *Economic Development*, 61.
41 United States Senate, "US Vulnerabilities to Money Laundering, Drugs, and Terrorist Financing: HSBC Case History" (Washington, DC: US Senate Permanent Subcommittee on Investigations, 2012), 190.
42 Wilson et al., *Economic Development*, 61.
43 US Embassy, Riyadh, to US Department of the Treasury et al. (diplomatic cable), "Saudi Royal Wealth: Where Do They Get All That Money?", 30 November 1996, Wikileaks (doc. no. 96Riyadh4784_a), https://wikileaks.org/plusd/cables/96RIYADH4784_a.html.
44 Field, *Merchants*, 120.
45 Ibid., 85–6.
46 Ulrichsen, "Saudi Arabia," 69.
47 Ibid.
48 Ibid., 70.
49 Esther van Eijk, "Sharia and National Law in Saudi Arabia," in *Sharia Incorporated*, ed. Jan Michiel Otto (Leiden, Netherlands: Leiden University Press, 2010), 156.
50 Ibid.
51 Ibid.
52 Gilles Kepel, *Jihad: The Trail of Political Islam* (Cambridge, MA: Harvard University Press, 2002), 72. See also: Jessica Stern and J.M. Berger, *ISIS: The State of Terror* (New York: HarperCollins, 2015), 265–9.
53 See UN Security Council, "Letter Dated 27 December 2001 from the Chairman of the Security Council Committee Established Pursuant to Resolution 1373 (2001) Concerning Counter-terrorism Addressed to the President of the Security Council," 27 December 2001, S/2001/1294, p. 5, para. 2, https://www.refworld.org/docid/46d571361e.html; and UN Security Council, "Letter Dated 31 July 2002 from the Chairman of the Security Council Committee Established Pursuant to Resolution 1373 (2001) Concerning Counter-terrorism Addressed to the President of the Security Council," 1 August 2002, S/2002/869, p. 4, subpara. 1, https://www.refworld.org/docid/46d6b9f10.html.
54 Financial Action Task Force, *Anti-Money Laundering and Combating the Financing of Terrorism: Kingdom of Saudi Arabia, Middle East and North Africa* (Paris: FATF Secretariat, 2010), 146.
55 Jean-Charles Brisard, *Terrorism Financing: Roots and Trends of Saudi Terrorism Financing*, report prepared for the President of the UN Security Council (New York: United Nations, 2002), 16.
56 Ibid., 17.

57 Ibid., 20.
58 Ibid., 24.
59 Steve Barber, "The 'New Economy of Terror': The Financing of Islamist Terrorism," *Global Security Studies* 2, no. 1 (2011): 5–6.
60 Ibid.
61 "In re Terrorist Attacks on September 11, 2001," 349 F. Supp. 2d 765 (SDNY 2005), 18 January 2005, sec. 832.
62 Jimmy Gurule, *Unfunding Terror: The Legal Response to the Financing of Global Terrorism* (Cheltenham, UK: Edward Elgar: 2008), 126.
63 US Department of the Treasury, "Additional Al-Haramain Branches, Former Leader Designated by Treasury as Al Qaida Supporters Marks Latest Action in Joint Designation with Saudi Arabia," media release, 2 June 2004, https://www.treasury.gov/press-center/press-releases/Pages/js1703.aspx.
64 Rohan Gunaratna, *Inside Al Qaeda* (New York: Berkeley Books, 2002), 5.
65 US Secretary of State to Central Intelligence Agency et al. (diplomatic cable), "Terrorist Financing – Updated Nonpaper on Al Haramain," 28 January 2003, Wikileaks (doc. no. 03State23994_a), https://wikileaks.org/plusd/cables/03STATE23994_a.html.
66 US Department of the Treasury, "Additional Al-Haramain Branches."
67 Ibid.
68 John B. Taylor, *Global Financial Warriors* (New York: W.W. Norton, 2007), 22.
69 Robert Windrem, "US knew of bin Laden Kenya cell," *NBC News*, 24 October 2003, http://www.nbcnews.com/id/3340668.
70 Ehrenfeld, *Funding Evil*, 46.
71 Burr and Collins, *Alms for Jihad*, 98.
72 Douglas Farrah, *Blood from Stones: The Secret Financial Network of Terror* (New York: Broadway Books, 2004), chap. 4.
73 Burr and Collins, *Alms for Jihad*, 98.
74 Juan Zarate, *Treasury's War* (New York: PublicAffairs, 2013), 80.
75 Matt Taibbi, "Gangster Bankers: Too Big to Jail," *Rolling Stone*, 22 February 2013, 3.
76 Steven Emerson, *Jihad Incorporated* (New York: Prometheus Books, 2006), chap. 10, loc. 4580.
77 Burr and Collins, *Alms for Jihad*, 279.
78 Ibid., 280.
79 Ibid., 281.
80 Ibid.
81 Stephen Schwartz, *The Two Faces of Islam: Saudi Fundamentalism and Its Role in Terrorism* (New York: Anchor Books, 2003), loc. 4951.

82 Douglas Farah and John Mintz, "US Trails Va. Muslim Money Ties," *Washington Post*, 7 October 2002, https://www.washingtonpost.com/archive/politics/2002/10/07/us-trails-va-muslim-money-ties/11fed21c-9928-40a4-845e-78b60c37f645/.
83 Mark Hosenball, "Attacking the Money Machine," *Newsweek*, 6 November 2001, http://www.newsweek.com/attacking-money-machine-149693.
84 Ibid.
85 US Department of the Treasury, "SDGT Designations," 7 November 2001, https://home.treasury.gov/policy-issues/financial-sanctions/recent-actions/20011107.
86 Farah and Mintz, "US Trails."
87 Ibid.
88 Craig Unger, *House of Bush, House of Saud* (New York: Scribner, 2004), 260.
89 Ibid., 261.
90 Naif bin Hethlain, *Saudi Arabia and the US since 1962: Allies in Conflict* (London: Saqi Books, 2010), 279. See also: Maurice R. Greenberg, William F. Wechsler, and Lee S. Wolosky, *Terrorist Financing* (New York: Council on Foreign Relations, 2002), 8.
91 Bin Hethlain, *Saudi Arabia*, 280.
92 William Simpson, *The Prince: The Secret of the World's Most Intriguing Royal* (New York: HarperCollins, 2006), 332.
93 Alfred B. Prados and Christopher M. Blanchard, "Saudi Arabia: Current Issues and U.S. Relations" (Washington, DC: Congressional Research Service, Library of Congress, 2006), 6.
94 Zarate, *Treasury's War*, 76.
95 Ibid.
96 Ibid., 82.
97 Gerald Posner, *Secrets of the Kingdom: The Inside Story of the Saudi-U.S. Connection* (New York: Random House, 2005), 171.
98 Glenn R. Simpson, "US Tracks Saudi Bank Favored by Extremists," *Wall Street Journal*, 26 July 2007, https://www.wsj.com/articles/SB118530038250476405.
99 Ibid.
100 US Embassy, Riyadh, to US Secretary of State (diplomatic cable), "Terrorist Financing: Al-Rajhi Bank", 27 September 2004, Wikileaks (doc. no. 04Riyadh5103_a), https://wikileaks.org/plusd/cables/04RIYADH5103_a.html.

101  US Secretary of State to US Embassy, Riyadh (diplomatic cable), "Joint Examination of Al Rajhi Bank through the Joint Terrorist Financing Task Force," 25 November 2004, Wikileaks (doc. no. 04State251768_a), https://wikileaks.org/plusd/cables/04STATE251768_a.html.
102  Ibid.
103  Ibid.
104  Carrick Mollenkamp and Brett Wolf (Reuters), "HSBC to pay record $1.9-billion fine in U.S. money laundering case," *Globe and Mail*, 11 December 2012, https://www.theglobeandmail.com/report-on-business/international-business/hsbc-to-pay-record-19-billion-fine-in-us-money-laundering-case/article6189108.
105  United States Senate, "US Vulnerabilities to Money Laundering, Drugs, and Terrorist Financing: HSBC Case History" (Washington, DC: US Senate Permanent Subcommittee on Investigations, 2012).
106  "Opening Statement of Sen. Carl Levin: US Vulnerabilities to Money Laundering, Drugs, and Terrorist Financing: HSBC Case History," media release, US Senate Permanent Subcommittee on Investigations, 17 July 2012, 4–5.
107  Bin Hethlain, *Saudi Arabia*, 306.
108  Egmont Group, "Saudi Arabia Financial Intelligence Unit (SAFIU)," accessed 2 February 2018, https://egmontgroup.org/en/content/saudi-arabia-saudi-arabia-financial-investigation-unit.
109  Posner, *Secrets*, 181.
110  US Embassy, Riyadh, to Central Intelligence Agency et al. (diplomatic cable), "The Saudi Financial Intelligence Unit I: Stab at 2007 Egmont Membership," 22 October 2006, Wikileaks (doc. no. 06Riyadh8401_a), https://wikileaks.org/plusd/cables/06RIYADH8401_a.html.
111  US Embassy, Riyadh, to Central Intelligence Agency et al. (diplomatic cable), "The Saudi Financial Intelligence Unit II: Power Struggle with SAMA," 22 October 2006, Wikileaks (doc. no. 06Riyadh8404_a), https://wikileaks.org/plusd/cables/06RIYADH8404_a.html.
112  US Embassy, Riyadh, to US Department of the Treasury (diplomatic cable), "Treasury DAS Presses Terror Finance Cooperation in Riyadh," 22 June 2009, Wikileaks (doc. no. 09Riyadh828_a), https://wikileaks.org/plusd/cables/09RIYADH828_a.html.
113  Ibid.
114  Ibid.
115  Simon English, "Saudi threat to withdraw billions in US investments," *Telegraph* (UK), 20 August 2002, http://www.telegraph.co.uk/news/

worldnews/middleeast/saudiarabia/1404928/Saudi-threat-to-withdraw-billions-in-US-investments.html.
116 Payton Smith, "US judge orders Saudi officials to testify in September 11 attacks lawsuit," *Jurist*, 13 September 2020, https://www.jurist.org/news/2020/09/us-judge-orders-saudi-officials-to-testify-in-september-11-attacks-lawsuit.

CHAPTER FOUR

1 Originating in 1933 as a credit union founded by a conglomerate of smaller collectives, Halk Bank became a bank formally only in 1938. See: "Company Profile: Foundation and Transformation Story of Halkbank," Halk Bank, accessed 7 March 2021, https://www.halkbank.com.tr/en/investor-relations/corporate-information/company-profile.html.
2 Abdullah Takim and Ensar Yilmaz, "Economic policy during Ataturk's era in Turkey (1923–1938)," *African Journal of Business Management* 4, no. 4 (2010): 551.
3 Dilek Barlas, *Etatism and Diplomacy in Turkey: Economic and Foreign Policies in an Uncertain World, 1929–1939* (Leiden, Netherlands: Brill, 1998), 42.
4 Germa Bel, "Against the Mainstream: Nazi Privatization in 1930s Germany," *Economic History Review* 63, no. 1 (2010): 34–55.
5 Barlas, *Etatism*, 62. See also: *Atatürk'ün Söylev ve Demeçleri I–III* (Ankara: Türk Tarih Kurumu Basımevi, 1989), 295.
6 "Company Profile: Foundation and Transformation Story of Halkbank."
7 Thomas Marois, "The Lost Logic of State-Owned Banks: Mexico, Turkey, and Neoliberalism," paper presented at the Canadian Political Science Association 79th annual conference, University of Saskatchewan, 31 May 2007, 7.
8 "Company Profile: Foundation and Transformation Story of Halkbank."
9 Ibid.
10 Tevfik F. Nas and Mehmet Odekon, introduction to *Liberalization and the Turkish Economy*, ed. Tevfik F. Nas and Mehmet Odekon (New York: Greenwood Press, 1988), 2.
11 Ziya Öniş, "Turgut Özal and His Economic Legacy: Turkish Neo-Liberalism in Critical Perspective," *Middle Eastern Studies* 40, no. 4 (July 2004): 117. See also: Ersin Kalaycıoğlu, "The Motherland Party: The Challenge of Institutionalization in a Charismatic Leader Party," *Turkish Studies* 3, no. 1 (Spring 2002): 41–61.
12 Öniş, "Turgut Özal," 126.

13 Ibid.
14 Çağa Ökten, "Privatization: What Has Been Achieved?", in *The Turkish Economy: The Real Economy, Corporate Governance and Reform*, ed. Sumru Altuğ and Alpay Filiztekin (Abingdon, UK: Routledge, 2006), 232.
15 Ibid., 240–1.
16 Marc C. Palmer, "The Turkish Privatization Experience, 1984–2009," *Perspectives on Business & Economics – Turkey: Bridging Two Worlds* 28, no. 9 (2010): 80, http://preserve.lehigh.edu/perspectives-v28/9.
17 Ibid., 83–4.
18 Muhittin Ataman, "Leadership Change: Özal Leadership and Restructuring in Turkish Foreign Policy," *Alternatives: Turkish Journal of International Relations* 1, no. 1 (Spring 2002): 124, 127.
19 Ibid., 127.
20 Ökten, "Privatization," 234.
21 "Our History," Halk Bank, accessed 7 March 2021, https://www.halkbank.com.tr/en/about-halkbank/halkbank-in-brief/History.html.
22 Banks Association of Turkey, *Banks in Turkey 2016*, Publication No. 322 (Istanbul: Banks Association of Turkey, 2017), II–242.
23 Izak Atiyas, "Recent Privatization of Turkey: A Reappraisal," in *Turkey and the Global Economy: Neo-Liberal Restructuring and Integration in the Post-Crisis Era*, ed. Ziya Öniş and Fikret Şenses (Abingdon, UK: Routledge, 2009), 101–22, 107.
24 Ibid.
25 Yener Altunbaş, Alper Kara, and Özlem Olgu, *Turkish Banking: Banking Under Political Instability and Chronic High Inflation* (Hampshire, UK: Palgrave, 2009), 54. See also: C. Emre Alper and Ziya Öniş, "Financial Globalization, the Democratic Deficit, and Recurrent Crises in Emerging Markets: The Turkish Experience in the Aftermath of Capital Account Liberalization," *Emerging Markets, Finance, and Trade* 39, no. 3 (2003): 5–26.
26 Altunbaş et al., *Turkish Banking*, 138.
27 "Milestones," Halk Bank, accessed 7 March 2021, https://www.halkbank.com.tr/en/investor-relations/corporate-information/milestones.html.
28 Mahmut Cengiz and Mitchel P. Roth, *The Illicit Economy in Turkey: How Criminals, Terrorism, and the Syrian Conflict Fuel Underground Markets* (Lanham, MD: Lexington Books, 2019), 33.
29 Halk Bank, offering memorandum, 29 May 2014, 82, http://www.ise.ie/debt_documents/Prospectus%20-%20Standalone_bf28fe49-51f6-4fcf-ac89-7a803aede994.pdf.
30 Halk Bank, offering memorandum, 4–5.

31 Cem Baslevent and Ali Akarca, "Micro Evidence on Inter-Party Vote Movements in Turkey: Who Voted for AKP in 2002?", 20 November 2008, 2, http://dx.doi.org/10.2139/ssrn.1304982.
32 Ibid., 10.
33 Ergun Özbudun, "From Political Islam to Conservative Democracy: The Case of the Justice and Development Party in Turkey," *South European Society and Politics* 11, nos. 3–4 (2006): 547.
34 Ahmet Insel, "The AKP and Normalizing Democracy in Turkey," *South Atlantic Quarterly* 102, nos. 2–3 (2003): 298–9.
35 Ibid., 298.
36 Atila Eralp, "Turkey and the European Union in the Post-Cold War Era," in *Turkey's New World*, ed. Alan Makovsky and Sabri Sayari (Washington, DC: Washington Institute for Near East Policy, 2000), 173.
37 Anti-Terror Law Act No. 3713: Law to Fight Terrorism, *Official Gazette* (Turkey), 12 April 1991, article 1.
38 "Duties and Powers," MASAK (Financial Crimes Investigation Board), accessed 10 April 2018, http://www.masak.gov.tr/en/content/duties-and-powers/148.
39 Prevention of Laundering the Proceeds of Crime Law, Law No. 5549, 2006, article 2
40 "Executive Summary," sec. 17, in Financial Action Task Force, *Third Mutual Evaluation Report: Anti-Money Laundering and Combating the Financing of Terrorism – Turkey* (Paris: FATF Secretariat, 2007).
41 "Chronology," MASAK (Financial Crimes Investigation Board), accessed 10 April 2018, http://www.masak.gov.tr/en/content/chronology/173.
42 See: Ziya Öniş and Caner Bakır, "Turkey's Political Economy in the Age of Financial Globalization: The Significance of the EU Anchor," *South European Society and Politics* 12, no. 2 (June 2007): 147–64.
43 "Executive Summary, sec. 7, in Financial Action Task Force, *Third Mutual Evaluation Report*.
44 "Executive Summary, sec. 5, in Financial Action Task Force, *Third Mutual Evaluation Report*.
45 Law No. 6415: Prevention of the Financing of Terrorism, 7 February 2013, article 3, item A.
46 Law No. 6415, article 5.
47 Law No. 6415, article 6.
48 Law No. 6415, article 6, sec. 2
49 Law No. 6415, article 6.

50 Financial Action Task Force, *Mutual Evaluation of Turkey: 15th Follow Up Report* (Paris: FATF Secretariat, 2014), 26.
51 Ibid., 24.
52 Financial Action Task Force, *Politically Exposed Persons (Recommendations 12 and 22)* (Paris: FATF Secretariat, 2013), 4–5.
53 FATF, *Mutual Evaluation of Turkey*, 24.
54 Ibid.
55 "High-risk and other monitored jurisdictions," Financial Action Task Force, accessed 10 April 2018, http://www.fatf-gafi.org/countries/#high-risk.
56 Benjamin Weinthal, "Iran secured as much as $20b. from Turkey breaking sanctions," *Jerusalem Post*, 24 July 2015, https://www.jpost.com/Middle-East/Iran/Iran-secured-as-much-as-20b-from-Turkey-breaking-sanctions-410057.
57 Nihat Ali Özcan and Özgür Özdamar, "Uneasy Neighbors: Turkish-Iranian Relations since the 1979 Islamic Revolution," *Middle East Policy* 17, no. 3 (2010): 105.
58 Philip Robins, *Suits and Uniforms: Turkish Foreign Policy Since the Cold War* (Seattle: University of Washington Press, 2003), 57.
59 Ataman, "Leadership Change," 124.
60 Ibid., 136.
61 Ibid., 138.
62 Robins, *Suits and Uniforms*, 57.
63 Ibid., 58.
64 Nader Habibi, "Turkey and Iran: Growing Economic Relations Despite Western Sanctions," *Middle East Brief* 62 (May 2012): 4.
65 US Department of Energy, "Natural Gas Exports from Iran: A report required by section 505(a) of the Iran Threat Reduction and Syria Human Rights Act of 2012" (Washington, DC: Energy Information Administration, 2012), 7.
66 Ibid., 1.
67 Ibid.
68 Matthew Levitt, *Hezbollah: The Global Footprint of Lebanon's Party of God* (Washington, DC: Georgetown University Press, 2013), 12.
69 Ibid.
70 Ibid.
71 Daniel Byman, *Deadly Connections: States that Sponsor Terrorism* (Cambridge: Cambridge University Press, 2005), 87–8.
72 Levitt, *Hezbollah*, 14.

73 Byman, *Deadly Connections*, 87–8.
74 Ibid.
75 Larry Rohter, "Argentine Judge Indicts 4 Iranian Officials in 1994 Bombing of Jewish Center," *New York Times*, 10 March 2003, https://www.nytimes.com/2003/03/10/world/argentine-judge-indicts-4-iranian-officials-in-1994-bombing-of-jewish-center.html.
76 Ibid.
77 Loretta Napoleoni, *Terror Incorporated* (New York: Seven Stories Press, 2005), 114–15.
78 Ibid., 115.
79 BBC News, "Hezbollah linked to Burgas bus bombing in Bulgaria," 5 February 2013, http://www.bbc.com/news/world-europe-21342192.
80 Levitt, *Hezbollah*, 265.
81 Ibid., 265–6.
82 Byman, *Deadly Connections*, 107–8.
83 See Iran and Libya Sanctions Act of 1996, H.R. 3107, 104th Congress (1995–96), secs 4–5.
84 Byman, *Deadly Connections*, 109.
85 Alireza Nader, "Influencing Iran's Nuclear Program," in *Sanctions, Statecraft and Nuclear Proliferation*, ed. Etel Solingen (Cambridge: Cambridge University Press, 2012), 214.
86 Ibid., 214.
87 Juan Zarate, *Treasury's War* (New York: PublicAffairs, 2013), 336.
88 James Rickards, *Currency Wars: The Making of the Next Global Crisis* (New York: Portfolio/Penguin, 2011), 261.
89 Zarate, *Treasury's War*, 48–60.
90 Ibid., 49–50.
91 Rickards, *Currency Wars*, 261–2.
92 Ibid.
93 Timothy Wittig, *Understanding Terrorist Finance* (Basingstoke, UK: Palgrave Macmillan, 2011), 10.
94 Cengiz and Roth, *Illicit Economy*, 132.
95 Glen Johnson and Richard Spencer, "Turkey's politicians, gold dealer, and the pop star," *Telegraph* (UK), 29 December 2013, https://www.telegraph.co.uk/news/worldnews/europe/turkey/10540423/Turkeys-politicians-gold-dealer-and-the-pop-star.html.
96 *Business Year*, "All About SMEs: TBY talks to Süleyman Aslan, CEO of Halkbank, on supporting SMEs, foreign investment, and regional expansion," 2012, https://www.thebusinessyear.com/turkey-2012/all-about-smes/interview.

97  US Embassy, Ankara, to US Department of the Treasury et al. (diplomatic cable), "Turkey: U/S Levey on the Dangers of Doing Business with Iran," 27 February 2008, Wikileaks (doc. no. 08Ankara379_a), accessed 2 April 2018, https://wikileaks.org/plusd/cables/08ANKARA379_a.html.
98  Ibid.
99  Ibid.
100 Ibid.; and Türkiye Halk Bankasi A.Ş. (Halkbank), "Statement of Anti-Money Laundering & Counter Terrorist Financing & Anti-Bribery-Corruption & Sanctions," 2008. The compliance officer mentioned in the latter document is Duran Uğur, who is referred to as "Dur Oglan" in the 27 February 2008 Wikileaks cable.
101 Ibid.
102 US Embassy, Ankara, to US Secretary of State (diplomatic cable), "Treasury Official on Fight against Terrorist Financing," 4 December 2009, Wikileaks (doc. no. 09Ankara1725_a), accessed 2 April 2018, https://wikileaks.org/plusd/cables/09ANKARA1725_a.html.
103 Johnson and Spencer, "Turkey's politicians."
104 Jonathan Schanzer, "The Biggest Sanctions-Evasion Scheme in Recent History," *Atlantic*, 4 January 2018, https://www.theatlantic.com/international/archive/2018/01/iran-turkey-gold-sanctions-nuclear-zarrab-atilla/549665.
105 Ibid.
106 Jonathan Schanzer and Rachel Ziemba, "The Anatomy of Turkey's 'Gas-for-Gold' Scheme with Iran," policy brief, Foundation for the Defense of Democracy, 14 June 2014, http://www.defenddemocracy.org/media-hit/the-anatomy-of-turkeys-gas-for-gold-scheme-with-iran.
107 *BBC News*, "Turkey corruption inquiry: More senior police 'fired,'" 20 December 2013, http://www.bbc.com/news/world-europe-25462121.
108 *BBC News*, "Hundreds of Turkish police officers dismissed," 7 January 2014, http://www.bbc.com/news/world-europe-25634542.
109 Orhan Coskun and Ece Toksabay, "Hit by scandal and resignations, Turk PM names new ministers," Reuters, 24 December 2013, https://www.reuters.com/article/us-turkey-corruption/hit-by-scandal-and-resignations-turk-pm-names-new-ministers-idUSBRE9BN0D720131225.
110 *Financial Times*, "Turkey's business sector hit by scandal fallout," 23 December 2013, https://www.ft.com/content/b4bda6de-6bee-11e3-85b1-00144feabdc0.
111 *BBC News*, "Turkish president signs off on new controls over judiciary," 26 February 2014, http://www.bbc.com/news/world-europe-26351258.

112 Daren Butler and Nick Tattersall, "Turkish judicial purge brings corruption investigation to halt," Reuters, 22 January 2014, https://www.reuters.com/article/us-turkey-corruption/turkish-judicial-purge-brings-corruption-investigation-to-halt-idUSBREA0L1G220140122.
113 Ibid.
114 Ibid.
115 *Hurriyet Daily News*, "Cash found in shoeboxes at Halkbank ex-manager's home not bank's money: Turkish PM," 11 February 2014, http://www.hurriyetdailynews.com/cash-found-in-shoeboxes-at-halkbank-ex-managers-home-not-banks-money-turkish-pm-62314.
116 David L. Phillips, *An Uncertain Ally* (Abingdon, UK: Routledge, 2017), 49.
117 Ibid.
118 Ibid., 50.
119 *Hurriyet Daily News*, "Turkey's massive corruption case dropped by prosecutor," 17 October 2014, http://www.hurriyetdailynews.com/turkeys-massive-corruption-case-dropped-by-prosecutor-73149.
120 Ibid.
121 Tracy Connor, "Turkish banker Hakan Atilla convicted in U.S. sanctions case," NBC News, 3 January 2018, https://www.nbcnews.com/news/us-news/turkish-banker-hakan-atilla-convicted-u-s-sanctions-case-n832181.
122 Phillips, *An Uncertain Ally*, 50.
123 Isobel Finkel and Christian Berthelsen, "U.S. Arrests Top Turkish Banker in Iran Sanctions Probe," Bloomberg, 23 March 2017, https://www.bloomberg.com/news/articles/2017-03-28/halkbank-deputy-g-m-arrested-in-u-s-in-iran-financing-probe.
124 United States v. Reza Zarrab, 15 Cr. 867 (SDNY 2016), sec. 4, pp. 35-40.
125 US Department of the Treasury, "Treasury Designates Iranian Commercial Airline Linked to Iran's Support for Terrorism," media release, 12 October 2011, https://www.treasury.gov/press-center/press-releases/Pages/tg1322.aspx.
126 Assaf Moghadam, *Militancy and Political Violence in Shiism: Trends and Patterns* (Abingdon, UK: Routledge, 2011), 87. See also: Levitt, *Hezbollah*, 9.
127 US Treasury Dept., "Treasury Designates."
128 Phillips, *An Uncertain Ally*, 52.
129 "Statement of Anti-Money Laundering and Counter Terrorist Financing and Anti-Bribery-Corruption and Sanctions," Halk Bank, 2016, 1. https://www.halkbank.com.tr/content/dam/halkbank/en/international-banking/compliance/statement_of_aml_ctf.pdf.
130 Ibid., 2.

131 *TurkishMinute*, "Jailed police chiefs who led 2013 corruption ops taken to police HQ," 14 January 2018, https://www.turkishminute.com/2018/01/14/jailed-police-chiefs-who-led-2013-corruption-ops-taken-to-police-hq/.

132 Dilara Zengin and Kubra Chohan, "Halkbank in clear in Turkish banker Atilla case in US," Anadolu News Agency, 4 January 2018, https://www.aa.com.tr/en/economy/halkbank-in-clear-in-turkish-banker-atilla-case-in-us/1022288.

133 Reuters, "Halkbank not Turkey will pay any US fine, deputy PM says," 11 January 2018, https://www.reuters.com/article/us-turkey-halkbank/halkbank-not-turkey-will-pay-any-u-s-fine-deputy-pm-says-idUSKBN1-F1O1Z.

134 Ibid.

135 *BBC News*, "Turkey anger as US convicts banker Atilla over Iran sanctions case," 4 January 2018, http://www.bbc.com/news/world-europe-42564833.

136 Reuters, "RPT – Update 2 – Halkbank shares surge after US seeks jail term for banker," 5 April 2018, https://www.reuters.com/article/usa-turkey-zarrab-spokesman/rpt-update-2-halkbank-shares-surge-after-us-seeks-jail-term-for-banker-idUSL5N1RI4GD.

137 Jonathan Stempel, "US seeks big contempt fines against Halkbank," Reuters, 21 January 2020, https://www.reuters.com/article/us-usa-turkey-halkbank-idUSKBN1ZK2JB.

138 Stewart Bishop, "Feds Say Halkbank's Immunity Claim is Bogus," *Law360*, 1 September 2020, https://www.law360.com/articles/1306336/feds-say-halkbank-s-immunity-claim-is-bogus.

139 Ibid.

140 Benjamin Weiser, "Turkish Banker in Iran Sanctions-Busting Case Sentenced to 32 Months," *New York Times*, 16 May 2018, https://www.nytimes.com/2018/05/16/world/turkish-iran-sanctions-trial.html.

141 Ibid.

142 Kadhim Shubber and Laura Pitel, "Turkish Banker Sentenced in US Court Over Iran Sanctions Violations," *Financial Times*, 16 May 2018, https://www.ft.com/content/a0b6ac1c-593d-11e8-b8b2-d6ceb45fa9do.

143 Ibid.

144 Ahval News Service, "Turkey withdrew gold from Fed amid crisis – analysis," 17 April 2018, https://ahvalnews.com/us-turkey/turkey-withdrew-gold-fed-amid-crisis-analysis.

145 Ibid.

146 Uğur Gürses, "Early elections and reserves held in the US," *Hurriyet Daily News*, 21 April 2018, http://www.hurriyetdailynews.com/opinion/ugur-gurses/early-elections-and-reserves-held-in-the-us-130648.

## CHAPTER FIVE

1 M.B. Malik, *Double Standards: The Forced Closure of the BCCI Bank* (Leicester, UK: Matador-Troubador Books, 2016), 12.
2 Peter Truell and Larry Gurwin, *False Profits: The Inside Story of BCCI, the World's Most Corrupt Financial Empire* (New York: Houghton Mifflin, 1992), 11.
3 James Ring Adams and Douglas Frantz, *A Full Service Bank: How BCCI Stole Billions around the World* (New York: Pocket Books, 1992), 29.
4 Truell and Gurwin, *False Profits*, 2.
5 See: Paul N. Doremus, William W. Keller, Louis W. Pauly, and Simon Reich, *The Myth of the Global Corporation* (Princeton, NJ: Princeton University Press, 1998).
6 Ronen Palan, Richard Murphy, and Christian Chavagneux, *Tax Havens: How Globalization Really Works* (Ithaca, NY: Cornell University Press, 2010), 119.
7 Ibid.
8 Nicholas Shaxson, *Treasure Islands: Uncovering the Damage of Offshore Banking and Tax Havens* (New York: Palgrave Macmillan, 2011), 16–17.
9 Peter Hall, *Governing the Economy: The Politics of State Intervention in Britain and France* (Oxford: Oxford University Press, 1986), 77.
10 Eric Helleiner, *States and the Reemergence of Global Finance* (Ithaca, NY: Cornell University Press, 1996), 84.
11 Ibid.
12 Gary Burn, "The State, the City, and the Euromarkets," *Review of International Political Economy* 6, no. 2 (1999): 226.
13 Shaxson, *Treasure Islands*, 89.
14 Ibid., 90.
15 Palan et al., *Tax Havens*, 137.
16 Jonathan Beaty and S.C. Gwynne, *The Outlaw Bank: A Wild Ride into the Secret Heart of BCCI* (New York: Random House, 1993), 113–14.
17 Shaxson, *Treasure Islands*, 90.
18 Ibid., 91–2.
19 Ibid., 92.
20 Ibid., 93.

21 Nicholas Ryder, *Money Laundering: An Endless Cycle? A Comparative Analysis of the Anti-Money Laundering Policies in the United States of America, the United Kingdom, Australia, and Canada* (Abingdon, UK: Routledge, 2012), 80.
22 Ibid., 79.
23 Beaty and Gwynne, *Outlaw Bank*, 114.
24 Ibid., 113.
25 Ibid., 114–15.
26 Adams and Franz, *A Full Service Bank*, 14.
27 Truell and Gurwin, *False Profits*, 18.
28 Ibid., 29.
29 Ibid., 48.
30 Adams and Franz, *A Full Service Bank*, 42–3.
31 Truell and Gurwin, *False Profits*, 30.
32 Ibid., 29.
33 Ibid., 28.
34 Ibid., 84.
35 Ibid.
36 Ibid., 87.
37 Beaty and Gwynne, *Outlaw Bank*, 89–90.
38 Truell and Gurwin, *False Profits*, 93.
39 Beaty and Gwynne, *Outlaw Bank*, 290–1.
40 Truell and Gurwin, *False Profits*, 101.
41 Ibid., 328.
42 Rachel Ehrenfeld, *Evil Money: Encounters along the Money Trail* (New York: HarperCollins, 1992), 172.
43 Ibid., 194.
44 Ibid., 199.
45 Ibid., 204–6.
46 Ibid., 177–8.
47 US Senate, "The BCCI Affair: Report to the Committee on Foreign Relations, US Senate, prepared by Senators John Kerry and Hank Brown," 102nd Congress (Washington, DC: US Senate Committee on Foreign Relations, 1992), 76.
48 Rohan Gunaratna, *Inside Al Qaeda* (New York: Berkeley Books, 2003), 17. See also: Rachel Ehrenfeld, *Funding Evil* (Chicago: Bonus Books, 2005), 58.
49 US House of Representatives, "Subcommittee Staff Report Regarding Federal Law Enforcement's Handling of Allegations Involving the Bank

of Credit and Commerce International" (Washington, DC: House Judiciary Committee Subcommittee on Crime and Criminal Justice, 1991).
50 Beaty and Gwynne, *Outlaw Bank*, 324.
51 Ibid., 325.
52 Ibid.
53 US Senate, "The BCCI Affair," 320–1.
54 Ibid., 353.
55 Shaxson, *Treasure Islands*, 17–18.
56 US Senate, "The BCCI Affair," 354.
57 Ibid., 355.
58 Ibid.
59 Ibid., 356.
60 Beaty and Gwynne, *Outlaw Bank*, 105.
61 Ibid., 105–6.
62 Adams and Franz, *A Full Service Bank*, 295.
63 Beaty and Gwynne, *Outlaw Bank*, 98.
64 Ibid., 107.
65 US Senate, "The BCCI Affair," 357.
66 House of Commons, "Minutes of Evidence Taken Before the Committee on Treasury and Civil Service," 23 July 1991, Fourth Report, Banking Supervision and BCCI (London: HMSO, 1992), 104.
67 House of Commons, "Inquiry into the Supervision of The Bank of Credit and Commerce International" (BCCI [Bingham Report]), *Parliamentary Debates*, Commons, 6th series, 6 November 1992, vol. 213, cols 523–94, paras 2.544–55.
68 Ibid., paras 2.544–55, 2.547–8.
69 Truell and Gurwin, *False Profits*, 283–4.
70 US Senate, "The BCCI Affair," 358–9.
71 Truell and Gurwin, *False Profits*, 311.
72 Ibid., 311.
73 Ehrenfeld, *Evil Money*, 201–2.
74 Raj K. Bhala, *Foreign Bank Regulation after BCCI* (Durham, NC: Carolina Academic Press, 1994), 9.
75 Ibid., 134–5. See also: House of Commons, "BCCI (Bingham Report)," paras 2.213–15.
76 Bhala, *Foreign Bank Regulation*, 134–5.
77 Rodney Wilson, *Banking and Finance in the Arab Middle East* (New York: St Martin's Press, 1983), 44.
78 Abdulhameed Shoman, *The Indomitable Arab: The Life and Times of Abdulhameed Shoman (1890–1974)* (London: Third World Centre, 1984), 142.

79 Ibid., 119, 67.
80 Ibid., 154.
81 Ibid., 149.
82 Ibid., 309.
83 Ibid.
84 Ibid., 220.
85 Ibid.
86 Herbert Feis, *Europe: The World's Banker, 1870–1914* (New Haven, CT: Yale University Press, 1930), 320–30.
87 Raymond F. Mikesell, "Sterling Area Currencies of the Middle East," *Middle East Journal* 2, no. 2 (1948): 167.
88 Tariq Moraiwed Tell, *The Social and Economic Origins of Monarchy in Jordan* (New York: Palgrave Macmillan, 2013), 77–8.
89 Shoman, *Indomitable Arab*, 173, 233.
90 Ibid., 234.
91 "Our History," Arab Bank, accessed 28 May 2018, https://www.arabbank.jo/smartmenu/smart-menu/about-us-2/our-history.
92 Shoman, *Indomitable Arab*, 354.
93 "Our History," Arab Bank.
94 Curtis R. Ryan, "Hashemite Kingdom of Jordan," in *The Government and Politics of the Middle East and North Africa*, 6th edition, ed. David E. Long, Bernard Reich, and Mark Gasiorowski (Boulder, CO: Westview Press, 2011), 301.
95 Timothy J. Piro, *The Political Economy of Market Reform in Jordan* (Lanham, MD: Rowman and Littlefield, 1998), 27–9.
96 Ibid., 29, 31.
97 Zayd Sha'sha, "The Role of the Private Sector in Jordan's Economy," in *Politics and the Economy in Jordan*, ed. Rodney Wilson (London: Routledge, 1991), 71.
98 Ibid., 73–4.
99 Ibid., 74.
100 "The Association's Organizational Structure: General Assembly," Association of Banks in Jordan, accessed 28 May 2018, http://abj.org.jo/en-us/The-Associations-Organizational-Structure.
101 Sha'sha, "Role of the Private Sector," 78. See also: Rodney Wilson, "Islamic Banking: The Jordanian Experience," in *Politics and the Economy in Jordan* (London: Routledge, 1991), 115.
102 Piro, *Political Economy*, 37–58.
103 "The Arab Bank's Place in Jordan and the Region" (diplomatic cable), 24 November 2002, Wikileaks (doc. no. 02Amman6852_a), para. 5,

accessed 28 May 2018, https://wikileaks.org/plusd/cables/02AMMAN 6852_a.html.
104 Ibid., para. 6.
105 Ibid., para. 4.
106 Ryan, "Hashemite Kingdom," 323.
107 Ibid., 325.
108 Yitzhak Reiter, "The Palestinian-Transjordanian Rift: Economic Might and Political Power in Jordan," *Middle East Journal* 58, no. 1 (2004): 78.
109 Ibid., 79.
110 Ibid.
111 Laurie A. Brand, "Palestinians and Jordanians: A Crisis of Identity," *Journal of Palestine Studies* 24, no. 4 (1995): 48.
112 Ibid.
113 Ryan, "Hashemite Kingdom," 302.
114 Matthew Levitt, *Hamas: Politics, Charity, and Terrorism in the Service of Jihad* (New Haven, CT: Yale University Press, 2006), 20.
115 Muhammad Muslih, *The Foreign Policy of Hamas* (New York: Council on Foreign Relations, 1999), 15.
116 Ibid., 17.
117 Russell E. Lucas, "Democratization in Jordan," *Journal of Democracy* 14, no. 1 (2003): 138.
118 Ali E. Hillal Dessouki and Karen Abul Kheir, "Foreign Policy as a Strategic National Asset: The Case of Jordan," in *The Foreign Policies of Arab States*, ed. Bahgat Korany and Ali E. Hillal Dessouki (Cairo: American University of Cairo Press, 2008), 264.
119 Lucas, "Democratization in Jordan," 139.
120 Glenn E. Robinson, "Defensive Democratization in Jordan," *International Journal of Middle East Studies* 30, no. 3 (August 1998): 387.
121 Lucas, "Democratization in Jordan," 139.
122 Levitt, *Hamas*, 44.
123 Ibid., 44.
124 Ibid., 45–6.
125 Ibid., 45.
126 Neven Bondokji, "The Muslim Brotherhood in Jordan: Time to Reform," policy briefing (Washington, DC: Brookings Institution, 2015), 2.
127 Glenn E. Robinson, "Hamas as a Social Movement," in *Islamic Activism: A Social Movement Theory Approach*, ed. Quintan Wiktorowicz (Bloomington: Indiana University Press, 2004), 117.
128 Gilles Kepel, *Jihad: The Trail of Political Islam* (Cambridge, MA: Harvard University Press, 2002), 336–7.

129  Ibid., 338.
130  Levitt, *Hamas*, 49.
131  Ibid.
132  US Department of State, "Designation of Foreign Terrorist Organizations," Public Notice 2612, *Federal Register* 62, no. 195 (8 October 1997).
133  Levitt, *Hamas*, 157.
134  Ibid., 158.
135  Ibid., 68–9.
136  Yuval Azoulay, "IDF Clears Ramallah Bank of Terror Involvement," *Haaretz*, 13 April 2010, https://www.haaretz.com/1.5101503.
137  Ibid.
138  Karen Krebsbach, "Arab Bank's $24 Million Lesson: Your Clients' Clients are Yours, Too," *American Banker*, 2 December 2013. See also: Juan Zarate, *Treasury's War: Unleashing of a New Era of Financial Warfare* (New York: PublicAffairs, 2013).
139  Zarate, *Treasury's War*, 148.
140  Ibid.
141  Financial Crimes Enforcement Network and Office of the Comptroller of the Currency, "FinCEN and OCC Assess $24 Million Penalty against Arab Bank Branch," media release, 17 August 2005, https://www.fincen.gov/sites/default/files/news_release/20050817.pdf.
142  Ibid., 6–7.
143  "U/S Levey Bilats Address Arab Bank and AML Law" (diplomatic cable), 17 February 2005, Wikileaks (doc. no. 05Amman1356_a), https://wikileaks.org/plusd/cables/05AMMAN1356_a.html.
144  Ibid.
145  *Yaffa Lev et al. v. Arab Bank*, PLC, No. 08-CV-3251, 47–8 (EDNY 2008).
146  "U/S Levey Bilats Address Arab Bank and AML Law," para. 3.
147  Ibid., para. 4.
148  Ibid., para. 5.
149  Ibid., para. 13.
150  Ibid., para. 6.
151  Ibid., para. 7.
152  *Joseph Jesner et al. v. Arab Bank*, PLC, 200 L Ed 2d 612 at 49–50 (S. Ct. 2018).
153  *Courtney Linde et al. v. Arab Bank*, PLC, 269 FRD 186 at 193–4 (EDNY 2010).
154  Ibid.
155  Diplomatic cable, "Israelis Brief U/S Levey on Terror Finance Steps against Hamas and Hizballah and Views on PA Welfare Reform" (diplomatic

cable), 18 February 2005, Wikileaks (doc. no. 05TelAviv1013_a), https://wikileaks.org/plusd/cables/05TELAVIV1013_a.html.

156 Ibid., paras 7–8.

157 "Assistant Secretary Wayne's July 10 Meetings with Jordan's Central Bank Governor Touqan and Finance Minister Al-Kodah" (diplomatic cable), 19 July 2005, Wikileaks (doc. no. 05Amman5725_a), https://wikileaks.org/plusd/cables/05AMMAN5725_a.html.

158 Ibid., para. 4.

159 "Scene Setter for Visit of Treasury Acting A/S Glaser to Amman" (diplomatic cable), 21 September 2005, paras 6–7, Wikileaks (doc. no. 05Amman7547_a), https://wikileaks.org/plusd/cables/05AMMAN7547_a.html.

160 Ibid.

161 Ibid., para. 1.

162 Lu'ayy Minwer Al-Rimawi, "Money Laundering in Jordan: A Positive Example of Middle Eastern Country Earnest About Catching Up with International Financial Standards," *Journal of Money Laundering Control* 7, no. 1 (2004): 15–17.

163 Ibid.

164 Ahmed Adnan Al-Nuemat, "Money Laundering and Banking Secrecy in the Jordanian Legislation," *Journal of International Commercial Law and Technology* 9, no. 2 (2014): 121.

165 Alfred B. Prados and Christopher M. Blanchard, "Saudi Arabia: Terrorist Financing Issues," Congressional Research Service Report RL32499, 14 September 2007, 6, Wikileaks, https://wikileaks.org/wiki/CRS:_Saudi_Arabia:_Terrorist_Financing_Issues,_September_14,_2007.

166 *Jesner*, 138 S. Ct. 1386 (2018) 200 L. Ed 2d 612 (Brief for Respondent, 6).

167 "Arab Bank Litigation," Motley Rice LLC, accessed 22 May 2018, https://www.motleyrice.com/anti-terrorism/arab-bank-litigation.

168 Reuters, "Arab Bank Settlement Over Israel Attacks May Hit Snag in US Appeals Court," *Jerusalem Post*, 17 May 2017, https://www.jpost.com/Middle-East/Arab-Bank-settlement-over-Israel-attacks-may-hit-snag-in-US-appeals-court-490976.

169 Stephanie Clifford, "Arab Bank Reaches Settlement in Suit Accusing It of Financing Terrorism," *New York Times*, 14 August 2015, https://www.nytimes.com/2015/08/15/nyregion/arab-bank-reaches-settlement-in-suit-accusing-it-of-financing-terrorism.html.

170 Arab Bank Group, *Annual Report 2015*, p. 5, https://www.arabbank.com/docs/default-source/annual-reports/arab-bank-group-annual-report-2015.

171 Ibid.

172 Yonah Jeremy Bob, "US Supreme Court ends second Arab Bank case," *Jerusalem Post*, 24 April 2018, https://www.jpost.com/Arab-Israeli-Conflict/US-Supreme-Court-ends-second-Arab-Bank-case-552643.
173 *Jesner*, 138 S. Ct. 1386 (2018) 200 L. Ed 2d 612 (Brief for the Hashemite Kingdom of Jordan as *Amicus Curiae* Supporting Respondent, 8).
174 Ibid.
175 Reuters, "US plans to boost aid to Jordan to $1 billion per year," 3 February 2015, https://www.reuters.com/article/us-jordan-aid-idUS-KBN0L72ET20150203. See also: Jeremy M. Sharp, "Jordan: Background and U.S. Relations" (Washington, DC: Congressional Research Service, 2018), 9–10.
176 *Jesner*, 138 S. Ct. 1386 (2018) 200 L. Ed 2d 612 (Brief for the Hashemite Kingdom of Jordan as *Amicus Curiae* Supporting Respondent, 8).

# Index

Page numbers in *italics* denote illustrative material.

9/11 and financial regulation propagation, 3, 17–18, 83–4; 9/11 survivors' prosecution, 90–1; Counter-Terrorism Committee, 22; FATF recommendations, 23; international laws, 23; UN Security Council resolutions, 22. *See also* Al Rajhi Bank – regulatory concerns
2008 financial crisis, 11, *159*

Abedi, Agha Hasan, 122
Afghanistan: Afghan Services Bureau (Makhtab al-Khidamat), 82–3; in Middle East context, 30, 128; as regulatory target, 22; and Soviet Union, 76, 80–1, 129
Agricultural Bank of China, 53
AKP. *See* Justice and Development Party (Turkey) (AKP)
Al-Barakat Bank, 38, 41
Al-Haramain Islamic Foundation (AHIF) (Saudi Arabia), 82–3, 86
Al-Qaeda: 9/11 survivors' prosecution, 90–1; and Al Rajhi Bank, 70, 78, 80–3, 86, 90–1; BCCI, support from, 128–9; organization structure, 3, 19, 22. *See also* Al Rajhi Bank – historical context; Al Rajhi Bank – regulatory concerns
Al Rajhi Bank
 – Al Rajhi family wealth and society context, 78
 – case study framework: blocked regulatory enforcement, 84–90; case study context, 7, 35, 38, 41; case study evaluation, 155–6, 162; counterterrorist financing, 79–84; enforcement case against, 70–92; legitimacy and regime building, 71–4; Saudi regulatory system, 74–8
 – historical context, 70–4; Hejaz (western Saudi Arabia), tensions in, 73–4, 90; Ibn Saud, 73–4; international tensions, 76; King Fahd, 77, 79; King Faisal assassination, 77; Nejd region, 74; oil industry impact, 77–8

– regulatory concerns: 9/11 hijackings, role of, 82, 85; Afghan Services Bureau (Makhtab al-Khidamat), 82; Al-Haramain Islamic Foundation, 82–3; Benevolence International Foundation, 83; charity structure, impact of, 81–2, 89–90; el-Hage, Wadih, 83; Huber, Albert F.A., 84; Ibn Taymiyyah, influence of, 80; international governments, scrutiny by, 84–6; international involvement, 82–3; legal institutions and religious influences, 79–81; motivation of terrorist cooperation, 91; Nairobi attack (1998), 83; Nasreddin, Ahmed Idris, 84; Operation Green Quest (US), 83–4; role of monarchy, 79–81, 84; Safa Group, 83–4; suspicious activity reports (SARS), 78–81; and terrorist groups, 80–3; Youssef, Nada, 84; and *zakat*, 81–2, 90–1

– regulatory enforcement: Anti-Terrorism Act of 1992 (US), 90; bank officials' risk exposure, 87–8; Basic Law of Saudi Arabia (1992), 79–80; FATF, 86; financial intelligence units (FIUS), 86, 88–9; HSBC Bank, 88, 90; regulatory reform efforts, 85–92; SAAR Foundation, 82–4; Saudi Arabian Monetary Agency (SAMA), 74–8, 80–1, 87–91; security interests superseding regulatory enforcement, 92; US court response, 90; and US officials and agencies, 85–9, 92; Western regulatory influences, 79, 82–4

– structure: Al Rajhi Banking and Investment Corporation, 77; Al Rajhi Company for Currency Exchange and Commerce, 78; Al Rajhi Trading and Exchange Company, 78; Al Taqwa Bank, 84; Department of Zakat and Income Taxes, 81; HSBC Bank, 88, 90; IMF assessment, 76; Saudi regulatory system, 74–8; Sharia-compliant framework, 75–7, 79–81

Al Rajhi Banking and Investment Corporation, 77

Al Rajhi Company for Currency Exchange and Commerce, 78

Al Rajhi Trading and Exchange Company, 78

Al Taqwa Bank, 38, 84

Amidror, General Yaacov, 67

AML/CTF rules: adoption of, 5, 8–9, 12–13, 20, 24, 26–9, 30; antecedents and models for, 18, 30–2, 35; bank-government linkages and blocked enforcement, 5–6, 25–7, 31–2; and corruption, 33–4; cultural context in financial affairs, 23; effectiveness of, 5–6, 13, 18, 21–4, 27–8, 31, 35–7; FATF, 17, 42–3; gaps in research literature, 28; and local conditions, 31, 41; security motivations of apolitical criminals versus terrorists, 28–9; and state power in financial sector, 13, 31–2; and state power in regulatory propagation, 26–7; and state security, 4, 17–18;

and tax havens, 27; theoretical gaps, 4–5, 37
AML Monitoring and Analysis Center (CAMLMAC) (China), 59–60
Annunzio-Wiley Anti-Money Laundering Act (US, 1992), 16–17
Anti-Drug Abuse Act (US, 1988), 17
anti-money-laundering (AML) and counterterrorist finance (CTF) rules. See AML/CTF rules
Antiterrorism Act (US, 1990), 17
Arab Bank
- case points: diplomacy by home state, 152; fortified finance emergence, 149, 151–2; multinational orientation, 150; private sector structure, 149; regional independence, 149; relationship to home state, 149–52
- case study framework: context, 7, 38, 41–2, 162; evaluation, 155–8, 162; enforcement case against, 134–49; institutional independence framework, 121–2
- historical context: antisemitism and nationalism, role of, 135–6; Arab Nationalism, 136–7; client base, 136–7; Hariri family, 139–40; Ottoman Bank, 136–7; private sector development, 139; Shoman, Abdul Hameed, 135; Western security interests, 141
- regulatory concerns: destruction of evidence, 145–7; funds reallocation, 143; Hamas and Arab Bank, 146; terrorist financing, 143–4; US investigations, 143–4

- regulatory enforcement: civil litigation results, 148–9; defence strategy, 145; litigation by terrorist victims, 145; penalties, 149; US response, 144–5
- structure: British context, 137; private bank (American model), 135; international branches, 137; private sector framework, 136, 139–40; shareholders (Arab nationals), 136; shareholders (international), 139
Atatürk, Mustafa Kemal, 94–5

bank coup of 1935 (China), 49
banking institutions: and data and monitoring activities, 17–18, 20–1; and financial economies, 31, 33; and home state regulatory enforcement, 5–7, 18, 24–7, 31, 41; and national security, 5, 11–12, 20, 24–5, 31; role in organized crime and terrorism, 4, 13–14, 19–20, 24; social contexts of, 13–15, 23–4, 32–3; and threat finance, 4, 8
Bank of China
- case study framework: blocked regulatory enforcement, 61–7; case study context, 7, 33, 35, 38, 42; and China's fortified finance regime, 57–61; development of Bank of China, 45–6; enforcement case against, 44–69; evaluation, 154–6, 162; monobank era, 53–5; origins of state ownership, 46–53; reform and continued state control, 55–7
- historical context: Article 191 (Chinese penal code), 58–9; bank

coup (1935), 49; bank structures, 46; "Big Four" banks, 55–6; Chiang Kai-shek government, 50–2; Civil War, 52–3; currency (silver standard), 47, 50, 52; Deng Xiaoping government, 44, 46, 49, 53–4, 68; Feng Guifen, 46; foreign exchange pressures, 45–6, 49; *fuguo qiangbing* (state and military power), 46; intelligence apparatus, role in, 61; Li Chao-chih, 54; Mao Zedong, government of, 48, 52, 54, 55; Nationalist government, 47–9, 51, 56–7; Nationalist Kuomintang, 48–9, 54; Republican government, 45, 47, 48–9; in Second World War, 52; "self-strengthening" philosophy, 46; US antagonism, 62; Yuan Shikai government, 49–50

– regulatory concerns: Amidror, General Yaacov, 67; bin Laden, Osama, 63; Dagan, Meir, 64; Palestinian terrorism financing, 65; Said al-Shurafa, 63–6; Secret Intelligence Service (China), 62; Shaya, Uzi, 66–7

– regulatory enforcement: anti-money-laundering bureau, 58; anti-money-laundering regulatory adoption in China, 59; confidentiality clauses (Article 7), 60–1; defence strategy, 65–9; deficiencies strategy (US), 66; financial intelligence units (FIUs), 58–60; fortified finance regime, 57–61; "know your customer" (KYC) stipulations, 58; reform and continued state control, 55–7; suspicious activity reports (SARs), 60; *Wultz v. Bank of China Ltd*, 63–7; Xi Jinping, 67; Xu Junping, 62–3

– structure: and Communist Party of China, 45, 48–9, 52–4, 68; foreign exchange expertise, 49–51, 53–5; initial public offering, 56–7; managerial staff, 54; Ministry of Finance, 48, 50, 53, 55; origins of state ownership, 52–3, 56–7; overseas presence, 54; People's Bank of China, 48, 53–66; public-private ownership model, 48, 50; Shareholders' Association (private equity interests), 47–8; state linkage replicated at local level, 53–4; Treasury Bank, 47

Bank of Commerce and Credit International. *See* BCCI

Bank of International Settlements, 19, 56, 120

Bank Secrecy Act (US, 1970), 12, 16, 125, 143–4, 153

Basel Accords (1996), 56

Basel Committee on Banking Supervision, 18–19, 131

Basic Law (Saudi Arabia, 1992), 79–80

BCCI (Bank of Commerce and Credit International)

– case points: British context and response, 152; disparate jurisdictions, 133; fortified finance emergence, 134, 149, 151; geopolitical diplomacy, 134; international financial backing, 133–4; offshore tax havens, use of, 133, 149–50; private sector

structure, 149; stateless ownership, 133, 150–2
- case study framework: context, 7, 38, 41–3; enforcement case against, 122–34; evaluation, 148–59, 161–2; institutional independence framework, 121–2
- historical context: Abedi, Agha Hasan, 122–3; Al Nahyan, Sheikh Zayed bin Sultan, 127; Bank of America, 127; Bank of England regulatory role, 125–7; Bhutto, Zulfikar Ali, 122–3; British Cayman Islands, 124–6; Euromarket impact, 124–5; monetarism, international shift to, 124; National Bank of Oman, 127; United Bank Limited, 123; Zia-ul-Haq, Muhammad, 122–3
- regulatory concerns: Bank of America, 127; Bank of England, 127–8; CIA, 130; loan management, 127; Middle East financing, 128–9; US and UK intelligence, 129; US politicians and agencies, 130
- regulatory enforcement: Al Nahyan, Zayed bin Sultan (Abu Dhabi Sheikh), 131; Bank of England, 130–3; FinCEN, 130; Manhattan District Attorney, 130, 132–3; multinational response, 133; Price Waterhouse, 131, 133; tax havens, continued risk from, 133; UK–Abu Dhabi collaboration, 132; UK agencies, 130–1
- relationships: CIA, 129–30; terrorist organizations, 128–9; US and UK intelligence, 128–9
- structure: Abedi, Agha Hasan, 122–3; "global" stateless framework, 121–4, 132–3; ICIC overseas subsidiary, 126; Luxembourg, 124, 133; motivation for institutional independence, 122–3; non-state jurisdictions (Abu Dhabi, Pakistan), 133; offsite ledgers, 126; Pakistani regulation, avoidance of, 122–3; tax haven framework, 122–3; vulnerability of "global" orientation, 123–4

Benevolence International Foundation (Saudi Arabia), 83
Berger, Suzanne, 31
Bhutto, Zulfikar Ali, 122–3
"Big Four" state banks (China), 44
bin Laden, Osama, 63, 82, 83
blocked regulatory enforcement –
case examination: authoritarianism hypothesis, 38; cases and method, 35–7; competing logics of finance and national security, 10–13; conceptual separation of states, banks, and terrorism financiers, 24–5; data framework, 42–3; enforcement blockage, 36; hypothesis testing, 25–35; institutional linkages, 34; negative and positive variables, 7; regulatory policy hypothesis, 37; rival hypothesis and case coding, 37–42; rule-of-law and regulatory quality data, 39–40; terrorist financing and fortified finance regulation, 13–24; variables and conceptualizations, 32–5
BNP Paribas banking group, 38

Bretton Woods Agreement (1971), 9, 12–13
Burn, Gary, 125
Bush, George H.W., 56
Bush, George W., 85, 87, 88

CAMLMAC. *See* AML Monitoring and Analysis Center
Cassara, John, 63
Cayman Islands: and BCCI, 124–6, 133; Caymans Protection Board, 125–6; Confidential Relationship Law (1976), 126; regulatory context and British structure, 126
CDD (customer due-diligence) rules, 4, 19
Cengiz, Mahmut, 100
Central Huijin Investment Ltd, 57
Central Reserve Bank of China (Wang Jingwei regime), 52
Chang Kia-ngau (Zhang, Jia'ao), 51
Chen Jintao, 48
Chiang Kai-shek, 50–2
China: China Investment Corporation (CIC), 57; Civil War, 52–3; Communist Party of China, relationship to Bank of China, 45, 48–9, 52–4, 68; Secret Intelligence Service, 62; State Council, 53–4, 56–8; State Planning Commission, 53. *See also* Bank of China
City of London, 124–6
Clunan, Anne L., 21
Cohen, Benjamin, 10
Cold War, 16; international economy after, 30–1; optimism in international institutions, 29

corruption: and bank-state linkages, 34–5; definitions, 33–4; and institutional linkages, 33; variability in regulatory enforcement, 34
Council of Europe, 17
Counter-Terrorism Committee (UN), 22
counterterrorist finance (CTF) and anti-money-laundering rules (AML). *See* AML/CTF rules
cultural context in financial affairs, 23, 27
currency transaction reports (CTRS), 16, 21
customer due-diligence (CDD) rules, 4, 19

Dagan, Meir, 64
Da Qing Bank, 47–9
deflection of enforcement (contrasted with veto of enforcement), 35
Deng Xiaoping, 44, 49, 53, 55, 68
Department of Zakat and Income Taxes (Saudi Arabia), 81
Doremus, Paul N., 11
Drezner, Daniel W., 11
drug trade: and development of AML regulations, 18; and illicit activities, 16
Drug Trafficking Offences Act (UK, 1986), 17
DZIT. *See* Department of Zakat and Income Taxes (Saudi Arabia)

Economic Congress (İzmir, 1923), 94
economic sanctions (contrasted with financial regulation), 22

Egmont Group, 28, 88–9, 103, 144
Ehrenfeld, Rachel, 70
Erdoğan, Recep Tayyip, 98, 100, 102, 114–15

Fahd, King, 77, 79
Faisal, King, assassination, 77
FATF. *See* Financial Action Task Force
Federal Reserve (US): domestic context, 10, 19; international activities, 120, 129–30, 133
Feis, Herbert, 12
Feng Guifen, 46
Financial Action Task Force (FATF): Forty Recommendations, 19; history, 4–5, 17–19; international partnerships, 22–3, 27–8; regulatory enforcement outcomes, 41–2; trade-based money laundering, 63. *See also* Al Rajhi Bank; AML/CTF rules; Halk Bank
Financial Crimes Enforcement Network (FinCEN) (US): domestic context, 20–1, 130; enforcement actions, 143–5, 149; structure, 20–1, 130
financial crisis (2008), 11, 159
financial deregulation (US and UK), 17–18
financial institutions, international: effectiveness of increased regulation, 18; national security goals, 11, 24–5, 29–30; and state linkage, 26–7; and state political economies, 30
financial intelligence units (FIUS), 4, 19–21, 28, 30, 86

financial regulation, international: economic sanctions, 22; evolution in response to self-funded organizations, 22; evolution of deregulation, 9–10; global harmonization impact, 4–5, 22; liberalization, 8–11; national security interests, 3, 5–6; terrorism response, 4–10; universal adoption and divergent results, 13
FinCEN. *See* Financial Crimes Enforcement Network (US)
FIUS. *See* financial intelligence units (FIUS)
fortified finance
– evaluation of fortified finance regime effectiveness: case studies, comparative, 153–7; enforcement outcomes, 153; fortified finance regulatory status, 154; political conditions, 154–5, 156–7; privatization status, 155; state ownership status, 155–6; state ownership as variable, 153–4; surveillance capabilities, 155–6; terrorist financing, 154
– general: definition, 10; evolution of, 27–9; institutional linkages, 32; standard policies in diverse contexts, 30
– implications of, 157–63; economic statecraft, impact of, 160; financial systems, risk forewarnings, 159; geopolitical and security interactions, 158–9; institutional configurations, strength of, 157; multinational interests, 159; offshore tax havens, continued risk from,

158–9; regulatory ineffectiveness, 157; state ownership variable, 157–8; targeted disincentives, 159–60; terrorist financing, risk of, 158
Forty Recommendations (FATF), 19, 23, 104
*fuguo qiangbing* (Chinese state and military power), 46
Fukuyama, Francis, 29

globalization of finance and national security, 9–13
*gongsi lu* (Chinese corporate statute), 47
gravity model for estimating money laundering (John Walker, 1999), 16
"great powers" governments, 4, 11–13, 22, 163; China as, 61, 69
Group of Seven (G7): creation of Financial Action Task Force (1989), 4–5, 134
Gurule, Jimmy, 24

Hage, Wadih el-, 83
Halk Bank
– case study framework: context, 7, 33, 35, 38, 41–3; evaluation, 117–20, 154–6, 161–2; fortified finance regime, 102–7; partial liberalization and domestic coalition building, 96–102; statist legacies, 94–6; and Turkish government, *101*
– historical context: Atatürk, Mustafa Kemal, 94–5; bank acquisitions, 98–9; domestic politics, 107, 109; Economic Congress (İzmir, 1923), 94; energy dependencies, role of, 108–9; enterprise focus, advantages of, 95–6, 98, 100, 102; Erdoğan, Recep Tayyip, 98, 100, 102, 114–15; European integration, 102, 104; failed privatization and legal positioning, 97, 99–100; Fascist economic influences, 95; geopolitical orientation, 102–3, 107–8, 117; international treaties, 103–5; Islamic context, 98; Justice and Development Party (AKP), 97; Özal, Turgut, 96–8, 102–3, 107–9; People's Fund, 96; political economy, 93–7; Privatization Administration, 97; Privatization High Council, 97; privatization process, 97–100; state ownership, impact of, 99–100, 107, 118–20; US partnership in Syria, 120; Zarrab, Reza, 115
– regulatory concerns: Atilla, Mehmet Hakan, 114–17, 119; corruption, 98–100, 102, 105–6; defence strategy, 113–15, 117, 120; FATF compliance, 105–7; financial corruption crackdown, 113; gold standard, use of, 105, 107, 112, 114, 120; money laundering, 112–15; retaliation against law enforcement and judicial officials, 114–15, 118–19; retaliation against witnesses, 116, 118–19; suspicious activity reports (SARs), 103–4; US allegations, charges, and arrests, 115–17; Zarrab, Reza, 114–15
– regulatory enforcement: antiterrorism laws, 105; Banking

Regulation and Supervision Agency, 113; compliance claims, 116; corruption, response to crackdown on, 114–15; dismissal of charges, 115–16; economic repositioning, 120; Egmont Group, 103; Financial Action Task Force, 103, 104–6; Implementation of Privatization Law 4046, 97, 99; international repercussions, 118; Law 3713, 103; Law 4208, 103; Law 4603, 99; MASAK, 103, 104; Prevention of Laundering Proceeds of Crime Law 5549, 103; punishment, absence of, 117, 119–20; and Syrian civil war, 120
– structure: and Turkish government, *101*, 102
Hamas: and Arab Bank, 135, 140–3, *146*, 147; and Bank of China, 61–4, *65*
Hanbali Islamic juridical tradition (Saudi Arabia), 71, 79–80
Helleiner, Eric, 10, 124
Hong Kong and Bank of China: as operations centre, 54; repossession by China (1997), 56; role in money-laundering operations, 62
HSBC Bank, 88, 90
Huber, Albert F.A., 84
Huijin Corporation, 57

Ibn Saud, 73–4
Ibn Taymiyyah, 80
institutional linkage: blocked regulatory enforcement, 25–7; characteristics of, 32–3; corruption contrast, 34–5; fortified financial regulations impact, 28, 32, 42; as independent variable, 25–6, 34; institutional independence, 121–2; state ownership variable, 41
International Convention for the Suppression of the Financing of Terrorism (United Nations, 1999), 22–3, 104–5
International Currency Control Agency, 17
International Monetary Fund (IMF), 20, 76, 111
international relations, state versus global cooperation motives, 29–30
Iran: and Halk Bank, 105–17, 119; nuclear weapons program, 111–12; tensions with US and sanctions, 111–12, 116
Irish Republican Army (IRA), 17
Israel and Bank of China: Amidror, General Yaacov, 67; Dagan, Meir, 64; Israeli National Security Council, 64; Matalon, Shlomo, 63–5; Middle East relationships, 61–9; Mossad, 64; Netanyahu, Benjamin, 66–7; Shaya, Uzi, 66–7; Terrorist Financing Task Force, 64;
Israeli and Arab Bank, 141, 143

Japan and Bank of China, 46–7, 52
Japanese invasion of China (1937), 52
Jordan: and Arab Bank, 137–40, 142–3; Association of Bankers, 139; and fortified finance reform, 144–5, 147–8; Jordanian Social

Security Corporation, 139; and Palestinian tensions, 138, 140–1; response to Arab Bank enforcement, 140, 145, 147–9; and terrorist organizations, 141; US aid to, 148–9. *See also* Arab Bank
Justice and Development Party (Turkey) (AKP), 93, 97, 107, 162; influence of Erdoğan, Recep Tayyip, 100, 102–3, 115, 118–19

Kirshner, Jonathan, 12, 19, 31, 52
know your customer (KYC) stipulations, 18–20, 58, 113, 118
Kung, H.H. (Kung Hsiang-hsi), 52

Li Chao-chih, 54
Liang Qichao, 50
Luxembourg. *See under* BCCI (Bank of Commerce and Credit International)

Makhtab al-Khidamat (MAK) (Afghan Services Bureau), 82–3
Mao Zedong, 44, 48–9, 52–5, 62
MASAK (Mali Suçları Araştırma Kurulu), 103–4
Matalon, Shlomo, 63–5
Mearsheimer, John J., 29
Middle East: and Arab Bank, 134–5; and BCCI, 129
Ministry of Finance (China), 48, 50, 53, 55
Ministry of Finance (Saudi Arabia), 75
Ministry of Public Security (China), 58
monetarism theory, 10, 124
money "dirtying," 21

money laundering: comparison with terrorist financing, 21–2, 22
Money Laundering and Financial Crimes Strategy Act (1998), 16–17
Money Laundering Control Act (1986), 16
Money Laundering Suppression Act (1994), 16
monobanking era (China), 49, 53–5
Mossad, 64, 66

Nahyan, Sheikh Zayed bin Sultan Al, 127
Nasreddin, Ahmed Idris, 84
Nasser, Gamal Abdel, 62, 138
National Commerce Bank (Saudi Arabia), 38
National Criminal Intelligence Service (UK), 20
national security concerns: banking institutions impact, 20, 24–5; financial regulation impact, 13, 20; international finance system, 3; regulatory influence, 11–13
Netanyahu, Benjamin, 66–7
non-cash instruments: role in financing terrorism, 14–15
Northern Expedition (China, 1926–28), 51

offshore tax havens. *See* tax havens, offshore
Operation Green Quest (US), 83–4
Özal, Turgut, 96–8, 102–3, 107–9
Özbudun, Ergun, 102

Palan, Ronen, 126
Palestine and Arab Bank, 135–6, 139–41

Palestinian Islamic Jihad and Bank of China, 65
People's Bank of China (PBC), 48, 53–66
People's Construction Bank, 53
People's Liberation Army and Bank of China, 62
People's Republic of China (PRC). *See* Bank of China
Polanyi, Karl, 27
political economies as non-cohesive entities, 28–31
privatization: case study variables, 33

Qing dynasty and Bank of China, 45–6

Reagan, Ronald, 17
regulatory enforcement, blocked – case examination. *See* blocked regulatory enforcement – case examination
research opportunities: academic disciplines, integration of, 4, 162–3; American legal system, role of, 161–2; banking institutions, deferred prosecution, 161; banking institutions, governance and corruption, 160–1; financial systems, risk forewarnings, 161; geopolitical and security variables, 162; international dynamics, evolving context, 162–3; state entities, variation of motivations, 161; state ownership variable, 161; terrorist financing methods, 160
Roth, Mitchel P., 100
rule of law: case study variables, 41

SAAR Foundation (Saudi Arabia), 82–4
Safa Group (Saudi Arabia), 83–4
Said al-Shurafa, 63, 65
Salafism and Al Rajhi Bank, 71
SAMA. *See* Saudi Arabian Monetary Agency (SAMA)
SARs (suspicious activity reports), 16–17, 21. *See also* Al Rajhi Bank; Arab Bank; Bank of China; BCCI (Bank of Commerce and Credit International); Halk Bank
Saudi Arabia: monarchy and Al Rajhi Bank, 71–4, 76, 77–8, 86, 90–2; state and Al Rajhi Bank, 86, 88–92. *See also* Al Rajhi Bank
Saudi Arabian Monetary Agency (SAMA), 74–6, 77, 78, 80–1, 87, 88–91
Second World War and Bank of China, 45, 51–2, 62
Secret Intelligence Service (China), 62
Shapiro, Jacob N., 15
Sharman, Jason Campbell, 24, 27, 30
Shaxson, Nicholas, 124
Shaya, Uzi, 66–7
Shelley, Louise, 34
Shleifer, Andrei, 33
Shoman, Abdul Hameed, 135
Siegel, David A., 15
SOEs (state-owned enterprises) as bank model, 33, 41, 155–7
Soong, T.V. (Soong Tzu-wen), 51–2
Soviet Union: and Afghanistan, 76, 81, 129; and Bank of China, 51, 62; and China, 51, 62; collapse of, 107; terrorist and guerrilla organizations, aid to, 15–16

Standard Chartered (UK bank), 38
State Council (China), 53–4, 56–8
state-owned enterprises (SOEs) as bank model, 33, 41, 155–7
State Planning Commission (China), 53
Strange, Susan, 9–10
Suleiman, Sheikh Abdullah, 74
Sun Yat-sen, 49
Sunni Islam and Al Rajhi Bank, 38, 70–2, 76, 80–1, 91, 156
surveillance model in banking, 21, 26, 155–7, 159
suspicious activity reports (SARs), 16–17, 21. *See also* Al Rajhi Bank; Arab Bank; Bank of China; BCCI (Bank of Commerce and Credit International); Halk Bank
Svensson, Jakob, 34
Swiss regulatory model, 19, 23, 124

tax havens, offshore: adoption of AML/CTF statutes, 23; as money-laundering framework, 16, 27. *See also* BCCI – case points; BCCI – historical context; BCCI – structure; Cayman Islands
terrorism and financial regulation: contradictory literature on, 4, 8
terrorism financing: definitions and trends, 14, 16, 21–2, 37–42
Terrorist Financing Task Force (Israel), 64
Terrorist Financing Unit (UK), 17
terrorist organizations: financial operations, 13–16, 20, 25
Thatcher, Margaret, 10, 17–18, 128

threat finance regulation: definitions and trends, 8–9, 12, 23, 26–7, 29–30, 37–8
trade-based money laundering: FATF definition of, 63
Transparency International, 34
Turkey: Economic Congress (İzmir, 1923), 94; Erdoğan, Recep Tayyip and AKP influence, 100, 102–3, 115, 118–19; fortified finance regime, 102–7; Justice and Development Party, 93, 97, 107, 162; Turkey Wealth Fund, 100. *See also* Halk Bank

United Kingdom: Drug Trafficking Offences Act (1986), 17; financial institutions, evolution of, 9, 17–18 (*see also* BCCI – structure); National Criminal Intelligence Service, 20; Terrorist Financing Unit, 17
United Nations, 18, 22–3, 104; Convention for the Suppression of the Financing of Terrorism (1999), 22–3, 104; Counter-Terrorism Committee, 22
United Nations Security Council: resolution 1267, 22, 105; resolution 1373, 22, 86; resolution 1988, 105; resolution 1989, 105
United States: Bank Secrecy Act (1970), 12, 16, 125, 143–4, 153; financial institutions, evolution of, 9, 12–13, 19; legal system, influence of, 3, 17. *See also* Al Rajhi Bank; Arab Bank; Bank of China; BCCI (Bank of Commerce and Credit International); Halk Bank

United States Department of the Treasury: enforcement activities, 83–4, 86, 89, 113, 145–7; regulatory role, 16–17, 20

United States Federal Reserve: domestic context, 10, 19; international activities, 120, 129–30, 133

United States Financial Crimes Enforcement Network (FinCEN): domestic context, 20–1, 130; international activities, 143–5, 149

veto of enforcement (contrasted with deflection of enforcement), 35

Vienna Convention (1988), 18

Viner, Jacob, 12

Vishny, Robert W., 33

Volcker, Paul, 10, 19

Wahhabi Islam and Al Rajhi Bank, 71–4, 77–9, 82, 90–1

Walker, John: gravity model (1999), 16

Warde, Ibrahim, 23, 27, 30

"war on drugs" and regulation development, 18–19

Wikileaks data, 42–3, 113, 154

Wittig, Timothy, 14, 23, 27

World Muslim League, 73

World Trade Organization, 56

World War II and Bank of China, 45, 51–2, 62

*Wultz v. Bank of China Ltd*, 63–7

Xi Jinping, 67, 162

Xu Junping, 62–3

*yinhang* ("silver shops," China), 49

Youssef, Nada, 84

Yuan Shikai, 49–50

Zarate, Juan, 23–4, 83, 86–7, 143

Zhang Jia'ao (Chang Kia-ngau), 51

Zhu Rongji, 56

Zia-ul-Haq, Muhammad, 122–3

Zouaydi, Mohammed Galeb Kalaje, 70, 82